DEAD AIR

DEAD AIR
The Night That Orson Welles Terrified America

WILLIAM ELLIOTT HAZELGROVE

ROWMAN & LITTLEFIELD
Lanham • Boulder • New York • London

Published by Rowman & Littlefield
An imprint of The Rowman & Littlefield Publishing Group, Inc.
4501 Forbes Boulevard, Suite 200, Lanham, Maryland 20706
www.rowman.com

86-90 Paul Street, London EC2A 4NE

British Library Cataloguing in Publication Information Available

Library of Congress Cataloging-in-Publication Data
Names: Hazelgrove, William Elliott, 1959– author. | Koch, Howard. Invasion from Mars.
Title: Dead air : the night that Orson Welles terrified America / William Elliott Hazelgrove.
Description: Lanham : Rowman & Littlefield, 2024. | Includes bibliographical references and
   index. | Summary: "On Halloween Eve 1938, Orson Welles put on a radio play of 'War of the
   Worlds' and terrorized an uneasy American public on the brink of World War II, perpetuating
   the greatest hoax in history and changing media forever. This book brings to life this fateful
   night and follows the life and career of Welles before and after the historic broadcast"—
   Provided by publisher.
Identifiers: LCCN 2024014753 (print) | LCCN 2024014754 (ebook) | ISBN 9781538187166
   (cloth) | ISBN 9781538187173 (epub)
Subjects: LCSH: War of the worlds (Radio program) | Welles, Orson, 1915–1985—Criticism
   and interpretation. | Science fiction radio programs—United States. | Science fiction radio
   programs—Psychological aspects | Radio audiences—United States.
Classification: LCC PN1991.77.W3 H39 2024 (print) | LCC PN1991.77.W3 (ebook) | DDC
   791.44/72—dc23/eng/20240422
LC record available at https://lccn.loc.gov/2024014753
LC ebook record available at https://lccn.loc.gov/2024014754

♾™ The paper used in this publication meets the minimum requirements of American National
Standard for Information Sciences—Permanence of Paper for Printed Library Materials, ANSI/
NISO Z39.48-1992.

Once again to

Kitty, Clay, Callie, and Careen

We couldn't soap all your windows and steal all your garden gates by tomorrow night, so we did the next best thing. We annihilated the world before your very ears and utterly destroyed the CBS.
—ORSON WELLES ON *WAR OF THE WORLDS*

Contents

THE MAGICIAN

HARRY HOUDINI STARED AT THE BOY BACKSTAGE WITH OVAL EYES AND full-blown cheeks. His voice was that of a full-grown adult stuck in the charade of a ten-year-old. His guardian, Dr. Bernstein, had brought him to the great magician who had shown the boy a trick, and the boy had come backstage to perform it. Houdini watched him and sternly said, "You must practice a trick, Orson, a thousand times before you perform it."[1] Orson Welles would never wait that long. As soon as he mastered a trick, he wanted to show it to people. He wanted to see what effect his magic tricks had on people. He wanted to make things disappear and then reappear. All his life, he would perform sleight of hand. During television interviews, Orson would perform small tricks. It was a way of impressing people and having them stare at the magician in a way that made him feel he could conjure up a world and then make it disappear.

During a broadcast on a warm Halloween eve on October 30, 1938, a twenty-three-year-old man held his hands up for radio silence in CBS's Studio One in New York City while millions of people panicked; ran out into the night; grabbed shotguns; drove off in speeding cars; ran screaming down the streets; had heart attacks; contemplated suicide; committed suicide; fell down stairs; ran for the hills; hid in basements and attics; went to churches to beg for mercy; ran for the rooftops; spilled into the streets; jumped on trains, subways, and taxis. Any way they could find to get away from robotic Martians intent on exterminating the human race with flesh-destroying heat rays and poisonous gas. Orson Welles held up his hands to his fellow actors, musicians, and sound technicians and turned six seconds of radio silence into absolute horror, changing how the world would view media forever, and making Orson Welles one of the most famous men in America. Jittery from war news and weary from the concussive effects of a nine-year Great Depression, Americans were experiencing a new medium called radio that was pushing its way into their homes. Incredibly, on this warm Halloween eve, people would come to believe that Martians had invaded America and had begun to exterminate the human race.

There is nothing more taboo in radio than "dead air." Dead air ends careers, destroys reputations, and gets shows canceled. It is the monster in the closet of every broadcaster. The show runs too short or too long. These are issues that can be dealt with, but the mistake, the glitch, the unforeseen event that leaves dead air buzzing out on the airwaves feels like death. It is radio in its naked form. An electromagnetic field shoots out over the dark fields of the republic, beaming across the cities, the farms, the homes, the apartments, the stores, and the theaters. The wave generated by an electromagnetic disturbance, oscillated by vacuum tubes or transistors is devoid of the human voice. It hums. It buzzes. Sometimes, there's a dance of static. On the other end, the human waits for this awful dead moment to end because it suggests the world can be a dark and horrible place devoid of humanity. On October 30, 1938, it went on . . . *for six long seconds*—the dead air of our souls.

Soon after the broadcast, Princeton professor Hadley Cantril conducted a study of the impact of the *War of the Worlds* and, in 1940, published *The Invasion from Mars: A Study in the Psychology of Panic*. He and his researchers, in the months following October, conducted interviews and sent out surveys to people and concluded that a core group of six million people heard the broadcast with a possible twelve million joining in by the end. This is out of a voting-age population of seventy million people in 1938. From this core group of people, the information spread out and enveloped the war-jittery nation. Cantril's book provides invaluable evidence because it is the only study undertaken soon after the broadcast. The interviews Cantril and his researchers conducted recorded the visceral reactions to the terror Orson Welles's radio play generated.

Cantril also addressed the sharing of the news that went out exponentially and was spread by people, media, telephones, telegrams, letters, and notes. One person bursting into a church declaring *the end of the world* acted as a megaphone broadcasting to hundreds who went home and spread the news to loved ones, neighbors, bystanders. This happened over and over and over. People ran to the churches to pray and then announced to frightened congregations that the world was ending, and the congregations then became purveyors of the panic.

Cantril analyzed 12,500 newspaper clippings and found that "the volume of press notices took an unusually sharp decline the second and third days, considerable interest was maintained for five days, and had not fallen below 30 percent of the original volume by the end of the first week. . . . Interest did not begin to flatten until the end of the second week."[2] Big black headlines dominated papers from New York to San Francisco: "Fake Radio 'War' Stirs Terror through U.S."[3] . . . "US Probes Invasion Broadcast . . . Radio Play Causes Wide Panic"[4] . . . "Radio Fake Scares Nation."[5]

The woman who broke her leg going down the stairs, the people who ran up into the mountains and refused to come down, and the woman attempting suicide by poison are all there on the front pages of newspapers the day after. The headlines go on, with regional papers picking up the story from the Associated Press (AP) and United Press International (UPI) wires and spreading it across the hinterlands. The number of people who believed Orson Welles's broadcast was beyond the original six million who heard it because of the advent of mass media; telephonic and telegraphic communication; and the effect of rumor, fact, and innuendo. Today, we call it "going viral." In 1938, no one understood the tsunami that breaking news bulletins produced. Radio was too new, and people weren't used to the power of the nascent spiderish mass media.

Once the terror began, it swept the nation, reaching people who did not even hear Welles's broadcast. The fear of imminent death by invading Martians had its own synergy, and once that wave of terror reached shore, it washed over rational thought and left only terror. The revisionism of recent years skews the facts along these lines: The newspapers revved up the story to sell papers and take revenge on the new medium of radio that had been sucking away advertising dollars; most people did not believe Martians had invaded and were murdering humans.

But the newspapers did not "go after" radio. As John Gosling writes in *Waging the War of the Worlds*, "The *New York Times* of October 31, in line with every other newspaper in the country, led with reports of the broadcast and the anger of listeners, turning up irate residents such as a Mrs. Warren Dean, who was quoted as saying, 'I've heard a lot of radio programs, but I've never heard anything as rotten as that.'"[6] Or Samuel Tishman, last seen running down Broadway, who proclaimed it "the most asinine stunt I ever heard of." "However, a thorough reading of the *Times* and a further large story on November 1 reveals no overt signs of bias. Indeed in the story Welles is given considerable room to defend himself, '. . . none of the malicious allegations reportedly put to Welles and Houseman by a pack of baying journalists on the night of the broadcast were repeated in the *Times* the following day.'"[7]

Historians have stated there is no way Orson Welles planned to scare the nation with a fake broadcast about Martians invading, gassing, and burning thousands of people. They point to Welles after the broadcast in the famous news conference, looking like a chastised son and surrounded by journalists. His eyes are wide; his demeanor is that of Peck's Bad Boy. Pure Welles. He is the magician who pulls a rabbit out of his hat and apologizes for startling the old lady in the front row. The essence of Orson Welles is obfuscation, deflection, deception, the writer typing with his right hand while telling the story with his left, commanding you not to look at the man behind the curtain. Welles understood illusion very well as he thumped you on the back of the head and asked whether you saw stars through his telescope.

The day after the October 30, 1938, broadcast, people picked up the *New York Times* and began reading the front-page article: "A wave of mass hysteria seized thousands of radio listeners throughout the nation between 8:15 and 9:30 o'clock last night when a broadcast of a dramatization of H.G. Wells's fantasy, 'The *War of the Worlds*,' led thousands to believe an interplanetary conflict had started with invading Martians spreading death and destruction in New Jersey and New York."[8] Increasing telephone traffic quickly became roadmaps to the impact of the broadcast, with radio stations receiving as much as a 500 percent increase of calls over their usual Sunday night traffic.

UPI reported that operators in San Francisco were swamped with "requests for cross-continental telephone connections with New York and New Jersey."[9] People didn't care about the charges of a long-distance call suddenly; they just wanted to tell mothers, fathers, daughters, and sons that they loved them before being obliterated. Closer to home, "the *New York Times* took 875 calls that night, with the *Newark Evening News* receiving 1,000. The Newark police headquarters reported nearly a thousand calls. Some asked if the police had extra gas masks or if they needed to close their windows. It has been estimated that the New Jersey Bell company received 75,000–100,000 calls over their normal traffic during the 8:00 PM hour. Paul Morton, the City Manager for Trenton, NJ, wrote a curt letter to the FCC following the CBS broadcast. The broadcast had 'completely crippled communication facilities of our police department for about three hours,' wrote Morton, 'I am requesting that you immediately make an investigation and do everything possible to prevent a recurrence. The situation was so acute that two thousand phone calls were received in about two hours, all communication lines were paralyzed and voided normal municipal functions.'"[10]

The interpretation that the *War of the Worlds* broadcast was a local phenomenon restricted to the East Coast is false for several reasons. The first is that CBS-affiliated stations carrying the *War of the Worlds* were scattered all over the country. As John Gosling concludes in *Waging the War of the Worlds*, "The evidence certainly seems to point convincingly toward the broadcast touching every corner of the United States. Thousands of miles from New York on the West Coast, the same degree of concern was recorded by local newspapers. The switchboard of the *Seattle Daily News* was according to the October 31 edition, 'deluged for hours with calls from people trying to learn whether the alarming news was authentic.' Local CBS affiliate stations were overwhelmed with calls, with station KIRO receiving over 250 calls in one hour. The *Newark Evening News* rounded up several reports from the country, including accounts that newspapers and radio station switchboards in Toronto, Ontario, had seen a heavy load of calls from concerned citizens. Other reports came from San Francisco, Boston, Memphis, and Detroit."[11]

Affiliated stations of the CBS Radio Network all over the United States carried *Mercury Theatre on the Air* on the night of October 30, 1938. The assumption that the broadcast was a local radio phenomenon would only make sense if the broadcast had been restricted to the signal emanating from the studio at 485 Madison Avenue in Manhattan. The total number of radio stations in 1938 was 685, of which 110 were affiliates of CBS. The Golden Age of Radio was in full swing, with four out of five households having a radio in the living room. Experimentation, innovation, new programming, unheard-of listenership, and mass media all came together in the 1930s. Men such as Orson Welles found themselves in the giant petri dish of Hertzian waves beaming across a population born when horses and buggies were giving way to Model Ts. The Wright brothers had flown thirty-five years before, and the *Titanic* had sunk just a quarter century earlier. A hallmark of the twentieth century was becoming unheard-of change.

Another phenomenon that accounted for the dissemination of the broadcast to the far reaches of the country was the advent of the car radio. Up until 1930, few cars had radios. Congress passed the "AM Radio for Every Vehicle Act" in 1930, requiring automakers to offer "amplitude modulation" in every new vehicle. By 1938 the push-button AM radio was standard equipment in a car. The terror of *War of the Worlds* was accented as people listened to the broadcast in their cars and then drove in wild panic away from the Martians while the broadcast played on. The new mobile radio spread terror to people who then became Paul Revere messengers of the apocalypse.

The *War of the Worlds* broadcast is what Orson Welles created, but who was Orson Welles? Was he a magician who could pull a rabbit out of a hat and scare a nation into thinking Martians were invading and then play Peck's Bad Boy who let things get out of control? Or was he a calculating child prodigy who recited Shakespeare with a voice out of touch with his years and a cherub expression that made him look like a man-child well into his thirties? Welles believed he was a *changeling*, a child whom fairies had secretly substituted for the parents' real child in infancy. Like Mozart, Welles possessed strange talents as a boy that made him stand out. In his case, he believed only being the child of much grander parents could account for his prodigious talents.

Orson Welles produced and created the *War of the Worlds*, and that event is the key to the man. The comet that is Orson Welles left a smoking tail across the universe, and it's fitting that his greatest triumph was an invasion from space. So, let's go back to that night. It was his live concert, the moment Orson Welles became famous and able to follow his vision and go to Hollywood—magician, conman, literary savant, genius, director, huckster, destroyer of worlds. The questions and answers are all wrapped up in the night of October 30, 1938, when Orson Welles fooled the world . . . and then conquered it.

PROLOGUE

October 30, 1938

CARL PHILLIPS, THE ON-THE-SPOT REPORTER, HAD JUST BEEN INCINER-
ated by advancing Martians armed with a heat ray. There was a muffled
clunk as he dropped the microphone, and then . . . *silence*. Twenty-three-
year-old Orson Welles held up his hands in Studio One, on the twentieth floor of the high-rise at 485 Madison Avenue in New York, and
held the country hostage. His hands are straight up to the ceiling in the
black-and-white photo of that night. He demanded total silence from
his actors and the orchestra. His face was somber. Not a muscle moved.
Orson stared at the script on the music stand, headphone wires trickling
down the side of his white shirt. You could have heard a pin drop in that
CBS studio. Everyone was frozen by the magician/actor/director/writer/
conductor who had just unleashed nationwide panic.

Another black-and-white picture of the CBS studio tells us more
about that Sunday evening. There are two men wearing headphones,
surrounded by turntables, bells, whistles, and microphones. They have
wool pants with long-sleeved shirts and suspenders. They are the sound
effects men. Beyond them are six people, one woman and five men, holding scripts around a microphone. The men are in suits and the woman
in a long dress; one man wears a sport coat. Behind them are men in the
glass-enclosed control room. One man smokes a pipe. Orson Welles is up
on a podium in front of a music stand, wearing suspenders, headphones
clamped to his ears. Behind him is a conductor facing a crowd of musicians. The soundproof tiles on the walls resemble giant bathroom tiles.

Everyone is subordinate to the twenty-three-year-old director on the raised wooden platform.

The hum of the radio frequency beams out across America. That hum says more than all the words and music *Mercury Theatre on the Air* could muster. All over America, people listened in horror to the sound of death. *Dead air.* There was no accounting for it. The Martians had just killed a reporter on the air, and now the world was silent. Orson had the world transfixed in place.

One . . . two . . . three . . . four . . . five . . . six. Orson holds his hands up for six seconds, sweating, dark ovals appearing under his arms.

Orson then drops his arms and continues as the phone in the control room rings. CBS executive Davidson Taylor snatches it up. Welles is concentrating on actor Kenny Delmar's speech as the secretary of the interior (who sounds just like President Franklin Roosevelt), who has just announced America is under attack by Martians. If Orson saw Taylor rush out of the control room, he thought nothing of it. What mattered, the only thing that mattered, was making his *Mercury Theatre on the Air* production of H. G. Wells's *War of the Worlds* as realistic as possible.

Another actor, Ray Collins, was now narrating the destruction of New York City by the Martians using poison gas and an incinerating heat ray. Taylor rushed back into the control room and then tried to barge into the studio. Producer John Houseman blocked him from entering as the CBS executive told him the show must stop. Switchboards were swamped with calls from people frightened to death, believing New Jersey and New York were under attack by Martians. Taylor had "heard rumors that people were killing themselves because of the broadcast or trying to flee from the Martians in droves. They had to announce immediately that it was all a fake."[1] Houseman refused as Orson turned the corner on the far side of the broadcast.

A sweating, agitated Taylor pleaded with Houseman to stop Orson from reading the coda at the show's end. The executive knew this would implicate CBS if Welles read the ending speech in which he revealed the entire broadcast was a Halloween prank: "The Mercury Theatre's radio version of dressing up in a sheet and jumping out of a bush and yelling 'boo!'"[2] This night was turning into a disaster. Taylor had heard of suicides, heart attacks, mass flights, and people falling down stairs. If it were all true, CBS would be liable. John Houseman held Taylor off until the station break. The executive then rushed into the studio, ran up to Welles, and told him all hell was breaking loose. Orson Welles, the provocateur, the magician, would have none of it. He was all about creating controversy. Who else would stage Shakespeare with an all-Black cast in Harlem?

Orson now had the phone to his ear in the control room. The long-distance calls were ominous: "The first message was a threat of death from a chamber of commerce official of Flint, Michigan, who asserted that the population of Flint had been scattered and that it would take days to reassemble it. The next message gave statistics on the broken tibias and fibulas of Western Pennsylvania."[3] Other messages could not be repeated, but death was promised. Orson hung up, convinced he was a mass murderer. It was live radio. Whatever happened, happened. There were no second chances, and Welles kept his finger tightly pressed on the pulse of his play. His wife, Virginia Welles, had called in the first ten minutes to let him know it was "absolutely marvelous and hair-raising."[4] That was all he needed.

The phone in the control room rang again. "On the other end of the line, a group of angry listeners in Michigan, who claimed to be hunkered down in their basements with shotguns . . . threatened to shoot Welles if they ever met him face to face."[5] A CBS page brought the message to Welles and watched the blood drain out of his face. Orson stared at the other actors and realized they had just entered unknown territory in radio broadcasting. The CBS switchboard was overwhelmed with frantic calls. CBS night news manager Hal Davies was on the phone in the control room. "About 10 or 15 minutes into the broadcast, the phones started ringing. And I began to get hysterical calls, saying, 'Where are the invaders?' And 'What's happening?' And I said, come on, this is just Orson Welles' Mercury Theatre because I had the program on the monitor. Just a regular show, take it easy, don't panic, there are no invaders."[6]

The break ended, and Welles cued the orchestra leader to begin a slower piece for the latter half of the broadcast. The first half of *War of the Worlds* was dynamite; the second half fizzled from a dead script and lack of action. But it didn't matter; the fuse had been lit, and the explosion was shooting out shock waves across America. In the second half, Orson was the main character, Professor Pierson, who rumbled through the burned-over countryside, finding no humanity until he bumped into a lone philosophizing man. As Orson narrated the end, his blood ran cold. In the control room, two policemen entered and stared at him. His heart thumped; his mouth went dry. Orson lost his place in the script and then recovered as one of the cops tried to push his way into the studio. One of Welles's studio assistants pushed the officer back from the door, and Welles felt his voice tighten. His voice was his strongest asset. But now, while the police pushed on the door, he inadvertently rushed through the ending and flipped the line "the next best thing" to "the best next thing."

Orson then went ahead with the ending coda the CBS executives were dreading, admitting the entire broadcast was a prank.

"So, goodbye, everybody. And remember, please, for the next day or so, the terrible lesson you learned tonight. That grinning, glowing, globular invader of your living room is an inhabitant of the pumpkin patch, and if your doorbell rings and nobody is there, that was no Martian . . . it's Halloween."[7]

And they were off the air. The announcer, Dan Seymour, burst into the studio with an army of CBS employees who began grabbing "scripts and recording discs that were either locked away or destroyed on the spot."[8] The phones started ringing and never stopped as the police multiplied. Another call came into the control room that John Houseman later described in his memoir as "a shrill voice announcing itself as the mayor of some Midwestern city, one of the big ones. He is screaming for Welles. Choking with fury, he reports mobs in the streets of his city, women and children huddling in churches, violence, and looting. If, as he now learns, the whole thing is nothing but a crummy joke—then he, personally, is coming up to New York to punch the author of it in the nose."[9]

CBS's wasn't the only switchboard overwhelmed. Edna M. Bohn was working her operator job at the Princeton office of New Jersey Bell when "all of a sudden, I think every subscriber in Princeton lifted their receivers."[10] Edna described the entire switchboard lighting up and fielding one call after another about Martians landing. Radio operators became so overwhelmed they began to plug into the switchboard and, without any preamble, say, "It's *just a radio show*."[11] Anne O'Brian Lamb was an operator at the long-distance toll exchange at the Bell Telephone office in Trenton. A Trenton newspaper published a letter she had written, describing "a sudden massive flood of calls from people desperate to reach their children at Lawrenceville and Princeton schools. The calls came thick and fast and were extremely alarming. 'Do you know anything about this green gas that is coming from Grovers Mill? I'll pay any amount of money if you will get me through to my son at Princeton.'"[12]

The impact of the radio show was beginning to show up on the streets as well. At a police station on West 135th Street in Harlem, thirty people arrived with all their possessions packed and told officers they were ready to be evacuated. Traffic jams immediately formed across the city, and the *Newark Evening News* wrote of an incident at Hedden Terrace and Hawthorne Avenue in which twenty families had come out of their apartments in their underclothes, dragging children with wet towels and handkerchiefs around their heads. It would take three police cars, an ambulance, and an emergency squad of eight policemen to convince the tenants that poisonous gas was not in the air. Still, over a dozen people were sent to St. Michael's Hospital for shock. Orson Welles's broadcast was beginning to ricochet all over the country.

Meanwhile, in CBS's Studio One, a bomb threat was called in, and the cast of *War of the Worlds* was hustled into a bathroom while police searched the building for the bomb. Richard Wilson, one of the actors, would later write, "I distinctly remember a group of frightened men squeezed in the ladies' room of the bathroom."[13] Executives led Orson Welles and John Houseman to a back office in the building and closed the door while CBS and the police decided what to do with the two men. Orson heard the key turn in the lock. He slumped down against a filing cabinet and shut his eyes. He realized then that he might go to jail, be murdered by angry mobs, or be sued into oblivion. His brilliant career was over. Now there was silence. Just silence. Like the six seconds of dead air Welles had hurled at the world. Orson slumped down farther, wondering for the first time in his life whether he had gone too far—a very alien thought indeed.

I
THE SETUP

I

Who Is Orson Welles?

1938

IN BOX 24 OF THE UNIVERSITY OF MICHIGAN ARCHIVES, IN A FOLDER
marked "NYC boroughs folder 1 (33-54)," in the Orson Welles collection, is a letter from Estelle Paultz to Orson Welles written on October
31, 1938, a day after the broadcast. This fifteen-page letter is the Olym-
pian of Welles letters and has become the poster child for screaming
panic. Estelle and her husband John had been listening to the radio when
the *War of the Worlds* broadcast began around 8:00 p.m. Eastern Time.
It was a typical evening in their working-class neighborhood one block
from Union Square in New York City. John and Estelle Paultz probably
bought their radio for $10. They were not poor, but they used the radio
for entertainment. It was free. One did not have to go to the theater and
pay for tickets. In their apartment at 8 East Fifteenth Street, they sat
down to listen to WABC, an affiliate of the Columbia Broadcasting System. Outside their open window, cars streamed past with the fusty smell
of exhaust, the scent of burgers and fried food from the diner down the
street wafted in, a touch of fall was in the night air.

Much like televisions today, the radio provided soothing background
noise of music and the low, resonant voice of the announcer. The Paultzes
read the paper as a reporter talked about a meteorite that had landed on
a farm in the New Jersey town of Grovers Mill. "*The flash in the sky was
visible . . . and the noise of the impact was heard as far north as Elizabeth.*"[1]

John and Estelle drank coffee and chatted. Halloween pumpkins dotted stoops and porches and the windows of the tenements. Sally Rand was performing at the Chicago Theatre. The Paultzes had gone to the Chicago World's Fair in 1933, but they had not seen her then. The reporter on the radio competed with the sound of New York traffic. The announcer described a large crater and what landed in the pit. "*The object itself doesn't look much like a meteor . . . it looks more like a huge cylinder.*"[2]

Listeners of the Edgar Bergen and Charlie McCarthy show had begun channel surfing when the station went to break. Much like modern streamers looking for something to catch their interest, radio listeners in 1938 twirled the dial and landed on whatever interested them. Many had no idea what show they had stumbled on, and many assumed it was straight news. "*The end of the thing is beginning to flake off! The top is beginning to rotate like a screw! The thing must be hollow!*"[3] The Paultzes turned and looked at the radio.

The announcer described the top falling off the cylinder and a creature inside. "*They look like tentacles to me. . . . It's as large as a bear, and it glistens like wet leather. . . . The eyes are black and gleam like a serpent. The mouth is V-shaped with saliva dripping from its rimless lips that seem to quiver and pulsate.*"[4]

Millions of people were convinced they were listening to an actual news broadcast. The radio had taken control just as it had the week before when news from Europe moved the world closer, inch by inch, to a worldwide conflagration. The events in Grovers Mill, New Jersey, unfolded in real time. The Paultzes and the millions who dropped in from the Edgar Bergen and Charlie McCarthy show were transfixed. The excited reporter continued to describe the monster rising out of the pit. "*I'm pulling this microphone with me as I talk. I'll have to stop the description until I take a new position. Hold on, will you please? . . .*"[5]

The radio goes eerily to piano music in the Hotel Park Plaza dance room and then back to the reporter. The Paultzes, along with people all over America, were sitting close to their radio. The reporter returned and described the police arriving. "*Two policemen advance with something in their hands. . . . It's a white handkerchief tied to a pole . . . a flag of truce. If those creatures know what that means. . . . Wait! Something's happening!*"[6]

A loud sonic hum filled the Paultzes' apartment. It was terrifying as the agitated reporter cut back in: *"I can make out a small beam of light against a mirror . . . it [has leapt] right at the advancing men. . . . Good Lord, they're turning into flame!"*[7] Screams filled the apartment, along with unearthly shrieks. The Paultzes stared at each other as the reporter continued. An explosion blasted from the radio. *"The woods . . . the barns . . . the gas tanks of automobiles . . . it's spreading everywhere. It's coming this way. About twenty yards to my right."*[8]

Meanwhile, back in CBS's Studio One, Orson Welles stared at the script on his music stand: (CRASH OF MICROPHONE . . . THEN DEAD SILENCE . . .). The silence dragged on for six long seconds. Radio itself had just been killed. The silence was horrifying. A man had just died on the radio, and then there was only the awful vacuum of space, of death—six long seconds of nothing. Finally, an announcer returned. *"Ladies and gentlemen, due to circumstances beyond our control, we are unable to continue the broadcast from Grovers Mill."*[9] The Paultzes were now panicking as events accelerated on the radio. Time and space had been compressed. There was no logical way for the speed of events to unfold, but, like a good novel that can't be put down, suspension of disbelief had kicked in.

Then a man who sounded like the president made an announcement. He tried to calm the country. *"I wish to impress upon you—private citizens and public officials, all of you—the urgent need of calm and resourceful action. Fortunately, this formidable enemy is still confined to a comparatively small area, and we may place our faith in the military forces to keep them there."*[10]

The Paultzes were no longer sitting. Panic had them running from one room to the next, trying to decide—should they stay or leave? People across the nation were wondering the same thing. The *Seattle Daily Times* would later report that a woman in Boston had "called her brother to say she heard the broadcast and was leaving home immediately."[11] She went on to tell him everyone else in the neighborhood was also leaving. The *Hartford Courant* reported that a telephone operator "got a mind picture of hundreds of people frozen with horror at real and impending doom, agony at the imagined fate of relatives and friends." The paper described a woman so distraught she couldn't drive when she heard the broadcast and called the paper from a gas station. "She had been listening to the program on her automobile radio and was so unnerved, she was unable to drive farther and called the *Courant* for additional information."[12]

The *Courant* also reported on the actions of Samuel Tishman of Riverside Drive in New York. The article quoted Tishman: "I grabbed my hat and coat and a few personal belongings and ran to the elevator . . . joining hundreds who had begun running toward Broadway."[13] The impulse to run, get out, and drive was spreading like wildfire. The *Hartford Courant* reported on Margaret Leedom of Hamilton, New Jersey. "Her neighbors told her they had packed the car, woken the children, and set out for Philadelphia. Leedom's family was also caught up in the excitement. Her brother had gone out to put gas in the car, leaving her mother and sister alone. When a knock came at the door, it was opened to reveal an innocent gang of trick-or-treaters or, as Leedom's sister assumed, 'Martians!' When she recovered her wits, the trick-or-treaters were on the receiving end of the trick to end all tricks. 'Do you dammed fools know what's going on?' demanded Leedom's mother, and after she explained that the Martians were invading, the trick-or-treaters took to their heels."[14]

The Paultzes were not alone in their apprehension. Even the US military was aware of Orson Welles's broadcast. Marine Corps officials "were forced to issue denials that troops based at Quantico had been spooked." The *Washington Post* reported that Major General James C. Breckinridge said that "officers and enlisted men of his command understood a play was being broadcast and not an account of a foreign invasion."[15] Later, the *Newark Evening News* reported that "unnamed army and navy officials had been critical of the broadcast, voicing the concern that in the event of a real attack by a foreign power on the country, people might not heed the warnings, believing it to be just another radio fake."[16]

The military might have been angered as the broadcast veered into radio conversations between bomber pilots who were attacking the Martians. The Paultzes and people around the country believed they were hearing military communications.

"Ladies and gentlemen, we've run special wires to the artillery line in adjacent villages to give you direct reports. . . . We take you to the battery of the 22nd Field Artillery, located in the Watchung Mountains."[17]

If the Paultzes could have shaken their panic, they would have realized bombers with high explosives and artillery could not be in place in minutes. But terror paralyzes logic. They believed that, incredibly, they were listening to the bomber pilot in real time.

"The machines are close together now, and we're ready to attack. . . . Planes circling, ready to strike. . . . There they go! . . . Green flash! They're spraying us with flame! . . . No chance to release bombs. . . . Now the engine's gone!"[18]

The pilot lost communication with the tower. John and Estelle stared at each other. The Martians were headed for New York. The military scored direct hits on the machines, but they just kept advancing with a poisonous black smoke choking the soldiers who coughed and died. A cacophony of voices began to build: "GAS MASKS USELESS. URGE POPULATION TO MOVE INTO OPEN SPACES. . . . SMOKE NOW SPREADING OVER RAYMOND BOULEVARD."[19]

The radio was now a backdrop. The Paultzes were leaving. New York City was next. The announcer narrated from the roof of a building. *"A bulletin is handed to me. Martian cylinders are falling all over the country. . . . Now the first machine reaches the shore. . . . His steel, cowlish head is even with the skyscrapers. . . . People in the streets see it now. They're running toward the East River, thousands of them dropping in like rats. . . . It's reached Times Square."*[20]

The Paultzes were no longer listening. John ran up to the roof to see the Martian machines. He saw nothing, but it didn't matter. They were leaving as fast they could. "The horror of it all," Estelle later wrote in her letter. "I couldn't listen anymore. All the primitive fear of the unknown awakened within me, robbing me of all reason . . . only one thing remained to do—run, fly, get on the fastest thing on wheels, and go as far and as quickly as our last six dollars would take us."[21]

With the clothes on their back, the Paultzes ran down the stairs and spilled out into the street. They were amazed to find no commotion, no panic, except for one man leaning in a doorway. They explained that the Martians were coming, and the man ran down Fifteenth Street toward the subway station. John and Estelle ran after him and hopped a train uptown but missed their stop for Penn Station and got off at Forty-Second Street. "Then we remembered that the Pennsylvania station is on 34th Street . . . back we went running all the way—heeding nothing—stopping for nothing, flying for our lives—before this horrible unknown."[22]

While the Paultzes were running for the train, Lillian R. Ruder of Bordentown, New Jersey, was having a baby in Mercer Hospital. She had lost a previous baby from a miscarriage and was overjoyed when the baby was delivered. The *Trentonian* later reported that after the baby had been born, Lillian "started to hear a strange murmuring in the hallway. Buzzing the nurse to find out what was happening, she was told that people were coming into the hospital with the incredible news that the world was ending. With her newborn baby to care for and a whole future together to look forward to with her husband, she could only pray, 'Dear God, don't let it end like this.'"[23]

The head of Warner Brothers' location department in Hollywood was driving through the redwoods of California with his wife when he tuned in to the broadcast. The affiliates of CBS broadcast the radio play all over the country and into cars, spreading it like wildfire. The executive wrote, "Soon they [the Martians] were landing all over, even in California. There was no escape. All we could think of was to try and get back to LA to see our children once more. And be with them when it happens. We went right by gas stations, but I forgot we were low on gas. In the middle of the forest our gas ran out. There was nothing to do. We just sat there holding hands expecting any minute to see those Martian monsters appear over the tops of the trees."[24]

Traffic policemen on the highways between New York and New Jersey were used to speeding cars of gangsters running from a robbery or an assassination, but "at about 8:15 or 8:20 PM, most of the traffic over the roads suddenly went wild."[25] Hundreds of speeding automobiles careened down the highways as the bewildered policemen struggled to catch up. When they looked in the cars, they saw families, not gangsters. And the speeding cars would not even stop when the policemen hailed them to pull over. "The stampede was in all directions. . . . Now and then a traffic man would catch an incoherent shout that there was an 'invasion' or that the world was coming to an end."[26] The most disheartening thing for the policemen was that as they sped to catch one automobile, four others would pass at even faster speeds. The panic was spreading lightning fast. In New York, a young man who had left a party after it broke up in a panic over the broadcast later wrote, "I drove like crazy up Sixth Avenue. I don't know how fast—fifty, maybe sixty miles an hour. The traffic cops at the street crossings just stared at us; they couldn't believe their eyes, whizzing right past them, going through red lights. I didn't care if I got a ticket. It was all over anyway. Funny thing, none of the cops chased us. I guess they were too flabbergasted. My apartment was on the way, so I stopped just long enough to rush in and shout up to my father that the Martians had landed, we were all going to be killed, and I was taking my girl home. When I got to her place, her parents were waiting for us. My father had called them. Told them to hold me there until he could send a doctor as I'd gone out of my mind."[27]

Police officers in the local stations also had to handle an onslaught of calls.

"There were puzzled policemen in station houses all over the country as demands came over the telephone for gas masks and where were the safest places to hide from the enemy. The second most puzzled group was the switchboard operators as the telephones went wild and people began to rave deliriously. Next came the clergy; priests were startled by the rush to get confessions, and Protestant ministers were astonished at the interruption of their sermons by demands for prayers to avert the impending doom of the world."[28] A Midwesterner, Joseph Hendley, later said after he heard the broadcast, "That Halloween boo sure had our family on its knees before the program was half over. God knows we prayed to him last Sunday."[29] The *New York Times* reported the service at the First Baptist Church of Caldwell, New Jersey, "was interrupted by the arrival of a terrified parishioner with the fearful news that a meteor had fallen, showering death and destruction. Led by their pastor, Reverend Thomas, the congregants all prayed for deliverance."[30] The *Washington Post* described a similar scenario where Lolly Mackenzie Dey remembers she was playing the piano at the Plainsboro Presbyterian Church when "someone, I think it was a fella, came barging in and shouting, 'Martians have just landed at Grovers Mill!' So, I stopped playing the piano and I just bowed my head and I prayed to the Lord."[31]

The Paultzes knew none of this, though, as they ran eight blocks, made it to Penn Station, waited on the station platform, and then got on the train and sat with "nothing to do but sit tense—white-faced and wait."[32] They didn't know about John Wilkens, who had been gassed in World War I, and when his daughter called from William and Mary College in Virginia, convinced she was going to be gassed, he lost no time in removing the doors from his 1935 Studebaker and driving to the college. There, he loaded in as many girls as he could fit. "I packed them in like sardines and wrapped a rope around the car so they wouldn't fall out and even lashed a few to the hood."[33] He then drove one hundred miles home down the highway with girls crying inside and outside the car. The Paultzes might have found humor in the story reported in the *Newark Evening News* about the man who had asked his girlfriend to marry him but had been turned down several times. Then he convinced her it was the end of the world and what did it matter. She said yes.

The train finally left the station and the Paultzes wondered how others could be so calm. Surely, they had not been listening to the radio. Estelle was just glad they were "ahead of the panic-stricken mob that was sure to follow as soon as they heard."[34] When the train stopped in the countryside of Connecticut, they were sure the Martians had stopped them. John began to tell people on the train about the murdering Martians. College students relayed the information, and a slow panic spread through the train car. Someone asked a conductor why they had stopped, and word came back that a woman had fallen ill and had to be taken off in an ambulance. "The people began to wonder," Estelle continued in her letter. "Half fearing that what we were saying might be true."[35] The fear wasn't restricted to adults. Henry Sears was thirteen and working on his homework with the radio on. His mother ran a tavern called the Green Gables Inn, and Henry and his mother lived upstairs over the bar. When he heard the broadcast, his homework became a distant memory, and he went downstairs to the bar. Grovers Mill was a scant eight miles away, and Henry announced to his mother and the customers that Martians were invading. After he plugged in the radio and everyone in the bar heard the broadcast, "all the men leaped up and announced their intentions to go and fight the aliens." Grabbing his gun, Henry headed after them, the frantic words of his mother ringing in his ears: "Henry, you're not going."[36]

Meanwhile, the train the Paultzes were on had begun to move again. Someone shouted out the name Orson Welles, and Estelle turned. She had seen his theater productions, *Voodoo Macbeth* and *The Cradle Will Rock*. He put on literary classics for *Mercury Theatre on the Air* on CBS. Estelle knew he "was the one man capable of imagining and bringing to vivid life the kind of thing we had heard."[37] The radio back in the Paultzes' abandoned apartment droned on and then went to the break: "You are listening to a CBS presentation of Orson Welles and the *Mercury Theatre on the Air* in an original dramatization of *War of the Worlds* by H. G. Wells."[38] No one heard it, and no one cared. The bomb had exploded, and there was only the fallout now. A voice shouted somewhere in the train car above the din, voicing the question now gripping the nation. . . .

"*Who is Orson Welles?*"[39]

Something Deathless and Dangerous

1937

ORSON WELLES RODE IN THE FRONT OF THE AMBULANCE, WEAVING through the traffic of downtown Manhattan with the bell blaring. He was amazed at how the cars moved out of the way as he smoked a cigarette with the wind blowing back his hair. He smoked up to sixty cigarettes a day, and then he smoked cigars. Tobacco was his drug the way food was his drug, as were booze and then amphetamines. But he had to have food always. Prodigious meals of steak and potatoes; lobster and caviar; fat, juicy corned beef sandwiches from his favorite deli; cheesecake, chocolate cake, milkshakes, sundaes, and gallons of coffee. It was the fuel he needed to direct his plays and orchestrate his radio shows. Many times, he picked hotels for their room service. He always ate like a growing boy; he was a growing boy at age twenty-two. He grew into Orson Welles the radio personality, director of hit plays, and *Mercury Theatre on the Air* content creator. He was evolving at a frantic crisis-driven pace, where he was best with his back against the wall, only minutes before he went on live radio. It was the way he worked. The more chaos, the better. Out of that chaos came vision and, amazingly, even genius.

But he was running late, even with the ambulance he used to get from studio to studio, reading scripts for the first time minutes before he went on, improvising on air and then running to his show, *The Shadow*, at CBS, where he would wolf down a steak while making edits on a script he often had just read for the first time, frequently still making edits when the light flicked on. Then he was live, *live*, pitch-perfect once again. He was that perfectly modulated voice booming out across the land to people huddled by their radios who had no idea a twenty-two-year-old was behind the voice of *The Shadow.*

It was where he lived, really—on live radio. The organ would play as the deep, strange voice of Orson Welles, now the sinister voice of the Shadow, seeped out into the dusky living rooms from oversized radios all over America. In the dull yellow dials of radios in living rooms, Orson masqueraded as proper Lamont Cranston but then became a man never seen who possessed the ability to cloud the minds of others to make himself invisible. The Shadow *was* Orson Welles. It was what he did so well, making the rube from Kenosha, Wisconsin, disappear and replacing him with the dynamic man capable of playing any role, from a baby to a superhero who would never appear. *Who knows what lurks in the hearts of men? Only the Shadow knows.* Only Orson Welles knew . . . and he used it to his advantage every time.

After *The Shadow* was done, Orson would run out of the studio and back into the ambulance to make it to another studio to do a segment of his play for a show, *March of Time*, produced by *Time* magazine in 1931. The show had become the most popular news documentary show on the air. Tens of millions of people tuned in every Friday night, and the newsreels of the shows went out to theaters with the stentorian voice Orson would eventually use over and over in radio programs and later *Citizen Kane*. But the format of *March of Time* was the epiphanic moment for Orson.

"The radio show . . . was not that of normal news broadcasting but of *news acting*. Dramatic recreation touched upon the most significant and often hair-raising stories of the day. Such events as the eruption of Mt. Vesuvius and the assassination of Huey Long were performed by professional actors and accompanied by convincing sound effects and a full symphony orchestra. Originally, the shows were given free to radio stations across the country in exchange for publicity for *Time* magazine."[1]

Re-creation of live news is what *March of Time* did best. Technology had not caught up to live reporting yet, so *March of Time* reproduced the news with sound effects and actors. The serendipitous moment for

Orson Welles was when he was given a script for an excerpt of the stage play *Panic* in which he had starred. It was to be included in one of the segments of *March of Time*. But also on his script was a report on the Dionne quintuplets with a re-creation of a hospital scene in which "the words 'baby jabber' were crossed out on the script. *The March of Time* had hundreds of doubles, 'D-men' who could affect several accents, dialects, or personalities, but the baby voices expert was unavailable that night. Orson saw the deleted words of baby jabber. 'I can do baby voices,' he told the director, and after a short audition of gurgles, coos, and infant talk, he was hired."[2] Soon he became a regular on the most popular news show in America.

After the baby voiceover with "the acoustic joke of the booming cascading Orson transforming his voice and scaling himself down . . . into the coos and cries of five infants with his wife Virginia howling in the CBS control room,"[3] he was out again for the rehearsal for his play, *Danton's Death*. Actors jumped up as he strode into the theater and began barking orders about lighting direction, dialogue lines, shredding the script and putting it back together, having the set disassembled for the tenth time and then put back together again, and complaining about the music, the lead, the lighting, the whole play, throwing his hands up and saying it was all terrible and leaving the actors with their mouths open. He was once again in the ambulance that thundered across midtown to a projection studio where a writer waited in the darkness, silently brooding, slightly drunk, waiting for a man sixteen years his junior. He immediately disliked the cherub-faced, gangly man who came in with the rumpled hair and suit. The writer looked on as Welles was handed the script, which he immediately started to take apart as the projectionist rolled the film of the Spanish Civil War.

Welles read lines, shook his head, and said the dialogue was pompous and complicated. He saw it as trite, turning to the projectionist and complaining that the script read, "Here are the faces of men close to death."[4] Like any great dramatist, he found the line unnecessary when it was to be read "at a moment when one saw faces on the screen that were so much more eloquent."[5] Welles said he couldn't read something *this bad* when he heard a growl in the darkness, and a giant bearded man emerged with flashing eyes. "Hemingway was drinking a bottle of whiskey and sized up the young actor, annoyed that Orson was late and even more annoyed that he had dared to criticize his prose. Welles tried to reason with Hemingway. 'Mr. Hemingway, it would be better if one saw the faces all alone, without commentary.' Ernest Hemingway stared at the twenty-two-year-old. 'You effeminate boys of the theatre,' he shouted. 'What do you know about real war?'"[6]

Welles didn't skip a beat. He put one hand behind his head and began to swish his hips and bat his eyes. "Oh Mr. Hemingway you think because you're so big and strong and have hair on your chest that you can bully me!"[7] Welles continued swishing his hips, coming closer to Hemingway with the projector rolling on with soldiers fighting in the background on the screen. It was Hemingway's *The Spanish Earth*, his documentary to show the fight against fascism and promote the nationalist cause in the hope the United States would come to their aid. Hemingway had gone over to Spain, where he had an affair with Margaret Gellhorn (whom he was teeing up to be the third Mrs. Hemingway) while shooting at the fascists, steaming up his glasses in the torrential heat, interviewing soldiers, and exposing himself to danger along the way. He had brought back his film, but he needed a voiceover; someone had suggested Orson Welles, and Hemingway had hesitatingly agreed to the audition.

Hemingway did what the world expected of him. Orson later wrote, "That enraged him, and he picked up a chair, and I picked up another, and right there in front of the images of the Spanish Civil War as they marched across the screen, we had a terrible scuffle. It was marvelous, two guys like us in front of these images representing people in the act of struggling and dying."[8] Hemingway was a proficient boxer, and it is amazing he didn't knock Welles out cold, but according to Hemingway, he got the best of it, and according to Welles, he got the best of it. Still, the two men grappled and bear-hugged and cursed and grunted and groaned until the lights came up, and they faced each other. "We ended by toasting each other over a bottle of whiskey."[9] But that was Welles's summation years later. Hemingway had them sharing some whiskey, and then they parted as friends, but neither man liked the other, and they never saw each other again socially. Biographer Andrew Gear summed up their relationship by saying, "It was more of a slightly rivalrous, untrusting association. My reading is that Welles was being a little more generous. I've read from other sources that Hemingway didn't like him at all and was wary of him."[10]

Orson Welles left in his ambulance, and Hemingway decided to do the voiceover himself, with his nasally midwestern twang sounding more like a man selling Bibles door-to-door than a narrator. Orson would have been a better pick, but Hemingway wasn't about to give oxygen to an upstart named Orson Welles.

Back in the ambulance heading for another studio, Orson reminded himself to call his wife Virginia because he was in real danger of missing the birth of his daughter. The problem was that domesticity was not in Welles and never would be. Now he was that twenty-two-year-old man jumping into the ambulance, weaving across town to his next play, radio show, and audition. John Houseman, Welles's co-producer on *War of the Worlds*, would later write that "he was a restlessly constructive fellow who just won't leave the stage where he found it. I am afraid he is a genius but mighty good company nonetheless."[11]

Orson amazingly did make it to the birth of his daughter, and then he was off again. Hemingway was right about one thing: you could not be sure of Welles about anything. All his life there would be a question regarding his sexuality, with men coming on to him beginning at a very early age. Welles also had many affairs, including one with ballerina Vera Zorina, who was bedazzled. They dined at 21 in New York, and later Vera said she "never enjoyed anything more. If I never see him again, I shall always remember it. How we talked and understood each other. He is wonderful, and for the first time since Léonide Massine, I felt my heart pounding and hands trembling."[12] Tall, dark, and handsome with an ever-present cigarette and able to throw off a bender with some morning coffee and dive into a play or a radio script . . . everyone wanted to be around the young Mozart.

Elia Kazan, who worked with Welles on *The Shadow*, later wrote, "I remember Welles arriving for rehearsal one morning; he'd been up allnight carousing but looked little worse for it and was full of continuing excitement. A valet-secretary met him on the side of the stage with a small valise containing fresh linen and the toilet articles he needed. The rehearsal was never interrupted. Orson had unflagging energy and recuperative powers at that time, and he soon looked as good as new. . . . Seldom have I seen a man so abundantly talented or one with a greater zest for life."[13]

There was no script to his life, and he brought that chaos to his plays and later his broadcasts. Producer John Houseman immediately saw his odd way of working. "Orson Welles was a prodigious, if somewhat erratic, worker." Houseman was nothing if not a discoverer of talent. Welles was the spark in the coal mine of Houseman's stalled career that would eventually lead to the *War of the Worlds*, at which time the kinetic destructive force would be on full display for the world to see. But even Houseman had no idea of the hurt that powered Welles. It was played out on the stage many times. A reviewer for the *New York Post*, John Mason Brown, nailed it in writing about a Mercury Theatre production with Welles on stage: "The astonishing all impressive virtue of Mr. Welles' production is that magnificent as it is in the theatre, it is far larger than its medium. Something deathless and dangerous in the world sweeps past you down the darkened aisles of the Mercury Theatre and takes possession of the proud, gaunt stage. It is something fearful and turbulent."[14]

What Brown saw glimmering in the brooding man was something far more profound than talent—a man born out of time and ultimately alone, leaving only the burning sled of his life, Rosebud, as a talisman.

3

Rosebud

1915

THAT SCENE. THE SLED BEING THROWN INTO THE FURNACE. BY THE END of *Citizen Kane*, moviegoers knew no more than at the beginning of the film when the question was posed: What was the meaning of Charles Foster Kane's last word, *Rosebud?* The movie was a famous flop. There are no real characters to root for—no real love story. You don't even see the narrator's face. And in the movie, that dark, groundbreaking, understated, overstated, noir menagerie of light and sound, reporters fan out searching for the secret of that last word. *Rosebud.* Undoubtedly, people in 1941 left the theater scratching their heads. Some caught it. Most didn't. Let's run the film backward to the beginning—all the way back. We see George Orson Welles playing in the snow. We don't know it is him. We see a boy. He was born on May 6, 1915, a ten-pound baby howling from a long delivery in Kenosha, Wisconsin, a small town forty miles north of Chicago.

The name George doesn't stick. His father, Richard Welles, was an alcoholic and part-time inventor who earned his keep as founder, treasurer, and general secretary of the Badger Brass Manufacturing Company, a bicycle lamp manufacturer, when he wasn't visiting the fleshpots of Chicago. He didn't like the name George, saying, "Every Pullman porter in the country was named George,"[1] so the boy with the too-large feet, the cherubic cheeks, the broad forehead, the strangely adult Asian eyes, and the even more strangely adult voice (a baritone at ten) became

Orson. He was named after a discreet gay couple, George and Orson, by his mother, Beatrice, the musician, suffragette, teacher, artist, and activist.

So, let's start the film there. George (known as Charles in the movie) is out in the snow, and his mother (played by Agnes Moorehead) is staring at him. She calls for him, "Charles . . . *Charles!*" Charles (Orson) reluctantly abandons his sled and goes inside, where his life changes forever.

Orson, who as a boy could recite great reams of poetry to adults, had an older brother, Richard, who, though recognized today as possibly autistic, was institutionalized. When Orson arrived in this world, he was the light to Richard's darkness. His mother reveled in his intellect, strange ability to recite facts, and epicurean delight with food. Orson later told a family friend and interloper in the Welles marriage, Dr. Bernstein, at age two that "the desire to take medicine is one of the greatest features which distinguishes men from animals."[2] Orson was named a genius early on. Dr. Bernstein became fascinated with the boy, and the lothario doctor, with one wife already under his belt and a history of having to leave Chicago after nearly beating a man to death, inserted himself into the precarious marriage of Beatrice and Richard Welles. A ménage à trois developed that is probably one of the strangest elements in the backstory of Orson Welles. In *Citizen Kane,* the character to whom the doctor lent his name is described as "an undersized Jew" in the words of the script, "spry with remarkably intense eyes."[3]

Richard Welles, the dreamy, alcoholic, part-time inventor who created a dishwasher that smashed dishes, a steam-powered plane that crashed, and a patented automobile jack, received $100,000 at the age of forty-six from the sale of the Badger Brass Company. After that, he declined to work anymore, becoming a fixture on the wallpaper of young Orson, who would lose both his parents by age sixteen. Richard died in the Bismarck Hotel in Chicago in 1930 from alcoholism. Beatrice died from stomach cancer in 1924. Orson's mother was the musician who encouraged Orson to live a life in the arts. She knew she had a prodigy after her first-born, Richard, stuttered; stared with dull, unimaginative eyes; and produced no spark intellectually. Orson later in life would view his parents through rose-colored glasses, responding to his portrayal of them in movies by saying, "My mother and father were both more remarkable than any story of mine can make them."[4]

Young Orson would often conduct imaginary orchestras for his mother, standing on a chair before a make-believe group of musicians. Richard would end up institutionalized for ten years with a suspected diagnosis of schizophrenia. The boy in *Citizen Kane* is treated as an only child, running in from the snow, and in real life, Orson rarely mentions Richard and will be treated as an only child who could play music, act, and move mountains with his encyclopedic Shakespeare recitation in that strangely deep voice. If he wasn't so impressive—this flat-footed boy with the strangely adult visage, a fat head, and long slender hands—he might have been considered odd.

Dr. Bernstein had steadily ingratiated himself with Orson's mother, Beatrice, while her husband Richard was traveling, drinking, and having affairs. When the Welles family moved to Chicago, Dr. Bernstein went with them. In *Citizen Kane*, a guardian, Mr. Thatcher, is waiting for Charles (Orson) to come in from the snow and take him away from his happy home. The boy's mother is staring out the window at the camera, her heart breaking. In real life, Orson's mother leaves him shortly after his tenth birthday after she tells him to blow out the candles and make a wish. Welles blew out the candles but never made a wish, and his mother died four days later. All his life, Orson Welles blamed himself for his mother's death because he hadn't made that wish.

In the movie, Charles is being told he is leaving the family home as his father stands ineffectually in the background. The boy cries that he doesn't want to leave. This scene was dredged up from Orson's soul. In reality, Orson had joined Dr. Bernstein at his home in Highland Park in 1930 after his father was found dead in the Bismarck Hotel. Bernstein treated him like a young Mozart, having Orson perform at parties, delighting adults with his poetry, deep voice, and strangely adult face. Men come on to him. He was just too pretty, too magnetic. "From my earliest childhood, I was the Lillie Langtry of the older homosexual set. Everybody wanted me," he later told an interviewer. He claimed to be demure by changing the subject or saying he felt ill whenever men came on to him. "I was like an eternal virgin."[5]

At this point in his life, Orson had had no formal schooling and was taken to Dr. Mueller in Madison, Wisconsin, for an evaluation. He was told he had "a profound disassociation of ideas" and that he was a genius. Dr. Mueller then made the boy "the object of homosexual advances."[6] Orson escaped out a window, or so he said. This was "nothing new to Orson who, having been frightened and ashamed the first few times it happened, soon knew just what to say when the bohemians who frequented his mother's salon made their move."[7] He went to see Mueller more than once, and the final time was when he climbed out the window to escape, ran to the train station, caught a train to Chicago, and ended up on Dr. Bernstein's doorstep.

The kids in the Bernstein neighborhood thought Orson odd, but he ended up in the Todd School for gifted children in Woodstock, Illinois. An artsy midwestern town forty miles west of Chicago, Woodstock had its own town square and theater and was a cultural oasis among the cornfields. The Todd School was run by a progressive, Roger (Skipper) Hill, who believed practical experience in life trumped all else. The school was set on a ten-acre campus. Opened in 1848 as Todd Seminary, the school advertised that it was "Near enough to Chicago to be easy access for parents desiring to place their boys with us from any part of the country . . . at the same time it is far enough from the city to be free from the interruptions of too frequent comings and goings, which are very demoralizing to a school of this kind." The school had a "gymnasium with a bowling alley; a music cottage; a library; a horse stable and riding track."[8] Todd boys wore a suit and tie, and the assembly hall was used for daily chapel services. Still, the atmosphere was more homelike, with an emphasis on nature. The curriculum covered first to tenth grade, by which time graduates were ready for college. The twelve years required by traditional high schools were often not the case at private schools. Orson's brother Richard had attended earlier, to dismal results, and stayed only a few years.

Roger Hill believed that young people were "created creators" and, in that vein, offered students a working radio station, a theater with a tour bus to take productions on the road, a motion picture theater, and access to a nearby airport. In 1938, the *New Yorker* described Todd as "a preparatory school of considerable antiquity, now run on severely progressive lines. The present headmaster, Roger Hill, a slim, white-haired, tweed-bearing man who looks as if he had been cast for his role by a motion picture director, has never let the traditional preparatory school curriculum stand in the way of creative work."[9] Orson and Dr. Bernstein toured the school and walked around the grounds, and Orson was not impressed until they reached the theater and assembly hall. "OK, this will do," Orson said. "This will do."[10]

He took the Binet-Simon Intelligence Scale to measure his intellectual development when he arrived. The test results put his IQ at 185. A note in the margin read, "140 is considered genius level."[11] Welles himself would promote this idea and sometimes play it down. "A genius," Welles told the *New York Post* after his Mercury Theatre production of *Julius Caesar*. "Perhaps. I'm either the genius they say I am or the world's godawfully ham. It's a fifty-fifty split."[12]

His first roommate, John C. Dexter, though, saw Orson as unique, writing, "We all recognized immediately that Orson was someone very different. Welles arrived with several suitcases and a large steamer trunk full of makeup, wigs, capes, magic equipment, candles, flashlights, and assorted stage wear. I was informed before he unpacked that he had been born in it, on stage. He inquired about my knowledge of the theatre, which was nil, and proceeded to relate what a wonderful medium it was. Switching the lights off, he retired into the bathroom, reappearing with a candle, hunchbacked and gruesomely made up. 'Who am I?' he demanded."[13]

Orson flourished under the tutelage of headmaster Roger Hill and his wife, Hortense. The Todd School was the only place Orson could call home throughout his life. He would never own a home and considered the rural midwestern town of Woodstock the closest he would ever have. The Hills became his unofficial family and saw his talent right away. Orson took to the theater and wowed the faculty. He assembled musicals and played in *Dr. Faustus, Everyman, Dr. Jekyll and Mr. Hyde, Richard III, Androcles,* and *Julius Caesar*. During this time, Ashton Stevens, a leading drama critic for the *Chicago American*, read an article about Orson Welles's performance in *Julius Caesar*, in which he played Cassius and

Antony and was accused of being an adult. In his article, Stevens makes an eerily prescient prediction.

"Given as good an education as will adhere to him at a good college, young and not ill-looking, Orson Welles is as likely as not to become my favorite actor. True, it will be four or five years before he has attained his majority and a degree, and I have yet to see him act. But I like the way he handles a difficult situation . . . I am going to put a clipping of this paragraph in my betting book. If Orson is not at least a leading man by the time it has yellowed; I'll never a make another prophecy."[14]

Before he died, Orson's father would appear drunkenly at his son's plays in the early years at Todd. "Orson used to hide from him when he did, saying he hated him. His drunkenness was impossible to ignore, an unbearable embarrassment in front of his fellow students . . . coming unannounced to a performance of *Wings over Europe*, he left before the end of the play because, as Welles later told biographer Barbara Leaming, 'he didn't want to admit he was interested in my acting career or some damn thing.'"[15] On a trip to the Orient, Richard Welles demanded that young Orson make sure he wasn't buried under the ground and that he was cremated or buried at sea. Orson realized he was on his own. "I was in my childhood determined to cure myself of childhood, a condition I conceived to be a pestilential handicap."[16] By 1930, he was cured, but, like the guilt Welles felt over his mother's death, the guilt he felt over his father's death stayed with him. He had chosen his mother over his father and had ignored the drunken man. He then chose Dr. Bernstein and Roger Hill and didn't see his father for the last six months of his life and heard of his death while at Todd.

Orson's time at the Todd School was invaluable to his development. His first radio encounter was at Todd, performing an adaptation of *Sherlock Holmes*. But Orson had no intention of going to college after the Todd School, where he had excelled in the theater and managed to get a few teachers fired for sexual advances. Orson had grown to his full height of six feet and lost all his childish, rotund qualities. He was a strapping young man with dark penetrating eyes, cheekbones, a full head of hair, and his stunning God-given voice. During this time, he slept over at a friend's house and shared a bed with his friend's father. When the man tried to seduce him in the middle of the night, Orson was shocked and fled the house.

At sixteen, he advertised himself in *Billboard* magazine as an actor:

ORSON WELLES—Stock, Characters, Heavies, Juveniles or as cast. Also, specialties, chalk talk, or can handle the stage. Young, excellent appearance, quick, sure study. Lots of pep, experience, and ability. Close in Chicago early in June and want a place in the good stock company for the remainder of the season. Salary is according to the late date of opening and business conditions. Photo on request. Address ORSON WELLES c/o H.L. Powers, Illinois Theatre, 65 E Jackson Blvd, Chicago, IL.[17]

There were no takers, and Orson put a second, more desperate notice in the paper:

Orson Welles is willing to invest a moderate amount of cash and own services as Heavy Character and Juvenile in good summer stock or repertory proposition. Reply to Orson Welles, Dramatic Coach, Todd Academy, Woodstock, Illinois.[18]

No one responded, and his guardian, Dr. Bernstein, pushed Orson hard to attend college. The issue arose with "three days of particularly domestic warfare . . . things went from bad to worse. Alternately, I defended and offended. My head remained bloody but unbowed, and my nose, thanks to the thoughtful blooming of some neighboring clover, began to sniffle hay-feverishly. The household was illusioned into the realization that something had to be done. . . . It was then that Dadda [Bernstein] arrived at a momentous decision and chose the lesser of two great evils in the spirit of true martyrdom. Going abroad alone is not quite as unthinkable as joining the theatre . . . and so . . . I was whisked out of the fire into the frying pan."[19]

Dr. Bernstein, who would later be the basis for the character of Mr. Bernstein in *Citizen Kane* in the role of lackey, assistant, and employee, was probably more the way Orson regarded his guardian in real life. Bernstein had taken over the distribution of Orson's inheritance, and financial duplicity leaked out in many later interviews. Orson would be heading for Ireland alone at the age of sixteen, financed by money inherited from his father and administered by Bernstein. And now we are back in the film, and it is a foregone conclusion that the boy has been given to Mr. Thatcher. A deal has been struck as Charles (Orson) stares out the open window of the cabin on the Colorado prairie with the wind howling in the background. He will never see his mother again. She might as well have died. We are to believe the deal that has been struck will make the boy and his parents wealthy, but he must leave his home. His mother, facing the camera, stoic and pained, says, "I've got his trunk all packed. I've had it packed for a week now."[20] The boy has been sold. Abandoned. He looks back at his family home from the black carriage taking him away from all that he has known. All that is left is his destiny as his sled is slowly covered with snow, obscuring the one clue to Charles Foster Kane. The secret Orson Welles carries, headed for Ireland all alone at sixteen.

Orson arrived in Ireland in August 1931. The wandering man-child painted landscapes, traveled in a donkey cart, and then just traveled, sending letters to Bernstein pleading for more money. "I am in desperate need of money!!! Unless financial aid awaits me in Dublin, I shall never be able to leave the city alive but will die a swift and painful death by starvation!"[21] Histrionics aside, Bernstein sent the money to the wandering scribe, who ended up outside the Gate Theatre in Dublin, where he knocked on the door and demanded an audition. Run by Hilton Edwards and Micheál MacLiammoir, the Gate was an established theater in Dublin, and when young Welles knocked on the door, Edwards answered and then went to find MacLiammoir, who later wrote, "Hilton walked into the scene dock one day and said, 'Somebody strange has arrived from America, come and see what you think of it.'

"'What,' I asked, 'is it?'

"'Tall, young, fat. Says he's been with the Guild Theater in New York. Don't believe a word of it, but he's interesting. I want to give him an audition.'"[22]

The two men went to the street, and MacLiammoir later wrote his impression of the sixteen-year-old who had been bumming around

Ireland painting landscapes: "A very tall young man with a chubby face, full, powerful lips, and disconcerting Chinese eyes. His hands were enormous and very beautifully shaped, like so many American hands; they were colored like champagne and moved with a sort of controlled abandon never seen in a European. The voice, with its brazen transatlantic sonority, was already that of a preacher, a leader, a man of power; it bloomed and boomed its way through the dusty air of the scene dock as though it would crash down the little Georgian walls and rip up the floor; he moved in a leisurely manner from foot to foot and surveyed us with magnificent patience as though here was our chance to do something beautiful at last—yes, sir—and were we going to take it?"[23]

Orson smoked a cigar and showed the two men American notices of his acting and got to the task at hand: lying. Why, of course, he was eighteen. While traveling Ireland he had become bored and was between engagements, and he would read for them that day as the archduke in Lion Feuchtwanger's *Jew Süss*, a part they were looking to cast, of course. The rendition of the audition by Orson for the two theater owners, as later written by MacLiammoir, is almost comedic.

> "Is this all the light you can give me?" he said in a voice like a regretful oboe. We hadn't given him any at all yet, so that was settled, and he began. It was an astonishing performance, wrong from beginning to end, but with all the qualities of fine acting tearing through a chaos of experience. His diction was practically perfect; his personality, in spite of his fantastic circus antics, was real and varied; his sense of passion, of evil, of drunkenness, of tyranny, of a sort of demonic authority was arresting; a preposterous energy pulsated through everything he did. One wanted to bellow with laughter, yet the laughter died on one's lips. One wanted to say, "Now, really, you know," but something stopped the words from coming. And that was because he was real to himself because it was something more to him than a show, more than the merely inflated exhibitionism one might have suspected from his previous talk, something much more.[24]

Later, they said he was awful as the archduke but magnificent as Orson Welles. They saw what adults saw in the boy: some preposterous mix of talent and brash ambition wrapped in a man masquerading as a boy masquerading as a man with a once-in-a-generation voice and pulling it all off amazingly. Afterward, Orson met Hilton Edwards in the theater.

"Terrible, wasn't it?" Orson said.

"Yes, bloody awful," Hilton replied. "But you can play the part. That is if you make me a promise. Don't obey me blindly, but listen to me. More importantly, listen to yourself. I can help show you how to play this part, but you must see and hear what's good about yourself and what's lousy."[25]

Then we are back in the film, and Orson is an adult and telling his benefactor, Mr. Thatcher, that he wants to run a newspaper, much to Thatcher's chagrin. In real life, he tells his guardian, Dr. Bernstein, that he is now a real actor in the theater and gives Bernstein a different version of Hilton Edwards's speech. It is much more laudatory, a real Orson Welles speech.

> You're already at the point a matinee idol arrives at when he's got on in years and people are writing plays around his little tricks and capers. But that won't do here. We have nobody to write nonsense for you to show off in. You have a gorgeous stage voice and a stage presence that is one in a million, and you're the first overactor I've seen in eons, but you couldn't come in and say "Milford, the carriage awaits," as well as Art our electrician . . . you couldn't say "How do you do?" behind the footlights like a human being. You handle your voice like a singer and there isn't a note of sincerity in it.[26]

There were supposedly two auditions, so maybe this speech was given after the second audition. Or maybe Orson Welles just made it all up. Either way, he had the part. Then they gave him some money and a place to stay and told him to be ready by October 13 to play the archduke. Years later, he would tell director Peter Bogdanovich, "I said I was a star already. I lied like a maniac . . . I was from America and in Ireland. I informed the owners of the Gate Theatre that I was the same Welles they must have read about."[27] Even though the theater owners saw right through the sixteen-year-old, Orson Welles had learned a valuable lesson: deception could push you a lot further than truth. But, of course, he knew this fact from the day he was born. It is what any great actor knows, and seven years later he would take it to its logical conclusion on Halloween eve. In the movie, Charles Kane writes up a series of principles, a manifesto he would use to guide his newspapers. Right away, on questioning by Mr. Bernstein, he replies, "You don't expect me to keep to any of those promises, now do you?"[28]

4

Something Dark and Brutal

1931

ORSON WAS SWEATING. HE WAS SIXTEEN AND ONSTAGE ON THE OPENING night of the Gate Theatre production of *Jew Süss*. The audience had just heckled him after an agonizing love scene in which he fell apart in embarrassment. As archduke, he was now delivering the line "A bride fit for Solomon! And Solomon had a thousand wives, didn't he?" And then that voice came sailing out of the black pit for the audience. "That's a black Protestant lie!"[1] It doesn't take much to knock off the bluff of the young man who had lied his way into one of the leading theaters in Dublin. Orson choked. His mind went blank. His throat was tight. It was a jumbling of the lines, and the character went away; Orson was naked on stage. He was dripping with perspiration, rivulets of sweat pouring down his forehead. The question can then be asked: Why had the two theater owners risked everything with this unknown American boy who had crashed into their orbit with no more credentials than the absurdly large cigar he had been smoking?

Let's leave Orson choking on the stage and back up. In his book *Wealth*, Andrew Carnegie figured the reason for his success was not one of hard work but basically being in the right place at the right time. The day Orson had chosen to barnstorm the Gate Theatre, the owner, play-wright, and director, Micheál MacLiammoir, needed someone to play the archduke in his upcoming play *Jew Süss*. He had been frustrated in his search and later wrote that "everywhere in Dublin among the younger members of the profession, among the students, the amateurs, the boys, and girls who want to go on the stage, one found the same complacent apathy, the same cheerful and careless approach, the same lack of passion."[2]

Now, enter this absurd American boy smoking a cigar outside his theater. To MacLiammoir, he was an answer to a prayer. The Gate Theatre was still only three years old and not beyond an experiment with two gay men at the helm. Rehearsals with Orson did not go well. MacLiammoir and Hilton Edwards often stared at each other with wagging heads, thinking, "This sort of thing will never do."[3] Still, they plowed on. The duke played a pivotal role, and the two owners kept Orson busy from dawn to dusk in the press room, the paint shop, and the rehearsal room. There was no going back, and on October 10, 1931, the play was announced, and Orson was introduced.

"A newcomer to the large cast will be Orson Welles, who served his apprenticeship to the Goodman Memorial Theatre in Chicago under the direction of Whiteford Kane, formerly of Ulster Literary Theatre."[4] Lie upon lie—Welles had never been in a production at the Goodman Theatre, and he certainly was never under the direction of Whiteford Kane, but the two owners had to give themselves some cover. In a letter to the head of the Todd School, Roger Hill, Orson wrote, "Tonight is the first dress rehearsal, and the day after tomorrow night, I make my professional debut (ahem) in a foreign country and the most accent-conscious city on the globe!"[5]

And now we are back to opening night. The Gate, which holds four hundred people, was packed. The show was a London hit, never seen in Dublin. Orson later claimed he had never known stage fright until that night, and he entered the stage "in a bliss of ignorance like a baby on a trapeze."[6]

Things moved along until the love scene with Betty Chancellor as Naomi. She later wrote that "his extraordinarily mature acting fell apart. He was then obviously embarrassed and unsure, and he tried to hide this by gripping me with such violence that I nearly lost my life but certainly not my virtue."[7] Welles seemed to find his footing, but in the second act he dropped his line "A bride fit for Solomon. He had a thousand wives, did he not?" And then came the heckling reply: "That's a black Protestant lie!"[8] And Orson lost all the bravado that got him on the stage in the first place. He was in that awful free fall every actor or public speaker knows in which a strange panic constricts thought and paralysis sets in. But Orson found his line—almost. The line should have been "Ring all the bells and fire the cannon," but the new actor in the Gate Theatre mangled it. Orson boomed out, "Ring the cannon and fire all the bells!"[9]

The silence of the theater constricted him further, as the gaffe settled on the audience. He was supposed to then perform the archduke's death by slumping onto his throne, but Welles instinctually reached for what would create his career and launch him to the stars. *Shock.* Orson flipped backward down a flight of stairs. The blunder was gone. The audience had been taken from one moment to the next, leaving them in awe of the newcomer to the theater. When the curtain call ended, Orson was anointed, and Micheál MacLiammoir recorded the moment in minute detail.

"Orson bows slowly, sedately, that they should realize him like this merits a bow, so slow and sedate the head goes down and quickly up again. . . . The people are still there, still applauding, more and more and more and back goes the big head and the laugh breaks out like fire in a jungle . . . it goes on and on. . . . Take that curtain up again . . . then the whole house again."[10]

His fellow actors were ignored. All eyes were on Orson Welles, who would later write Hortense Hill at the Todd School, "I took six curtain calls alone with the gallery and pit shouting and stamping and calling my name. This sounds like an appalling boast, and so it is."[11] Here, we are reminded that Orson Welles had no parents except for a dubious guardian in Dr. Bernstein. He had no one to tell of his triumphs but Roger and Hortense Hill. Orson wanted the Hills to be his guardians, not Dr. Bernstein, but they had turned him down. Still, they were as close to family as he would ever get. He had no mother to champion him, no father to encourage him. He was just a sixteen-year-old in a foreign country going through life on sheer audacity. His only biological family was his institutionalized brother. The world was really his only family now, and he had to be loved.

The notices pushed Orson Welles's ego to the sky. The *Dublin Opinion* "reported that 'the young American actor received nothing short of a personal triumph.' The *New York Times* correspondent in Dublin wrote, 'The Duke is played by a young American actor,18 years old, whose performance is astonishingly fine . . . Welles, who had appeared occasionally at the Goodman Theatre in small parts with the Theater Guild in New York.'"[12] Lies mixed in with laudatory praise. From deception comes something higher, something good. The truth is not enough. There must be more. Deception is a fine art; its greatest practitioner was just starting. He was launched, but the theater owners did not put him in the lead. He was the Ghost and Fortinbras in *Hamlet* and the Grand Vizier in *Magi*. He was a star in the theater community of Dublin, went to parties, and found himself the center of attention.

Attention became his drug for life. He was known as "Young Welles" around Dublin and became famous in that quicksilver way that spread through the community. But MacLiammoir saw the emptiness, if not cruelty, in Welles's pursuit of that fame. "'When the demon of showmanship was on him,' MacLiammoir later wrote, 'he would be intolerable; something dark and brutal swept through him when a stupid audience surrounded him, and he would use them mercilessly without shame or repulsion, blaring out his impromptu opinions and trumpeting his jungle laughter as one tinsel fable followed another and the circle of fish eyes watched his antics spellbound like children at a country fair.'"[13]

Eight years later, newspapers would run with the theory that Orson Welles had induced panic in America not because his rendition of *War of the Worlds* was so realistic but because the American people were so uneducated, gullible, or just plain stupid. Some reason had to be given for why panic had gripped the nation, but the truth was that Orson Welles instinctively knew how to play an audience early on. But the price for Orson, having come of age in the adult theater world at sixteen, was mighty. After commenting on his mercurial nature, John Houseman would later write of Orson, "In Dublin, when he started in the theatre, he was just sixteen, and claiming to be what he is now twenty-two. In effect, this was a pact with hell; he sold his youth for grown-up glory. As a result, we are inflicted with these flashes of that delinquent adolescence which he appears to have bartered away."[14] That sixteen-year-old change-ling drinking in the accolades didn't know a novel written five hundred miles away in Surrey, England, by a different Wells, would change his life forever.

5

The Shadow

1934

ON A DECEMBER NIGHT IN 1934, JOHN HOUSEMAN SAT IN THE DARK-
ness of the Martin Beck Theatre in Manhattan and stared at the actor
playing Tybalt in *Romeo and Juliet.* Writing thirty years later, Houseman
recorded his thoughts on first seeing Orson Welles: "His nodding attention was galvanized when the furious Tybalt appeared suddenly in the
sunlit Verona square; death, in scarlet and black, in the form of a monstrous boy, flat-footed and graceless, yet swift and agile; soft as jelly one
moment and uncoiled in the next, in a spring of such furious energy that,
once released, it could be checked by no human intervention. What made
this figure so obscene and terrible was the pale, shiny child's face under
the unnatural growth of dark beard, from which there issued a voice of
such clarity and power that it tore like a high wind through the genteel
modulated voices of the well-trained professionals."[1]

Houseman hurried backstage to congratulate the young actor, but
he was nowhere to be found. One cannot consider the *War of the Worlds*
without considering the role John Houseman played in the broadcast,
which leads us back to the role he played in Orson Welles's life. Orson
would look for father figures his entire life. A dubious figure in many
ways, Dr. Bernstein was the first contender and became Orson's guardian
and then the executor of Richard Welles's will. Once Orson was clear of
Bernstein, he found Roger Hill, headmaster of the Todd School, whom
he would return to many times and keep apprised of his triumphs like a

proud son. But the man who would be Orson's partner and just as responsible for getting *War of the Worlds* on the air was undoubtedly Welles's longest-serving surrogate father.

Failure begets failure begets success. John Houseman knew this all too well. He also understood the adage of those who can't do . . . teach. And those who can't create . . . produce. John Houseman understood that desire was not enough and that talent trumps all. The grain merchant turned playwright turned director turned nothing was considering that his days in the arts were numbered. Houseman had lost his first business in the crash of 1929 and turned toward the arts much like a man who retires and then does what he really wanted to do. But he did not have the fire of creativity that allows one to produce art. "Against all conviction, I continued to cherish the conviction that once again, any day now, some golden opportunity would present itself," he later wrote, "and I must be alert and resourceful enough to grasp it when it appeared."[2] The man who admires art is not an artist per se, but Houseman had a unique ability to see a diamond in the rough, and he saw it in the monstrous boy who had captivated him with his voice and the bubbling rage inside him.

Like a man looking for water in the desert guided only by instinct, Houseman went backstage to find Orson, but it would ultimately take him three weeks of searching backstages to find the nineteen-year-old Orson Welles. He found him, "half in and out of costume and character, beardless and naked to the waist, but still covered in greasepaint, still falsely nosed." Houseman noticed the discarded costume, "stiff with sweat," and the "extraordinarily beautiful hands with enormous white palms."[3]

John Houseman didn't know that after Orson had left Ireland, he had gone to look for theatrical work in London and found that his high reviews did not follow him. Returning to the States with no real prospects, he traveled back to his home base of the Todd School in Woodstock, Illinois, for some local theater work. It was here that Orson had bumped into Thornton Wilder at a cocktail party in Chicago, who arranged an audition with Katharine Cornell's traveling company in New York. After two seasons with the Cornell's company, Orson once again returned to his alma mater, the Todd School in Illinois. Here he held a drama festival; made a dark brooding film, *The Hearts of Age*; and married Virginia Nicolson, an actress from a good family. He returned to New York and the Cornell touring company, where he drank too much, talked too much, was late for rehearsals, and was demoted from Mercutio to Tybalt.

It was at this point that John Houseman, the dapper, tweed-wearing, thirty-two-year-old producer, went backstage and asked Orson to meet him at a bar across the street from the theater. When Welles walked into the bar, Houseman was struck dumb by the young man walking toward him with the "pale pudding face with the violent black eyes, the button nose with the wen to one side of it and the deep runnel meeting the well-shaped mouth over the astonishingly small teeth."[4] It was love at first sight. That was how Orson put it years later, but he always said that everyone fell in love with him. The voice "that made people turn at the neighboring tables struck John Houseman more than anything else."[5] He noticed the strange vibration of Welles's voice in the lower range. It was something he had not heard before. Houseman wanted Welles for Archibald MacLeish's play *Panic*, and when he pitched the play to Welles, he glossed over the fact that he wanted him to play a sixty-year-old man. When Houseman introduced Orson Welles to MacLeish, the older playwright was skeptical, feeling Orson was too young to play the main character. Then Orson read.

"Hearing that voice for the first time in its full and astonishing range . . . it was an instrument of pathos and terror, infinite delicacy and brutally devastating power."[6] Welles got the part of McGafferty, the ruthless tycoon destroyed in the 1933 banking crisis. However, the play was poorly received, and the reviews were tepid at best, with a run of only three nights. It would seem Houseman was not going to get his foothold in the arts after all with his young protégé.

Orson returned to Woodstock for the summer with Virginia, where they stayed in a cabin in Lake Geneva. Roger Hill fed Orson money while he worked on new play ideas, but nothing came out of the summer except tans, rest, and relaxation. "Mainly, he worked on the old standby, an Irish travel book," Hill remembered. "Also, he turned out a long and rambling piece which was planned for magazine use entitled 'Now I am

21' or something of the sort."[7] Virginia's father, Leo Nicolson, tried to persuade Orson to pursue a career as a stockbroker, but the young actor turned him down. Nicolson didn't want his daughter married to a failure. This was a crossroads for Orson. He had talent, maybe even genius, but he was drifting, and the pressure from Virginia's family was growing on the young couple to settle down. Orson decided to return to New York.

Roger and Hortense Hill gave the couple a used Essex motorcar to drive east, and by the fall, Orson and his young wife, Virginia, started for New York from Woodstock in a car that would only go twenty-five miles an hour. The trip took two weeks and Virginia drove since Orson could not drive and never would. Virginia tired quickly, so they were forced to stop many times. Orson kept a steady performance of jokes and stories while navigating as "they snailed across Indiana, Ohio, and through the Alleghenies in low gear."[8] They drove through the newly opened Holland Tunnel. They emerged in Manhattan where they abandoned the jalopy in a garage by the Waldorf Astoria and checked their bags at the baggage counter in Grand Central Station. They found a seven-dollar-a-week apartment on West Fourteenth Street.

The Great Depression produced staggering unemployment, and with no firm commitments, Virginia and Orson were reduced to a hand-to-mouth existence in New York. They ate whatever they had at home but mostly went to "New York automats, cafeterias where, without the interference of waiters or waitresses, they could concoct marvelously ingenious combinations of mustard-catsup soups and relish sandwiches, paying only for bread and taking advantage of the free condiments provided. . . . Virginia was forced to pawn a matching fur scarf and muff and then, one by one, virtually all of her best dresses to pay the rent."[9] Orson made the rounds, but there were no theater roles.

Then John Houseman arranged for MacLeish's play *Panic* to be on *March of Time*, the most popular news show on the radio, one week after the play closed on March 22, 1935. This was the night the other actors couldn't reproduce the sound of five babies babbling. Welles impressed the producers when he went from playing the gruff McGafferty in *Panic* to creating the cooing of five babies. Voice actor Dwight Weist was there when Welles went to record *Panic*: "I saw this bizarre guy dressed in a strange ill-fitting suit, and he walked very funny. He never moved his shoulders, arms hanging limply by his side, and getting off in a corner by himself. And he was a strange-looking man. He looked like a Eurasian with a head too big for his shoulders and a mouth almost too small for his face . . . and I thought: What will this guy sound like in front of the microphone? Then all of a sudden, he gets in front of the microphone, and you get the famous Orson Welles voice, and I thought, Oh, OK."[10]

The regular cast of *March of Time* couldn't successfully impersonate Sir Basil Zaharoff with his deep voice and accent. Dozens of actors tried for the part and failed and then Orson read for the part. He "captured Zaharoff's tone, mood, and accent in what sounded like an exact duplication of the man. He was hired immediately and, in a short time, played King Victor Emmanuel, Charles Laughton, Horace Greeley . . . and dozens of extra voices."[11] Orson had advantages over the other *March of Time* performers; he not only had an incredible voice but also was an excellent actor. Early on, Orson took his job of being an impersonator seriously.

When he was offered a principal part, he would visit Hendrik Booraem, the program director, be given a 78-rpm record of the character's voice, and cram his substantial frame into a small soundproof chamber just large enough for himself and a phonograph. After carefully listening and studying the timbre, inflection, and accent a few times, he would then be ready to test his impersonation by making a trial transcription and then comparing it with the original voice. . . . This process would be repeated time after time if necessary. Still, Orson often emerged from the booth in short order with a voice so like its owners that it was difficult to distinguish it from the original.[12]

If Orson couldn't find a voice recording, he would go to the *March of Time* newsreel library "and study screened film footage of the subject. Occasionally, he would have to go to a commercial theatre to listen to his subject speak in rival newsreels."[13] It is hard to understand how fortunate Orson was to live at a time when the Golden Age of Radio was beginning. His and Virginia's living situation had improved; they were not eating condiment sandwiches any longer. One might compare it to our current gold rush of streaming quality drama. Shows were hiring hundreds of actors, with programs like the *Cavalcade of America* drama-tizing American literature, and this situation drew hundreds of actors to New York for the easy money of working in front of a microphone. With the right voice and a range of dialects and voices, actors found themselves in hot demand for the new medium. Sixty million people tuned in to different shows, with *Amos 'n' Andy* being the front-runner. Even movies had to step aside when *Amos 'n' Andy* came on. People weren't going to the film if the show was scheduled, so theater owners offered not only to show a movie but also to allow people to hear *Amos 'n' Andy*.

"At 7 PM, the film was stopped, a large console radio placed on the stage in front of the screen, and for fifteen minutes, the audience would be treated to the misadventures of the redoubtable duo and their involvement with the Kingfish and Madame Queen."[14] Radio power over people was something new. "The utility companies reported that people didn't flush toilets or run water during 'Amos 'n' Andy' time. Bus lines and taxis had virtually no passengers when the show was on the air."[15] It was during this time of incredible growth and experimentation in radio that Orson Welles stepped in. No one yet understood the power of radio and what it could do for the careers of unknown actors. "Such programs as the *Kraft Music Hall*, the *Rudy Vallee Show*, *Buck Rogers in the Twenty-fifth Century*, the *Burns and Allen Show*, *Death Valley Days*, and *Easy Acres* had millions of regular fans, while people such as Robert Ripley and Will Rogers were promoting their names and talents through quick mastery of the medium."[16] Movies, plays, operas, concerts, novels, and vaudeville could now be covered by radio with the correct adaptation skills. "Radio had become one of the most effective sales mediums and news reporting vehicles in the world; by the late 1930s, it was obvious that people could be made to march or work, save or fight, by listening to radio."[17]

Orson Welles's practical radio education occurred during his *March of Time* years. Welles had a natural voice, but the radio was a technical medium with its own tricks and methods of using the medium to con-vey the story. "He quickly grasped how to improve his performance by mastering such techniques as distance from the microphone, when or when not to overlap the dialogue of others, how to do group scenes, how long to pause, control of breathing, and attention to entrance and exit cues."[18] The microphone became Orson's friend, tool, device, and creative link to convey the story to an unseen listener. Not tied down by an audience before him, Orson could morph into any character he felt like. During this time, he became aware of the basics that moved radio drama, which included "sharp, simple, direct characterizations, singleness of theme; unity of dramatic effect; crisp dialogue, instant captivity of the audience, swift movement of the plot."[19]

Orson was a sponge, absorbing the new world. *March of Time* was strict in its requirement of two five-hour rehearsals before each show, but this was nothing compared to the number of rehearsals Welles was used to in the theater. Before it was all over, Welles would not rehearse at all, showing up minutes before going on the air and reading his part cold. He understood the medium so well he didn't need rehearsals to develop his timing. Now he made good money for the first time and became known in the industry. And while no one in the public knew his name, America heard his voice. He was now "one of the privileged few allowed into the private side of the public media where the control booth became the proscenium and the microphone the stage and the invisible audience was tens of thousands of times larger than any he had acted for, all sitting obediently in front parlors, bedrooms, Ford sedans, and lonely diners in every city of the land, all listening to his splendid voice."[20]

His first real break came about as CBS raided its own program for talent. *The Shadow* was a mystery show with Frank Readick's voice introducing each episode. The Shadow was not a character but a narrator of the program. Ratings slipped, and CBS scrambled around for a new format, turning the Shadow into an actual character named Lamont Cranston, "a sophisticated playboy and criminologist, who, because of a secret he had learned when living in the Orient, had the power to cloud men's minds—making himself invisible."[21] Auditions were held for the new Shadow, and Orson read for the part using his deep, booming voice. He was hired along with Agnes Moorehead from *March of Time*, who would be the Shadow's assistant on the show. For the first time on a Sunday, the voice invading homes at 5:00 p.m. across America would be identified as Orson Welles. He was out of the anonymous mosh pit of impersonators and actors who made up the *March of Time* thespians.

Millions of Americans tuned in as *The Shadow* quickly became the most popular mystery show. Fan mail flooded CBS, and Shadow Clubs formed across the country. Orson was in demand in department stores and at sponsored events where he would appear in a black hat, cape, and mask. The theme song and introductory moniker became a staple of American culture: "Who knows what evil lurks in the hearts of men? The Shadow knows!"[22] The menacing laugh (strangely, Welles could not do the laugh) and building music became instantly recognizable.

It was a dream job: the sawdust sophisticated carny character of the Shadow. It was a light role that paid well, and Orson was the star. The script was sent to Welles each week, where he marked it up and then returned it. Also part of the job were the commercials. Ever the barking ad man, Welles brought gravitas and enthusiasm as he pitched whatever product was in front of him. After he had the routine down, Orson began showing up without even reading the final script or knowing the mystery's outcome. He often showed up just when the red light blinked on at 5:30 p.m. "with his usual bounce and roll, just as the mysterious music faded away, to the infamous opening; 'Who knows what evil lurks in the hearts of men . . .'"[23]

Orson played the part with a lighthearted satirical attitude infectious to the other actors, and he seemed to enjoy the hokey dialogue and cardboard plots. Once, having not read the script, he turned to writer Sidney Slon on a break: "Hey, this is a hell of a script. How does it end?"[24] Ever the prankster, Orson came in at the last minute with his script when it flew out of his hands and ended up on the floor. "There was consternation in the control room," recalled series announcer Ken Roberts. "Fear on the faces of the musicians. Everybody was upset. Suddenly, Orson merely smiled, reached into his pocket, and took out another script . . . the whole thing had been planned to frighten the director."[25]

Orson Welles had broken through with money and building fame. But more than that, he was using *The Shadow* and *March of Time* as test tubes to experiment with the powerful new medium of radio. He could split his time between shows because he was unknown to audiences from *March of Time*.

Now began the ambulance period of Orson Welles's life, in which he rushed from one studio to another. The recording technology was in its infancy, and radio had to go live. Inevitably, Orson's later theater work and radio commitments collided. "He would often appear at the radio stations in his makeup for *Faustus*, including his beard, but wearing a tuxedo. After delivering his speech on the air, just a few minutes before nine, he would jump into the ambulance . . . and speed to Maxine Elliott's Theatre. As the chorus recited its passage in the opening scene, he would climb into his costume and enter the stage with barely an instant before his cue."[26]

The quality of Orson Welles's voice was perfect for the radio and kept him working for years. "Standing before the microphone as though it were a mirror, he would seemingly be able to gesture with sound and move himself in space, creating illusions of intimacy or distance by employing only certain voice changes, an audible pantomime. He could play Iago as well as Hamlet, Othello not less than Prospero; a newsboy or a tyrant, a child or a patriarch. . . . He knew how to give his performance just enough light and shade to prevent monotony or sameness."[27]

Paul D. Zimmerman, a *Newsweek* critic, said Welles's voice was "full of elegance and easy virility."[28] The case could be made that Orson Welles was better suited for radio than any other medium. His voice was front and center on the radio, and no other sounded like Orson Welles. Many of the shows had studio audiences that Welles could play to, but he preferred to be alone with the microphone. He worked seven days a week, and the story is true of an elevator being held up for him so that "he could soar to the upper floors in seconds and in a dramatic entrance make airtime in one of the studios with perhaps a second to spare."[29] Orson had the good fortune to come to radio during significant expansion. In 1937, ten million radios were being sold annually, with improvements in clarity and range coming rapidly. In addition, world events pushed radio to new heights. "The marriage of the Duke of Windsor . . . the destruction of the *Hindenburg*, the Lindbergh kidnapping, the Braddock-Louis fight for the heavyweight championship of the world, the funeral of John D. Rockefeller, Franklin D. Roosevelt's second inaugural."[30] Now millions could follow the events of the day in real time and get their entertainment.

But, more critically, radio was in an age when boundaries were pushed further each day. Producers and actors found different ways to convey reality to the listeners of the programs. Orson was hired by producer Irving Reis, who wanted to create the effect of a vast city square and hired two hundred college drama students to play people in the crowd. Reis turned the two hundred students into a crowd of ten thousand listeners through new techniques. Later, he explained how he did it to a reporter for the Herald *Tribune*. "At a given cue in the script, the crowd would be given a signal to cheer. When the people around the microphone stopped cheering, the recordings of their voices were brought in. These sounds took about three seconds to reach the microphone. With careful timing of both on-stage sounds and off-stage recordings, the resulting aural effect, as interpreted by listeners, sounded exactly like the cheers of a great crowd, echoing in the distance."[31]

Now, in an eerie foreshadowing of the format Orson would use for the *War of the Worlds* broadcast, Welles's role in Reis's production was to give the listener "an eyewitness view of the proceedings in the square."[32] An on-the-spot reporter would be the main character of the H. G. Wells broadcast a year later, and here was where Welles got his on-the-job training on how to pull it off. Reis found that even Orson Welles's voice could not compete with the college students, and "so he constructed a small studio—actually an isolation booth . . . Welles sat inside with the microphone, and when Reis cued his turn to speak, the sounds of Welles's voice and the crowd mixed for better clarity."[33] The result was Orson's on-the-spot narration sounding like he was among a crowd of ten thousand. Critic Gilbert Seldes noted in *Scribner's Magazine*, "The technique created a symphonic effect as the selection of contrasting voices and the balancing of sound when the narrator spoke over and under the crowd voices."[34] This technique of an on-the-spot reporter would be used brilliantly when the Martians crashed in Grovers Mill, New Jersey, and in New York when the on-the-spot reporter died.

Welles was hired for the *School of the Air of the Americas*, a weekly half-hour educational series that CBS broadcast to public schools. Here, he met his future costar in *Citizen Kane*, twenty-nine-year-old Joseph Cotten. When Orson was introduced to Cotten by producer Knowles Entriken, he tapped out his pipe in the wastepaper basket and started a fire. They became quick friends.

Radio acting was highly lucrative, and Welles took every job he could get after word got around of the young man with the golden voice. Orson, who had been living hand to mouth, made $1,000 to $1,500 a week. As his popularity increased, he became more in demand. He used his voice like a fine instrument, changing it from Freud to a Southern sharecropper. Welles could do anything, and John Houseman took note.

Never had the Great Depression helped someone's career the way it would help Orson Welles. Under the New Deal, Congress "authorized the greatest single appropriation of its kind in history: the Emergency Relief Appropriation Act of 1935. Nearly five billion dollars was allotted for the grand and single purpose of helping 3.5 million people who were out of work."[35] The Federal Theatre Project, headed by Hallie Flanagan, was raw money pumped into the arts to bring culture to the American people who could barely afford the price of a loaf of bread. Flanagan's first project was a *Living Newspapers* series that dramatized news stories, similar to *The March of Time*. She focused on controversial issues that empowered the audience to become more involved. The right portrayed the Federal Theatre Project as a left-wing mechanism for Roosevelt's agenda. But Flanagan plowed on and created the Negro Theatre Project. There were "Negro Units" created in sixteen cities composed of Black actors and crew. Rose McClendon and John Houseman were appointed to head the New York unit. Houseman immediately put Orson forth to direct the first Negro Theatre project. He later recounted his reason for choosing Orson when he had no real experience heading up a theater:

> In my working relationship with this astonishing boy whose theatrical experience was so much greater and richer than mine, it was I the pupil, he the teacher. In certain fields, I was his senior, possessed of painfully acquired knowledge that was wider and more comprehensive than his, but what amazed and awed me in Orson was his astounding and innate dramatic instinct. Listening to him, day after day, with rising

fascination, I had the sense of hearing a man initiated, at birth, into the most secret rites of a mystery—the theatre—of which he felt himself, all times, right and undisputed master.[36]

Welles was now making good money from radio, and John Houseman was technically an illegal alien from Romania. They were not the type of men the Federal Theatre Project was designed to help, but it was a godsend for Orson's career. Orson initially rejected Houseman's offer, wanting to concentrate on his radio career, but Virginia urged him on. "Orson, I want you to take this job," she said. "It's a chance of a lifetime . . . *you must!*"[37] Virginia Welles also came up with the idea for the first play, *Macbeth*, which played in Harlem with its all-Black cast.

Voodoo Macbeth was born, and Orson, who had directed only a few plays at the Todd School, was now at the head of a cast of over twenty-five people who had never acted before. And this was when Welles was taking on more radio jobs and working eighteen-hour days. The ambulance rushed him from studio to studio, finally depositing him at the Harlem theater sometime after midnight for rehearsal, with Welles downing steaks and coffee, smoking one cigarette after another, and popping Benzedrine when needed. "Those close to him observed his trick of catnaps, collapsing for twenty minutes, then surging ahead . . . fueled by meals, liquor, and Benzedrine."[38] The rehearsals often ran until morning with Welles going out after and partying with the lead Jack Carter, who took Orson to brothels and jazz clubs in Harlem he could never have gone to by himself.

Orson was working at the edge of exhaustion and breakdown, but this is where he lived. "There seems to have been a need to keep high, the essential motivation of compulsive behavior. Anything—for the alcoholic, the drug addict, the glutton . . . not to lose adrenalin."[39] But it was a thrilling adventure for the cast as Orson's directorial style developed. He began experimenting with sound and would use sound effects to build up the delivery of dialogue followed by "thunder, wind, or lightning, coming in at the end of the line to make the force of delivery seem greater or more dramatic."[40] Experimenting all the time, he pushed people to their limits. Welles often lost his temper, hurling the script, screaming, and stomping around onstage. From the first rows of the theater, with his legs over the seat and wine in one hand, Welles would critique the acting. At the same time, Virginia or his young secretary, Augusta Weissberger, would scribble furiously the notes to give the actors. The notes were a compendium of the director-producer's stream of consciousness.

> You're not acting as though you have blood on your hands. . . . Lady MacDuff should look after Macduff. . . . Start the Voodoo drums very low on the scream by the women's "liar and slave" line. . . . Jack's tone of questions too high. . . . I can't hear the witches, "All hail Macbeth Thane of Cawdor." . . . JACK, FOR GOD'S SAKE, LEARN YOUR LINES AND TAKE THE WEARINESS OUT OF YOUR BODY AS YOU GO UP THE STAIRS. . . . Tommy, take the emotion out of your voice. . . . Ellis, your "gentle lady" is too disinterested. No one should exit left in "meet in hall together." The choir stinks. Jack isn't pleading a cause at all. . . . When are we going to start using the blood? Get a cushion for the crown . . . .[41]

Welles became imperious with the cast members who were older and rougher and looked on the young white boy with suspicion. Edna Thomas recalled later that "Orson began to get very abusive and said to me, 'Darling, come down here. I'm not going to have you standing there all this time while these dumbbells aren't catching on.' When I came down, I told him, 'Orson don't do that, those people will take your head off.'"[42]

Orson was getting no sleep and started drinking more and chewing amphetamines. Orson would later tell biographer Barbara Leaming that it was "the most sleepless period of my life. We rehearsed from midnight till dawn. And after dawn would rise I would walk through Central Park. Imagine what New York was like in those days; I'd walk through Harlem, through Central Park, and with that exercise under my belt, take a shower, and go to whatever studio I had to be at."[43]

Orson was oblivious to his personal safety. One night, four men attacked him in the foyer of the theater, one of them brandishing a razor. Jack Carter overpowered the men and saved Welles. Carter, who acted many times as Orson's bodyguard, stepped up during a rehearsal and called out the complaining actors. A brawl broke out with smashed scenery and injuries to cast members. This was the line Orson walked, pushing himself and others beyond the breaking point.

Orson would later tell director Peter Bogdanovich, "When you do that play (*Macbeth*), it has a really oppressive effect on everybody. Really, it's terrifying. Stays with you all day."[44] Houseman, for his part, moved behind the scenes and built up the buzz until the opening night on April 14, 1936. Ten thousand people jammed the streets of Harlem around the theatre, and when the curtain rang down for the last time, the crowd couldn't get enough. The *Daily News* the next day led with "Negro Theater Creates Something of a Sensation in Harlem."[45] The article by critic Robert Burns Mantle barely mentions Welles but centers on the spectacle created by the production: "There were floodlights on the marquee and mounted police in the street. There was a crowd of several hundred people trying to get into the theatre and a small crowd trying to get out when it was discovered that even the standing room was all taken. . . . It wasn't Shakespearean speech. It wasn't Shakespeare's Scotland. It wasn't Shakespeare at all. But it was weirdly fascinating in color and action." By the end of the article, the critic doesn't know quite what to think. "Orson Welles, with a fondness for experiment, and John Houseman did the staging. It was all quite unusual. And a little bewildering."[46]

Orson was flying in the face of convention, of race prejudice, and tearing Shakespeare out of the stodgy realms of the theatrical elite. The *Chicago Tribune* was not so enthralled with the Welles experiment, running a headline that read, "Colored 'Macbeth' Proves Charade and Little More."[47] The critic didn't believe Orson's cast could recite the Shakespearean lines in the end. "The production is rather weird . . . it is only when the colored actors begin to read the text of Macbeth. . . . Then you know something is wrong. This is not the speech of Negroes nor within their grasp. . . . The colored Macbeth becomes a charade and little more."[48]

Orson had pushed the envelope and might have noted that while some saw the brilliance of putting on *Voodoo Macbeth*, others saw only a failure. But after the first curtain call on opening night, Orson was dragged by the cast from the wings to a thunderous ovation. The one-hundred-seat theater was packed, and people gave the young direc-tor a standing ovation. Orson Welles had put on a Black *Macbeth*. The Lafayette Theater had sixty-four sold-out shows, and then the play went on tour. Many thought Welles's play might break some of the color bar-riers in the entertainment industry, but Hattie McDaniel proved them wrong. When *Gone with the Wind* premiered in Atlanta in 1939, the city requested she not come. When she won the Academy Award for best supporting actress, she rose from the table in the corner of the room where she and her husband sat quietly by themselves.

The Federal Theatre Project proved to be the gift that kept on giving. Houseman and Welles created Project 891, where they put on avant-garde plays and more Shakespeare. *Horse Eats Hat* and *Tragical History of the Life and Death of Doctor Faustus* were first up. It is here Welles developed his signature tricks where people would vanish on stage and props would be hurled through space. Welles took classical works and gave them a modern twist, a boilerplate he would perfect in his radio plays.

Even in reality, and even with his ambulance, Welles was pushing the limits of space and time. *Doctor Faustus* showed at 9:00 p.m., but Welles's radio show was at 8:00 p.m., so he would zoom across town in full stage makeup, doing the radio show in costume. He'd then zoom to Maxine Elliott's Theatre, where the curtain would be going up as he ran backstage and made his entrance. Once the play ended, he was back in the ambulance to broadcast to the West Coast audiences. Welles worked in chaos on *Doctor Faustus*.

Hallie Flanagan went to a rehearsal and later wrote her impression of Welles in action: "Going into the Maxine Elliott during rehearsal was like going into the pit of hell, total darkness punctuated by stabs of light, trapdoors opening and closing to reveal bewildered stagehands or actors going up and down or around in circles, explosions, properties disap-pearing in a clap of thunder, and Orson, muttering the mighty lines and interspersing them with fierce adjurations to the invisible but omnipotent Feder."[49]

The Shadow continued to bring the Wellesian voice into homes all over America. His on-the-job training continued with the *Columbia Workshop*. It was a CBS "sustaining program" with no sponsors, designed to build the CBS brand. Ratings were not important, but experimentation was. So they let a twenty-one-year-old radio actor try out *Macbeth* and *Hamlet* on a radio audience, something that had never been done before. Welles worked with CBS composer Bernard Herrmann. The two upstarts did not get along, with Welles throwing out Herrmann's composition for *Macbeth*, but they would later get along very well for a radio play called *War of the Worlds*. Welles then took on an Archibald MacLeish play, *The Fall of the City*. The plot is about an attack on a city by an invader that turns out to be an empty suit of armor. An allegory for fascism, MacLeish tailored the play for Welles and used the format of a news broadcast to make it seem natural to listeners. Orson Welles was taking careful notes in his school of one for radio broadcasting. He would use all the tools and tricks of the trade when the time came to graduate.

6

The Cradle Will Rock

1937

ORSON WAS SWEATING AS HE STOOD ON THE WOODEN BOX BEFORE Maxine Elliott's Theatre in New York. He had just been locked out of his theater by the government because of fear that his musical *The Cradle Will Rock* might foment unrest or even revolution. Armed guards took possession of the set and props and forbade anyone associated with the production to enter. Yet the crowd had arrived and milled around in front of the theater. That was when Orson jumped up and called for their attention. He faced the thousand people dressed for a night at the theater. They had paid to see *The Cradle Will Rock*, and Orson was determined they should. He announced that the play would be moved to the Venice Theatre twenty blocks north and there would be no charge if people wanted to bring friends. The crowd cheered. It was another last-minute save by Orson Welles.

And if a man who only attended prep school at the Todd School for Boys depended on life to fill in the rest of his on-the-job education, then we can begin to string together the checkers leading to that fateful broadcast on Halloween eve 1938. Each incident in Orson's life filled in another blank in the *War of the Worlds* broadcast novel. The Gate Theatre in Dublin had taught him to bluff his way into any situation by lying as far as it would carry him. The radio gave him on-the-job training and an opportunity to experiment as he developed the concept of spreading himself as thin as possible and pushing himself to the wall where the creative juices marinated the most. Then he put on a Black *Macbeth* in Harlem, showing the world that he could shock with his audacity and never apologize. If Orson was then looking to put on a controversial play that would get more headlines for audacity than content, then *The Cradle Will Rock* fit the bill.

The musical by Marc Blitzstein was a piece of political dynamite that championed the working man's plight in the labor strife of the 1930s with rising unions clashing with management and owners. Welles was smitten with the musical and felt it was worthy of the Federal Theatre Project. Houseman had doubts, but Blitzstein played pieces from the musical for him on the piano, winning him over. The Federal Theatre director Hallie Flanagan had to be won over, and "Marc Blitzstein sat down at the piano and played, sang and acted," she wrote later, "with the hard hypnotic drive which came to be familiar to the audiences, his new opera. It took no magic to see that this was not a play set to music nor music illustrated by actors, but music and play equaling something new and better than either."[1] Blitzstein later wrote, "Hallie Flanagan . . . is crazy for it, says the biggest best and is also terrified about it for the Project."[2] She had Blitzstein, Orson, and Houseman fly to Washington to help sell the project. The call for unionization was the message of the play at a time when labor was battling the steel industry, with the killing of ten workers in clashes with police in Chicago. The very controversy of the subject matter intrigued Welles, and he threw himself into the rehearsals after officials in Washington reluctantly signed off.

The conductor of *The Cradle Will Rock*, Lehman Engel, later wrote his impression of Welles: "Even during those early years, he was driven to being overly busy. When he wasn't busy, he was lonely and miserable . . . he was, always has been, and still is, a boy, a Peter Pan too heavy for flying . . . despite his youth, Orson was in full charge of whatever he understood. When he was inclined to lag, John Houseman sped him on his way. He was inventive, witty, alternately lazy, energetic, and knowledgeable. His thinking was bold, and his work usually produced sensational results. . . . He would start at ten in the morning and not leave the theatre. He might dismiss the cast at four the next morning, but when we would return at noon, we would find Orson sleeping in a theatre seat."[3]

Four days before the opening night, the Federal Theatre Project took a direct hit with funding cuts, the issuance of 1,700 pink slips, and a moratorium on any news productions. Houseman and Welles knew this ruling was aimed at *The Cradle Will Rock*. Indeed, Blitzstein's show seemed to have come from the daily headlines of labor upheaval throughout America, with many afraid that revolution might be around the corner. It was not inconceivable that the incendiary musical might be the match to the fire, much like Beaumarchais's *Marriage of Figaro* had a hand in fomentingthe French Revolution. Welles and Houseman had sold 1,800 tickets, and they were determined the play should open.

After two public dress rehearsals, WPAarmed guards closed the theater with orders to confiscate the set. But the audience gathered outside, and inside Welles and Houseman met with Blitzstein. "We have a production ready; we have a fully paid audience outside," announced Welles. "And we will have our premiere tonight."[4] They agreed to mount the show as an independent venture at that moment. At 7:00 p.m., they found the Venice Theatre at Seventh Avenue and Fifty-Ninth Street, and the truck that had been driving around with a piano was directed there as the cast and crew—and the audience—walked the twenty-one blocks to the new venue on a sticky, hot June night.

Blitzstein took his seat at the piano and now had to fill in for the orchestra and whatever missing actors whose roles he would play. The back was taken off the piano to increase the volume. Just past 9:00 p.m., Orson and Houseman walked on a stage lit by the single spotlight, and Orson "briefly explained the narrative meaning of the play and noted that he could see some but certainly not all the cast spread throughout the theatre. Since the cast was now the audience, he went on, in a manifesto for living theatre, the audience could become cast if they wanted: 'If you have the urge to act, just get up and do so.'"[5]

Then Welles dramatically paused and, in that voice so right for the theater, boomed out, "We have the honor to present—with the composer at the piano—THE CRADLE WILL ROCK!" Blitzstein began in his suspenders and shirt darkened from the intense heat inside the theater as Olive Stanton, playing the character of Moll, began to sing. The searchlight frantically looked for the actress and then found her singing bravely in the audience. "Blitzstein in his shirt sleeves belted out tune after tune, and the actors dutifully stood and performed their parts, the chorus answering from the first few rows. . . . Orson sat a few feet away from Blitzstein and occasionally explained to the audience the changes in scenes, the fact that a telephone just rang or that an explosion had occurred."[6]

Somehow, the magic that is live theater was caught, and suddenly they were at the end with Larry singing out to the audience the final lines, with Blitzstein playing furiously, wringing wet with sweat at his piano. The curtain fell, and there was stunned silence inside the theater. The audience exploded and jumped to their feet in ecstatic applause. The following day, newspapers all over the country carried "stories of the rousing and unconventional opening of *The Cradle Will Rock*."[7] In her review for *Stage* magazine, Ruth Sedgwick wrote, "At its angriest and best—at that high moment with the excitement mounting, mounting, a great art becoming a living crusade." Archibald MacLeish called it "the most exciting evening of theatre this New York generation has seen."[8]

The *Daily News* set the scene with "John Houseman and Orson Welles had rehearsed *The Cradle Will Rock* two months last Spring and had it all set for production at the Maxine Elliott Theatre when word came from Washington it should not be given. . . . Outside the theatre the night of the scheduled production a huge crowd of disappointed patrons of the people's theatre demanded a show."[9] Orson had once again challenged the odds, pulled a rabbit out of his hat when disaster seemed imminent, and took victory from the jaws of defeat. How many producers would have taken on a controversial play like *The Cradle Will Rock* when many thought the very system of government was in danger and then defied that government and taken the show to another theater and pulled off a brilliant musical with no orchestra, set, or costumes? It was a dry run for *War of the Worlds*. The lesson Welles took was that a car going off a cliff was not necessarily a disaster. Sometimes that car had to go off the cliff to get to the other side. The trick was to stay alive during the process.

The WPA government-inspired theater eventually ended for Welles and Houseman, and by the following August they had created their own company with the Mercury Theatre. Welles lost no time in taking *Julius*

Caesar and turning it into a monologue on the dangers of fascism with the cast dressed like fascists in the Hitler or Mussolini legions. He used a picture from Hitler's famous Nuremberg rally with lights shooting straight up into the sky and had the set mirror the lighting and starkness of a fascist regime. The back brick wall was painted blood red with bleak platforms for the actors to stand on. The Brooks Costume Company provided costumes with "khaki-brown, high-necked uniforms of the style worn by the doughboys in World War I."[10] Orson then had the uniforms dyed black. Orson once again took control, demanding the same level of dedication from this cast that he had for *Voodoo Macbeth*. "His rehearsals were long and arduous, and pieces of action and lines were practiced almost like acrobatic feats or balletic movements, over and over again until they were perfect. The crowds and mobs were not permitted to mumble their words as is customary on the stage, but each member had a specific line written for him that he had to memorize and speak."[11]

Welles played Brutus, and the play opened on November 11, 1937. Shortly thereafter, Italy joined Germany and Japan in the Anti-Comintern Pact, drawing up the battle lines for World War II. Immediately before the curtain went up, Welles demanded that all the theater's lights, including the exit signs, be put out. A stagehand pointed out that it was against the law. Welles simply replied, "We'll turn them back on immediately. I want complete darkness. Don't worry, I'll take total responsibility."[12] The exit lights went out, and then the house lights snapped off to a coal-mine darkness. The audience could not see their hands in front of their faces. The silence was oppressive, but then a lone voice cried, "Caesar!"[13]

The lights came up, and Julius Caesar stood on a bare stage in a black fascist uniform. The audience at that point "had no difficulty imagining him in the Roman Forum or accepting that this dictator with a jutting chin and head thrown back in characteristic arrogance, searching for the voice of the doomsayer, was, in fact, Benito Mussolini or Adolf Hitler or any other tyrant of the unfree world."[14] Welles dazzled the audience as Brutus with his leather gloves and "conservative blue serge suit and a green greatcoat."[15] John Mason Brown came to the preview. The leading New York critic later wrote, "The astonishing all-impressive virtue of Mr. Welles's production is that magnificent as it is as theatre, it is far larger than its medium. Something deathless and dangerous in the world sweeps past you down the darkened aisles of the Mercury and takes possession of the proud, gaunt stage. It is something fearful and turbulent that distends the drama to include the lives of nations as well as of men. To an extent, no other director in our day and country has equaled Mr. Welles."[16]

The high-energy play took a toll on Welles, and catastrophes occurred during the run. A real knife was used in a scene with Joseph Holland as Caesar. Welles lost his balance in the stabbing scene and plunged it into Holland's chest. An artery near the heart was severed and Holland bled all over the stage, refusing to move until the curtain came down. Actors slipped in the blood until the scene ended, and Holland was rushed to Roosevelt Hospital by ambulance. Another night, Welles, who was still performing his radio work, lost volume during his performance, and someone yelled "Louder!" from the audience. Welles lost the thread of his character and found himself searching the audience for the heckler. Another time, the sprinkler system of the theater dumped water all over him.

Still, the *Daily News* critic Robert Burns Mantle led off with "'Julius Caesar' in Overcoats Mercury's First Experiment." This time the critic singled out Orson Welles and John Houseman, who "achieve exactly what they set out to achieve, which is novelty plus sanity in a classic revival . . . they have tossed convention down the airshaft and brought in expediency and a marvelous battery of lights."[17] The *Vancouver Citizen* pronounced the first play of Orson's Mercury Theatre a blazing success: "All Hail Julius Caesar and William Shakespeare, but more especially producer-actor Orson Welles!"[18] Brooks Atkinson of the *New York Times* proclaimed the play to be "honest, swift, extraordinarily vivid. . . . To judge by their first production, the Mercury will be a theatre where enthusiasm for acting and boldness in production are to be generously indulged by young actors with minds of their own."[19]

Orson Welles, it seemed, could do no wrong. He started a theater and immediately had a hit. *Julius Caesar* was a critical and financial success for Welles and Houseman. *Bold. Innovative. Daring.* These were words now stuck to Orson Welles, the successful producer, director, actor, and radio personality. Orson was living large now. On May 9, 1938, Orson appeared on the cover of *Time* magazine in full makeup and beard as Captain Shotover of *Heartbreak House*. It was a home run with a lengthy profile on the actor-director. He was touted as an innovator of the stage and a real force in traditional entertainment, as his role in *The Shadow* proved. "The brightest moon that has risen over Broadway in years, Welles should feel at home in the sky, for the sky is the only limit his ambitions recognize."[20] The *Time* puff piece profile summed up his life and tremendous success: "In person. With a voice that booms like Big Ben's but a laugh like a youngster's giggle. . . . He loves the mounting Welles legend but wants to keep the record straight. Stories of his recent affluence—the Big House at Snedens Landing, NY, the luxurious Lincoln town car and chauffeur—annoy him."[21] Welles defended this statement by saying, "I'm one of those fellows so frightened of driving that I go 80 miles an hour—and the more frightened I get, the faster I go." Orson then played coy with the reporter: "I am essentially a hack, a commercial person. If I had a hobby, I would immediately make money on it or abandon it."[22]

Welles was making about a half million a year in today's dollars and living the life he thought a theater owner/producer/actor should live. He received an Outstanding Theatrical Achievement award from the New York Drama Study Group. But there were also early dissenters. Brooks Atkinson of the *Times* tossed a small cloud into Welles's blue sky when he wrote, "He is an intuitive showman. His theatrical ideas are creative and inventive. And his theatrical imagination is so wide in scope that he can give the theatre enormous fluency and power. . . . Plays have to give way to his whims, and actors have to subordinate their art when he gets underway, for the Shadow is monarch of all he surveys. It is no secret that his willfulness and impulsiveness may also wreck the Mercury Theatre, for he is a thorough egoist in the grand manner of the old-style tragedian."[23]

The Mercury, for all its success, was not profitable. Orson's lavish lifestyle was draining away funds as he pumped money into new projects. Orson and Houseman were both wondering whether one season would be all there was for the Mercury Theatre. In 1938, Welles began rehearsing *The Five Kings* but had to step away for the birth of his daughter on March 27. Welles raced to Presbyterian Hospital and met his daughter, who was promptly named Christopher. During this time, CBS had been watching Orson Welles's rise in the national press and considered him for "a prestige series of radio plays of classical or distinguished contemporary works." The network envisioned Welles "as the possible host, director, and star, together with his ensemble for their new series."[24]

CBS examined reviews of Welles's plays and the national coverage he had been receiving "as the most famous name of our time in the American drama."[25] Orson had unheard-of coverage in the media. United Press International had declared, "The meteoric rise of Orson Welles, Mercury Theatre continues unabated."[26] This item ran in thousands of newspapers, and syndicated writers such as Walter Winchell and Robert Benchley mentioned him continually. Soon after the *Time* cover story came out, CBS was on the phone with Orson, offering him "an hour-long dramatic series of dramatic broadcasts with himself as writer-director, producer, narrator and star."[27] He had just been handed the castle keys and raced to tell John Houseman. The producer saw a black limousine pulling up to his home with Orson's large face in the back window. Orson told him that CBS had offered him nine weekly radio programs to perform adaptations of famous books. It was called *First Person Singular* and would morph into *Mercury Theatre on the Air*. The program would be directed, written, performed, and produced by Orson Welles. All he had to do was find the right books for the episodes. In six months, Orson would find the book that would change his life forever.

7

Dummies

1938

THE SUN WAS SHINING ON THE HUDSON AS THE SPEEDBOAT CRESTED the waves with the wind blowing back Orson's hair while he leaned forward and watched the Manhattan skyline become larger and larger until he was under the buildings. Orson Welles had found a beautiful home at Snedens Landing for him, Virginia, and the baby on the west bank of the Hudson river. He had bought a speedboat that would serve the same function as the ambulance and get him into Manhattan in half the time. He would jump down from the dock into his new speedboat, like his new chauffeur, new clothes, and new assistants, and jet out across the Hudson River with the stars sparkling above while he headed back to his waiting wife and child. Except he rarely made it back, instead seeking out actresses, dancers, ballerinas, anyone who gave the man with the insatiable appetite what he needed. Virginia later wrote that his returning from Manhattan had "become such a rare event that I told him he might as well give up on the boat and swim across."[1]

So, Orson Welles, the twenty-three-year-old who had wowed the theater world, now had his radio show. No longer in the shadows playing the Shadow, Welles was front and center as the *New York Times* announced his new radio show with a flourish: "Orson Welles, the twenty-three-year-old actor-director who has introduced several innovations in the legitimate theater, has been invited with the Mercury Theatre to produce nine one-hour weekly broadcast dramas over the CBS network, beginning July 11, 1938."[2] Welles was quoted as saying, "We plan to bring to radio the experimental techniques which have proved so successful in another medium and to treat radio with the intelligence and respect such a beautiful and powerful medium deserves."[3] Welles planned an innovation for radio no one had tried, that of the omniscient narrator. This third-person technique of narrative would allow "direct contact between the narrator and listener; he becomes not merely a neutral storyteller, but the author himself of whom the characters are simply projections."[4] Welles no longer had to learn a script, put on a costume, and act. Now he could use his strongest asset on radio to create a story: his voice.

In a later interview in *Radio Annual*, Welles expands on the advantages of radio over theater, and we see breadcrumbs leading to the broadcast of the *War of the Worlds*. "The less a radio drama resembles a play, the better it is likely to be. . . . It must be . . . drastically different. . . . Images called up by radio must be imagined, not seen. And so, we find that radio drama is more akin to the form of the novel, to storytelling."[5] *Newsweek* summed up the new show by saying the program "will avoid the cut-and-dried dramatic technique that introduces dialogue with routine radio announcements. Welles will serve as genial host to his radio audience."[6]

Treasure Island was the first show for *Mercury Theatre on the Air*. John Houseman complained he knew nothing of radio. Orson had assumed Houseman would be working with him, but Houseman saw a fundamental shift in their relationship with the radio show. "Throughout my theatrical association with Orson over the past three and a half years, much of the initiative had been mine, strategically and artistically. While I had never hesitated to acknowledge Orson's creative leadership . . . I had managed to . . . maintain the balance of power in partnership. . . . With the coming of the radio show, this delicate balance was disturbed and, finally, destroyed. The formula 'produced, written, directed and performed by Orson Welles' was one that I approved and encouraged . . . but its effect . . . on the future course of Mercury was deep and irreversible. From being Orson's partner, I had become an employee."[7]

Houseman's first job was to come up with a script. For three weeks, he slaved over a script trying to convert the novel *Treasure Island* into a sixty-minute radio drama. Then Orson changed his mind and decided he wanted to do *Dracula*. Though Orson's selections for *Mercury Theatre on the Air* rarely came from his own reading material, Bram Stoker's *Dracula* was something he had read. Often, ideas for shows came to him from assistants, friends, listeners, and other actors. He would haunt bookstores and libraries looking for selections or scour anthologies "such as *Transatlantic Stories* and *Short Stories from the New Yorker* and constantly perused *Harper's*, the *Saturday Evening Post*, and the *Atlantic*." Once Orson settled on a story, he had to secure the rights unless it was in the public domain. Orson "wanted a story of a particular kind, a simple one that demands from the reader a certain acceptance of strange and extraordinary events, that he could transmit over the air the way an old vaquero of Mexico . . . might enthrall the villagers of remote towns night after night with tales of adventure and mystery."[8]

In typical Welles fashion, the script would be hashed out overnight. Over hash in Perkins' Restaurant, Houseman and his secretary Augusta Weissberger broke down the Bram Stoker novel. "Over several meals and without the benefit of sleep, awash with bottles of wine, balloons of brandy, and great pots of coffee in cyclical alteration, they gutted the book of its most striking moments, thrashed out a framework onto which they latched dialogue transcribed from the book, cobbled together narrative links, and finally staggered away from the restaurant with a script."[9] When dawn came, Welles celebrated "with eggs and bacon, kippered herring, coffee, and juice."[10] This would be their first radio play, and Orson, of course, would play the part of Dracula himself, but now he had the facilities of CBS and a twenty-three-piece orchestra led by Bernard Herrmann. Herrmann was the head of music at CBS and had to produce almost forty minutes of music for a fifty-seven-minute show. His ability to deliver the type of music fitting the show's mood made him invaluable.

Herrmann and the sound technicians assisted Welles in his quest for new and unusual sound effects. The chaos, restlessness, and pressure that Welles worked under infected everyone. Paul Stewart recalled the technicians trying to replicate the sound of leaves using newspaper. "Orson, in his usual way, heard it and said, 'That won't do. Leaves don't sound like that. It sounds exactly like a newspaper.' It didn't sound like a newspaper at all, but he always had to have his moments of bad behavior for his personal satisfaction. 'Go into Central Park,' he said. 'Find me real branches from a real bush.' The sound man looked at him. 'It's February . . . the bushes have no leaves.' 'You're right,' said Orson, 'Use the newspaper.'"[11]

Paul Stewart had been the director of *Cavalcade of America* and was called in because Orson had no experience producing a show. Stewart organized *Mercury Theatre on the Air* in a way Orson Welles never could. The script would be furnished Wednesday before the show and rehearsed in the studio without Orson; then a recording was generated on shellac discs that Stewart supervised. After that, Orson would listen to the recording and make notes, but it was on the Sunday of the show that Welles performed his trick of taking the ordinary and transforming it into the extraordinary.

Richard Barr, in an unpublished memoir, describes the Sunday rehearsal: "Orson did not direct his shows; he conducted them. Standing on a podium in front of a dynamic microphone, he waved his arms, cued every music and sound cue."[12] Paul Stewart later described the final dress rehearsal: "There was absolute chaos, absolute chaos every week. Welles is a very destructive man, he has to destroy everything and then put it back together again himself, and there were passionate discussions between him, Houseman, and me. Then someone would say, 'We're on the air in two minutes.' The ground was strewn with paper. That we got on the air at all was a weekly miracle because it was always like that."[13]

Orson quickly produced one drama after another. *Dracula, Treasure Island, A Tale of Two Cities, The Thirty-Nine Steps, The Affairs of Anatol, The Count of Monte Cristo, The Man Who Was Thursday, Julius Caesar, Jane Eyre,* and *Sherlock Holmes.* The new show was a success, and it was because of the talent, voice, and force that was Orson Welles. Simon Callow summed up the magic of Orson this way: "No matter what voice Welles assumes, it's always unmistakably him; he doesn't begin to rival Peter Ustinov, for example, in the virtuosity of pitch, accent, rhythm, character. He often brilliantly catches a color, a flavor, but he doesn't submit to its character. He manipulates it, usually to sonorous effect. Above all he creates atmosphere; it is his presence that dominates the entire show. His *Dracula* voice sounds artificially manufactured, like the controlled belches by which the late Jack Hawkins was able to find a substitute voice when his vocal cords had been destroyed by cancer—but it is his own special resonance that creates the effect. The camera is said to love certain actors, and the microphone positively adored Welles."[14]

People also recognized another famous voice on the radio. The Swedish ventriloquist Edgar Bergen and his dummy Charlie McCarthy played opposite *Mercury Theatre on the Air* and swept the ratings regularly. Edgar John Bergen taught himself the art of ventriloquism at age eleven from a book, *The Wizards Manual*, and so impressed ventriloquist Harry Lester that he gave the teenager a job as a projectionist in return for lessons for three months. Edgar then paid a woodcutter, Theodore Mack, to make him the head of a dummy based on a red-headed newspaper boy. Edgar spent all of $36 to create Charlie McCarthy and made the body himself out of a nine-inch broomstick with rubber bands and cords to make the jaw move. The most famous dummy in the world was born; inexplicably, Edgar and Charlie found their biggest audience on the radio, where no one could even see Bergen's skill as a ventriloquist. Playing as part of the *Chase and Sanborn Hour*, the *Charlie McCarthy Show* divided the audience with Jack Benny and *First Person Singular*. *Mercury Theatre on the Air* picked up only 3.6 percent of the total listening audience (32 million) on the night of October 30, 1938. The dummy and the Swedish ventriloquist took a whopping 34.6 percent.

The number of listeners sampling Orson Welles's new show that put classics on the air barely broke a million listeners. Welles pumped up his shows with his signature sparkle and chaos. "No one could have denied the desperate haste with which the shows were written or the mischievous use of music and lurid sound effects to paper over the cracks. But Welles had no shame about it. He took it as seriously as he took Shakespeare or Shaw—and was convinced that a radio show as much as a play relied upon its magic heat."[15] And Welles was still producing for the regular Mercury Theatre as they lurched from the disaster of *Too Much Johnson* to *Danton's Death*, which would be the theater's swan song. Welles had too many irons in the fire as usual, but like any young artist, he didn't know what would catch and propel him to the next thing.

The composer Bernard Herrmann, who worked with Orson on his radio shows, later wrote of his approach to theater on the air. "Welles's radio quality, like Sir Thomas Beechman's in music, was essentially one of spontaneity. At the start of every broadcast, Orson was an unknown quantity. As he went along, his mood would assert itself, and the temperature would start to increase till the point of incandescence. . . . Even when his shows weren't good, they were better than other people's successes. He inspired us all: the musicians, the actors, the sound effects men, and the engineers. They'd all tell you they had never worked on shows like Orson Welles's. Horses' hooves are horses' hooves—yet they felt different with Orson; why? I think it had to do with the element of the unknown, the surprise, and the uncomfortable excitement of improvisation."[16]

Saying that the two audiences listening to Orson Welles and Edgar Bergen were different would be an understatement. Bergen's audience expected lighthearted laughs. The show was rated number one for two years straight. On October 30, 1938, the show received its highest Hooper rating at 34.6 percent of the total audience. Orson Welles's audience never quite knew what to expect, and people tuning into the show for the first time were often bewildered at the slightly off-center, at timesalmost satiric, approach Welles took to his material. The show could be dark or light, but some strange, unknown element always broke through the landscape of 1930s radio. People listening to a dummy would not have known what to make of a radio play called the *War of the Worlds*.

In the summer of 1938, before the broadcast of *War of the Worlds*, Orson moved from his house at Snedens Landing to the St. Regis Hotel to oversee the creation of his first film. The play for the Mercury Theatre that summer was *Too Much Johnson*, and Orson had decided to film a forty-minute teaser to be inter-spliced with the play as a twenty-minute prologue and two ten-minute sequences for the second and third acts. The move to the hotel was for reasons of health as much as convenience. Orson suffered from asthma and hay fever, and the high pollen count pushed him toward the air-conditioning of the St. Regis. Virginia stayed behind with the baby.

As Orson sat cross-legged on his bed at the hotel, he issued directives. "Food deliveries from the hotel's kitchen or from either of his two favorite restaurants, Reuben's or Jack and Charlie's, arrived in a round-the-clock attempt to appease his insatiable hunger. Phone calls seeking money were made with alacrity, and incoming calls were received with tension. . . . Standing by were mini-legions of breathless messengers, note-scribbling assistants, and overly inquisitive reporters. Orson Welles was about to make his first film."[17]

John Houseman came up with $10,000 to finance the film, and Welles immediately threw himself into rehearsals and shooting the film. *Too Much Johnson* was a farce, and the film would augment the play's hilarity. Welles viewed genre films, focusing on Mack Sennett slapstick shorts. There was little rehearsal. Orson plunged into filming in Battery Park, Central Park, and Yonkers and on the Hudson River. He immediately developed a highly personal style on the set. Like in radio, "He constantly used his acting talents to show his actors what he wanted. During many of the action sequences, however, he would bellow his instructions—no megaphone needed—from camera to set, urging his actors in the chase scenes through New York streets to employ more daring attempts."[18]

True to form, Orson was frequently late, to the cast and crew's frustration, and came up with fantastic excuses when he arrived. The crew worked sixteen-hour days for no pay, holding pieces of flimsy scenery in the hot sun. One day, the crew rebelled and went to find something to eat, and Welles became furious and demanded to know what they were doing until actor John Berry explained that they had not eaten all day. Orson arranged for food immediately, offering Berry his director's chair. Orson's striving for the reality of Mack Sennett films often put his actors in danger. In one scene, Joseph Cotten jumped from a roof and stood on the edge of a ledge of a five-story building. A crowd gathered with people shouting, "Don't jump!"

"Squad cars, fire engines, and newspapermen fled to the scene. Filming stopped, and Welles climbed down from the top of the building where he had directed the action. Drenched in sweat, he explained, 'All we are trying to do is make a movie.'"[19] After ten days of shooting, Welles had accumulated twenty-five thousand feet of film, and the play was due to open in a few days. There was no more money, and Welles began editing at the St. Regis with a Moviola editing machine. He began cutting, splicing, and realizing what twenty-five thousand feet of film means in terms of time. He never left the room except for a rehearsal of his radio show or to rehearse the play. "Bits of film were scattered across the room, and, as Houseman recalled, Welles's assistants had to 'wade knee deep through a crackling sea of inflammable film.'"[20]

John Berry helped Orson in any way he could in making the short disastrous film. He would do anything to work with Orson Welles and had nearly passed out several times in Yonkers, holding flimsy scenery up in the blinding sun. He also lined up apartments where Orson would take his ballerina of the month. Welles had established fame with the Mercury Theatre and *Mercury Theatre on the Air* radio program, and Berry didn't ask any questions about these love nest arrangements. He just concentrated on his work with Welles on editing the film. He recalled one night when the film caught fire in the projector: "What I remember, most remarkably, is me running with the projector in my hand, burning, trying to get out the door into the Goddamn hallway and Houseman racing for the door at the same time . . . while Orson, with absolutely no concern whatsoever, was back inside, standing and looking at some piece of film in his hand, smoking his pipe."[21]

The job of editing the film in time for the opening quickly became insurmountable. When an attorney notified Orson that Paramount owned the film rights to *Too Much Johnson*, it was with relief that Orson realized the film couldn't be used. Welles had leased the dramatic rights but not the movie rights. If the film were used, Orson would have to pay a leasing fee that might be substantial. Then the laboratory processing the film refused to deliver the final footage until it was paid in full. Orson tried to lower the wages for his actors, but the union forced him to pay the total amount. The best he could do was cobble together a portion of the film to be played at Stony Creek Theatre for a prescreening. It did not go well. The missing footage made the film fragmentary, with no connecting dramatic cohesion. The auditorium had a low ceiling, which inhibited the projection of the film. Orson Welles's first film was a complete bust.

The play *Too Much Johnson* opened on August 16, 1938, without the prequel film. The play made no sense without the connecting movie and closed two weeks later without reaching Broadway. The boy wonder had stumbled badly. In 2008, a print of the film was discovered in Italy and set to music. *Too Much Johnson* is now a study in slapstick comedy. It is Orson's first effort, but there is no trace of the brilliance that would follow in *Citizen Kane*. But maybe *Too Much Johnson* was where Orson realized traditional filmmaking would not work—much the way traditional radio did not work for him.

Lying in his bed in the air-conditioned hotel room, Orson knew he had to come up with something bold and big. He had been on a long tear of success and didn't understand the concussive effect of a big failure. One day, John Berry rapped on the door of Welles's room and walked in. He stopped, mouth agog. Orson Welles was spread out naked on the bed. The blinds were down, and the room was dark. Orson had "retired into his air-conditioned room at the St. Regis, where he lay in darkness for a week, surrounded by 25,000 feet of film . . . convinced that he was going to die, racked by asthma and fear and despair."[22] Welles motioned Berry to a chair, where he stayed and later reported Orson's recitation of "self-vilification and the remorse for what he had done to those around him . . . for the cruelty and moral corruption with which he reproached himself." Welles began to talk about his failures. *Too Much Johnson*, the film and the play, had failed miserably, and it looked like his latest play, *Danton's Death*, was heading the same way, with a consensus among the cast and crew that it wasn't very good. Orson was in a dark place. During a crisis, his asthma came on, throwing him back to some dark days as a child when he heard "the inner voices, the ones spurring him on and those others saying that he was fundamentally worthless. . . . His self-accusations were terrifying to those who heard them, utterly negative and destructive."[23]

The orphan was depressed in a way at which John Berry could only guess. It had been only three months since the birth of his daughter, and Orson was having numerous affairs that threatened to end his marriage. Orson was questioning his life, dismissing his successes: the Mercury Theatre, *Mercury Theatre on the Air*, *The Shadow*, *March of Time*. He was complaining about his partner, John Houseman—the man who had become his surrogate father, keeper, confidant, partner, and consultant, the man who allowed the genius to dance and told him when he had spent all his money. And Welles had made good money—$1,000 a week—during the Great Depression, but, of course, it was all gone, gone into plays, films, and radio shows that didn't work out. Gone with the limousine that picked him up daily, his apartment on the Upper East Side, his prodigious meals, his prodigious drinking, partying to all hours, and the hotel rooms of his latest conquests.

In August 1938, Orson spoke to a group of educators at Columbia University, resulting in the *Cincinnati Enquirer* headline "Prodigy of New York Stage Bites Hand That Is Feeding Him during Course of Talk before Group of Educators—Orson Welles Asserts Movies Have It All Over Stage."[24] Orson disparaged his theatrical accomplishments, and the article stated, "Modern theatre was in a very low down condition indeed, that the movies had it all over the stage and that he saw no very good reason why audiences should come to see his revivals of old plays."[25] The article went on to note that "his *Julius Caesar* ha[d] been called a master-piece of production" and that "no one yet understands what made Welles say what he did. His outburst was put down as a mild brainstorm or as inspired by youthful emotionalism."[26] The article then mentioned Orson was presenting a weekly radio dramatization, broadcast every Monday during the summer, and that "Welles was experimenting with new techniques in these productions."[27]

Orson had dropped hints as to his future. He was no longer interested in the Mercury Theatre or theater at all. In perfect Welles fashion, he wanted to destroy his own work. He wanted to make films, but to get there he would use his radio show to experiment with new ways of presenting drama. Welles was doing what he did best: tearing down a medium and then moving on. His art was the art of self-destruction that brought forth brilliant ways of presenting dramatic stories. The reporter called Orson's tearing down of theater a "very puzzling reaction,"[28] but he didn't understand the man behind the play or the radio shows. Orson was at sea. He had gone as far as he could. He had lost his enthusiasm for the stage. He loved radio, but he loved film more, and he didn't see how he could get to Hollywood. David Selznick had sounded him out on playing Beethoven, but it had fizzled out. Orson wanted to do something great; he didn't know what it was, but he was a Roman candle burning very quickly and he must strike while he had the opportunity.

Time was running out on his personal life as well. One day Virginia surprised her husband by going to his room at the Algonquin in Manhattan to wait for him to return.

"The sun came up, and there was still no sign of Orson," Virginia ruefully confessed to her daughter, Christopher Welles Feder, many years later. "I decided there was little point in waiting any longer, but before going home, I wanted to leave a love note on his pillow. That's when I opened the desk drawer, looking for some notepaper." Virginia found love letters from various women to Orson. "That made the shock more terrible . . . my being so innocent and trusting. It seemed every ballerina in New York had written to him, and there were also letters from my good friend Geraldine. I couldn't believe at first that Orson would actually send Geraldine to stay with me when he'd been having an affair with her." Virginia then staggered over to the hotel window and tried to open it. She was going to commit suicide but couldn't get the window open. "God knows I tried," she later told her daughter.[29]

Like so many women of the time, Virginia eventually convinced herself the love letters didn't prove anything and stayed in her marriage. She was having a baby, and Orson was attentive and loving when he was around. She reasoned that he was so busy, he couldn't possibly have any time for an affair. But Orson *was* having multiple affairs. It was "my period of ballerinas," he later told biographer Barbara Leaming, "and none of them were a disappointment. . . . I didn't consciously go out to collect them, but life just worked out that way."[30] He couldn't settle down in his career or personal life. The ambulance was a perfect symbol of his life—bells clanging and the rushing through life to get to the next event, radio show, or play. Running, rushing, rushing, and then he would crash; suffocating doubt would overwhelm him. He was really nothing but a charlatan, a magician playing his last card. He knew this about himself.

Too Much Johnson did play at some smaller venues. The *Hartford Courant*, advertising a run at the Stony Creek Theatre, proclaimed, "*Too Much*

Johnson is a distinct departure from any of the past productions the keen theatrical organization has produced: *The Shoemakers Holiday, The Cradle Will Rock, Julius Caesar, Heartbreak House*. Four smash hits in succession, and every play is a different type for this young group, which is less than a year old."[31] But the fact Orson had four smash hits meant nothing to him now. He wanted to move on. He needed a bigger platform, a bigger stage, and that was movies. He was less than four months away from the broadcast that would change his life forever. Maybe in that darkness in that hotel room, the idea bubbled up. Orson would later say, "I had conceived the idea of doing a radio broadcast in such a manner that a crisis would actually seem to be happening and would be broadcast in such a dramatized form as to appear to be a real event taking place at that time, rather than a mere radio play."[32]

In less than four months, the naked boy wonder would eventually rise from his bed, bring H. G. Wells's novel to life, and unleash Martians on the land. From the darkest point came the most brilliant light. It had been this way all of Orson Welles's life.

8

The Perfect Setup

September 1938

THE PERFECT SETUP FOR ORSON WELLES CAME IN THE FALL OF 1938. People who awoke in Hackensack, New Jersey, on September 22, 1938, after a hurricane-fueled storm, read newspapers in shock. The *Bergen Evening Record* blared the headline "Hitler Boosts Price of Peace."[1] Below that was another article about the devastating hurricane that had hit the East Coast and Hackensack: "133 Known Dead in Hurricane, Damage in Millions; Property Loss Here Over 300,000; Relief Speeded."[2] Weeks before, Adolf Hitler had proclaimed that the Sudetenland in Czechoslovakia was part of Germany and that the Sudetenland Germans wanted to be part of the German Reich and the land must be immediately ceded to Germany. Hitler pointed out reports of abuse of the Sudetenland Germans, which would force his hand to occupy Czechoslovakia if his demands were not met. War seemed imminent.

A bold black headline in a Pennsylvania paper screamed, "Sudetenland or War, Says Hitler. Invasion Set for Saturday as Fuhrer Hurls Challenge. 'Hand us the territory by October 1st.'"[3] Hitler had put a gun to the head of the world. Radio bulletins broke in with blaring news that war seemed imminent in Europe. The natural barriers of the oceans had not kept America out of World War I and now the country's sense of safety had been pierced by the device Americans were relying on for their news: radio, which, at this point, was not yet even twenty years old.

The term "broadcast journalism" was born during the 1920 Harding-Cox presidential election when station KDKA reported on returns in East Pittsburgh from a hut on top of a factory. Real-time election results broke newspapers' stranglehold, with radio listeners skyrocketing from sixty thousand in 1921 to 16.7 million in 1930. The Lindbergh kidnapping in 1932 put radio front and center. Charles Lindbergh had flown across the Atlantic in 1925 and became a superstar celebrity. His marriage to socialite Anne Morrow set up a fairy-tale happy ending, with a son, Charles Jr., born in their Hopewell, New Jersey, mansion on June 22, 1930. On March 1, 1932, however, Charles Jr. was kidnapped, and a ransom demanded. The nation was riveted, and newspapers hit a wall, publishing numerous extra editions but unable to keep up with the public's hunger for news. Radio moved in and began broadcasting from New Jersey with real-time bulletins. Another boost came when the Great Depression decimated the banking system. Banks began to fail as people withdrew their money and put it under their mattresses or the running boards of their Model Ts. Many buried their life savings in their backyards.

Franklin Delano Roosevelt (FDR) inherited a country on edge, and his first order of business was to stabilize the banks. There was no insurance for people. No FDIC. If investors pulled out their money, the bank failed. The trick was to get people to have faith again in the economy, the government, and the banks. On March 12, 1933, FDR went on the air with the first of his "fireside chats." Sixty million people listened to the president using the new medium of radio as he made his case. He implored people to put their money back in the banks. This was the worst year of the Great Depression, and yet people returned $1.2 billion to the banks. Radio allowed the president to come into living rooms, homes, apartments, and farms. All over the country, people listened to FDR as if he were talking just to them.

The immediacy of radio had pushed newspapers aside. They were no longer the primary way people looked for news of a dramatic event. The speed of radio technology was akin to the Internet's emergence in the 1980s, when online news competed with television. "The intensity with which America listened to the radio reports from the Munich crisis was without parallel in radio history. Portable radio sets which had just been developed had tremendous sales. People carried them to wherever they went, to restaurants, offices, and on the streets. This was the day of the taxicab radios, and every standing cab was surrounded by crowds as on World Series days. Here was a World Series with a vengeance!"[4]

There was no reason not to trust implicitly what was coming over the radio. A *Fortune* magazine survey quoted in the Cantril report on the *War of the Worlds* broadcast asked listeners what they trusted more, radio or newspapers, and what gave them news more free from prejudice. Only 17 percent rated newspapers as reliable. Newspapers had taken a hit during the yellow journalism period of the late 1800s and early 1900s when William Randolph Hearst's *New York Journal* and Joseph Pulitzer's *New York World* battled it out for circulation.

In the fall of 1938, people listened intently as the prime minister of Britain, Neville Chamberlain, provided a way out of Hitler's ultimatum by giving the Sudetenland to the Germans. He returned to England and waved around the signed document proclaiming "Peace for Our Time." "Appeasement" would become a dirty word for all time, but the world had been pulled back from the brink. The BBC reported on the moment in a breaking news format: "Mr. Chamberlain is posing and waving his hat with the great air of nonchalance and gaiety which he adopted once before on the airplane and which I believe he adopted yesterday when he said 'It's all right' to people in Downing Street. He doesn't mind in the least being importuned by the photographers who sought Mr. Chamberlain, and he beams all over his face."[5]

Neville Chamberlain had sold Czechoslovakia down the river to preserve peace by giving Hitler the Sudetenland. A separate broadcast by the Czechoslovakian justice minister told a different, much darker story: "We faced a choice. Either war, a heroic struggle of our armies, but a war we could only lose, a terrible war, which would have ended, not just with the destruction of our valiant soldiers, but with the total annihilation of our nation, with the murder and violation of our women and children, to accept what the European powers dictated to us in Munich."[6]

In another broadcast, people heard journalist Jonathan Griffin's somber prediction of what Neville Chamberlain's appeasement really meant:

"For the moment you have peace, but you have got it for the moment on the cheap at others' expenses. . . . later on you will find that you have mortgaged the security of Great Britain and her position as a Great Power."[7] Radio had brought Chamberlain's sellout into living rooms all over America, which would soon become the bloody flag of appeasement.

By September 29, 1938, it seemed war might be averted, and radio had taken another significant step. Listenership increased a dramatic 40 percent during the crisis, with people glued to their radios as sales hit an all-time high. No one could afford to be out of touch with the storm clouds brewing as the peace began to feel like a Band-Aid on a horrible wound that was festering again. On October 1, the German army occupied the Sudetenland. By October 6, newspapers were already doubting the wisdom of appeasing Adolf Hitler.

United Press International (UPI) carried a story expressing doubt in the peace outlook in Europe. The reporter, Webb Miller, claimed access to Neville Chamberlain from sources who confirmed "the Nazi Fuhrer left no doubt in Chamberlain's mind that the third Reich expects to achieve complete political, military and economic domination of the continent. He was understood to have indicated to Chamberlain that he regarded this domination as Germany's inalienable right due to the population of 80,000,000, her political and industrial organization, and the 'genius' of the German people."[8] The war news was increasing, with more and more news bulletins breaking into regular programming. Radio had become a ticking bomb, and people clutched their hands and stared at the floor as they listened to the carnage. Then a devastating hurricane swept through New England, killing seven hundred people on September 21, 1938. It was the deadliest hurricane to have ever hit the East Coast. Twelve million people remained unemployed from the Great Depression, even as the economy picked up from the early demands of a brewing war. There was a feeling that the other shoe was about to drop in the United States as the cool air of autumn filtered down and windows were shut at night.

Children in London were evacuated to the countryside as the British fleet mobilized. President Roosevelt went on the radio and said, "The conscience and the impelling desire of the people of my country demand that the voice of their government be raised again and yet again to avert and to avoid war."[9] Another headline ominously reported, "U.S. Lines Ready to Bring Home All Americans." The article reported, "An American rush homeward from war-menaced Europe prompted the United States lines today to prepare for wholesale evacuation on ships with capacities augmented by hundreds of cots, lifeboats, and extra provisions. The lines moved quickly to meet an emergency like the exodus from abroad in 1914's chaotic World War days."[10]

The storm was approaching, and people hung on to news that might tell them when it was about to break. Halloween portended more than goblins and witches; it also portended a world slipping into the abyss. A bottled-up sense of panic was in the air and people could almost smell the fear. Orson Welles would open that bottle and let the fear run wild. And he had the perfect model. Four days before the broadcast, Orson Welles listened to *Air Raid*, a play presented on the show *Columbia Workshop*. It was by Archibald MacLeish and was a novel whose story was conveyed in news format. The play opens with an announcer on a tenement roof in a European border town. Welles had permitted the *Columbia Workshop* to use his Mercury actor Ray Collins as the reporter. The action quickly picks up with the reporter on the spot. "He can see everything around him; his microphone picks up the sounds of women chattering and children playing. It is early in the morning of the day when the next war breaks out. More description of the town—a microcosm of European condition—continues, and the play gives an unforgettable picture of the war at its inception and the confused psychology of modern warfare. . . . The whine of raiding planes can be heard. The populace is noisy and in confusion, running for shelter. Machine guns sputter, and antiaircraft guns fire explosively. Finally, a boy's voice is transposed into an agonizing scream as bombs begin to fall."[11]

Welles's broadcast would follow the same dramatic arc right up to the boy screaming as bombs fall. The audience assumed the boy died, and Orson used this assumption in his broadcast. The announcer telling the story was in the motif of Edward R. Murrow, who would later narrate the blitz over London. *Air Raid* had been very popular, and *Time* magazine gave it a full-page review. None of this success was lost on Orson. The crescendo of rising action and tension in his broadcast would be duplicated from the MacLeish script. Archibald MacLeish took seven months to produce his broadcast; Orson would take only seven days. Like the sampling that goes on today in music, Welles borrowed a good idea when he heard it.

But a horrible event had given Orson an even better roadmap to follow and would become a recording that Welles's team would study closely. The live broadcast of the burning and crash of the *Hindenburg* changed radio forever. On May 6, 1937, reporter and broadcaster Herbert Morrison of WLS Chicago watched the silver dirigible *Hindenburg* sail out of the clouds after crossing the Atlantic from Germany. The silver paint caught the filtered sun as Morrison and sound engineer Charlie Nehlsen squinted toward the sky.

They had flown in the day before from Chicago to report on the airship's arrival from Germany due to dock at Lakehurst, New Jersey. The day had clouded over as a gust of wind played havoc with the approaching helium-filled airship. Water ballast had been off-loaded for several hours to bring the ship level, but the downdraft from an approaching storm kept the nose up. The two-and-a-half-day trip across the Atlantic was becoming routine, but WLS wanted a recording of the landing. A disc would be made of Morrison's report and taken to Chicago. Radio depended on being live, so Morrison's recorded report on the *Hindenburg* would be given low priority. Nevertheless, Morrison had to make it as exciting as he could, and American Airlines sponsored WLS, so Morrison hyped the flight from Chicago as much as the landing: "We both flew down from Chicago yesterday afternoon aboard one of the giant new 21-passenger flagships of American Airlines. It took us only 3 hours and 55 minutes to fly nonstop from Chicago to New York. When we landed at Newark, we found another flagship of American Airlines waiting to take us to Lakehurst with our equipment when we were ready to go."[12] As the slow-moving dirigible circled the field and approached the mooring tower, Morrison had to fill the time with something. "Well, here it comes, ladies and gentlemen; we're out now, outside of the hangar. And what a great sight it is; it is thrilling, just a marvelous sight. It's coming down out of the sky, pointed directly toward us and the mooring mast. The mighty diesel engines just roared, the propellors biting the air and throwing it back into a gale-like whirlpool. No wonder this great floating palace can travel through the air at such a speed."[13]

Morrison went on with his description, painting mental pictures for his audience: "Now and then, the propellors are caught in the rays of sun. . . . the ship is riding majestically toward us like some great feather, riding as though it was mighty proud. . . . orders are shouted to the crew, the passengers probably lining the windows looking down at the field ahead of them." Then Morrison put in another plug for American Airlines: "And these giant flagships standing here, the American Airlines flagships, waiting to direct them to all points in the United States. . . . It's practically standing still now."[14] Morrison continued droning on in the sonorous voice of the announcer:

> They've dropped ropes out of the nose of the ship, and it's been taken hold of down on the field by several men. It's starting to rain again; the rain has slacked up a little bit. The back motors of the ship are just holding it, just enough to keep it from—*it burst into flames! Get this, Charlie! Get this, Charlie! It's burning and crashing. Oh, my, get out of the way, please. It's burning and bursting into flames and it's . . . and it's falling on the mooring mast and all the folks agree that this is terrible. This is one of the worst catastrophes in the world!*[15]

Morrison is crying as he is talking. There is no separation now from the broadcaster and the human being witnessing a horrific tragedy. Morrison is nowhere near Orson Welles's range and before the crash had rambled on in the droning tone of the staid announcer, stumbling over words with a slight downstate accent, chopping off the ends of words, and at times hesitating as he picked a word for the right description. Now he is a runaway train of emotion and rambling dialogue.

> *And oh, it's . . . crashing, oh, four or five hundred feet into the sky, and it . . . it's a terrific crash, ladies and gentlemen. It's smoke, and it's in flames now; and the frame is crashing to the ground, not quite to the mooring mast. Oh, the humanity! And all the passengers screaming around here. I told you; it . . . I can't even talk to people, their friends are on there! Ah! It's . . . It . . . It's a . . . ah! I . . . I can't talk, ladies and gentlemen . . . Honest, it's just*

laying there, a mass of smoking wreckage. Ah! And everybody can hardly breathe and talk and the screaming. I . . . I . . . I'm sorry. Honest, I . . . I can hardly breathe. I . . . I'm going to step inside, where I cannot see it. Charlie, that's terrible. Ah, ah . . . I can't. Listen, folks; I . . . I'm going to have to stop for a minute because I've lost my voice. This is the worst thing I've ever witnessed.[16]

What Herbert Morrison witnessed was the incineration of thirty-six people when the sixteen hydrogen bags in the *Hindenburg* ignited after a lightning strike. This was new territory—a recorded broadcast in which the broadcaster witnessed a horrific event that was so bad it overwhelmed the medium. The third wall of radio was pierced as Herbert Morrison became part of the story of the *Hindenburg*. The safe distance of radio vanished, and the listening audience was plunged into the hell of the moment as well. Charlie, the sound man, kept the recording going as Morrison returned. "Well, ladies and gentlemen, I'm back again. I've sort of recovered from this terrific explosion and the terrific crash that occurred just as it was being pulled down to the mooring mast."[17]

Morrison's composure didn't last long, however, and he was overcome again, unable to get his breath from emotion, shock, and the burning fumes of the hydrogen gas. "*I wish I could stop in just a minute and see if I can get my breath again. And Charlie, if you'll save it out just a minute. I'll come back with more description, ladies and gentlemen.*"[18] When Morrison comes back, he approaches the ship's tip and encounters a survivor. "*I met a man coming out, a dazed, dazed . . . he couldn't find his way. I grabbed hold of him. It's Philip Mangone, Philip Mangone, that's MANGONE of New York.*" Morrison has once again passed through the wall of separation and become part of the story, trying to get the man's name out to relatives. Morrison continues in an agonized voice: "*He's burned terribly in the hands, and he's burned terribly in the face. His eyebrows, all his hair is burned off but he's walking. . . . he told me he jumped, he jumped with other passengers.*"[19]

Herbert Morrison and his sound engineer rushed back to Chicago with their recording. Morrison had addressed the audience as if he were live the whole time. The forty-minute recording was played on WLS the next day at 11:45 a.m. and people thought it was live. Morrison had broken into a new dimension in radio, one in which radio became part of the event. There had been news bulletins on the radio fifteen minutes after the *Hindenburg* burst into flames, but Morrison's report was the only on-the-spot recording. NBC and CBS hesitated to play the recording because it was not live and re-created the events with sound effects and actors. *March of Time* had already broadcast a version of the *Hindenburg* tragedy with explosions and screaming voices all created in the studio. No one had heard the Morrison recording, and no one cared. Re-created news was just better. Orson Welles would listen to the Morrison recording and understand the significance of the *Hindenburg* disaster broadcast. Radio had become fair game for the storyteller.

9

Martians

October 1938

MANY STORIES SELECTED BY ORSON WELLES BEFORE *THE WAR OF THE Worlds* were written for children but hopped the fence and appealed to adults as well. The road to *War of the Worlds* ran through the novel *Lorna Doone* by R. D. Blackmore. It was a swashbuckling tale of John Ridd, who fights for the beautiful Lorna. Welles would play John Ridd, but he lost faith in the show after the script was nearly completed. "It now seemed dated and slow-moving. Further work and revision were needed, but the time for the next show was growing thin, and it began to appear doubtful whether an acceptable script for *Lorna Doone* could be prepared in time."[1] The only other novel the rights had been secured for was the science fiction novel *War of the Worlds* by H. G. Wells.

Orson loved science fiction, but radio had little of it to offer. Buck Rogers was popular, but children were the audience. Orson had two other science fiction tales in mind: M. P. Shiel's *The Purple Cloud*, an end-of-the-world dystopic story, and Arthur Conan Doyle's *The Lost World*, in which dinosaurs are discovered in the Amazon jungle. Eventually Orson settled on *War of the Worlds*. Mercury had paid a small amount of money for the rights, but when Orson read it over for an initial treatment, he feared it might be "too old-fashioned and too remote to sustain his audiences' interest."[2] It had to be modernized in language, and the location had to be moved from England to the United States.

A story in which aliens who would come to colonize Earth and destroy humans with heat ray guns and poisonous gas and use three-legged machines to accomplish their mission may seem preposterous, but the public had been fascinated by the idea of Martians ever since English astronomer Percival Lowell had declared canals on Mars evidence of a Martian civilization. In 1895, Lowell published three books detailing his thesis: "That the lines form a system that, instead of running anywhither, they join certain points to certain others, making thus not a simple network, but one whose meshes connect centers directly with one another, is striking at first sight, and loses none of its peculiarity on second thought. For the intrinsic improbability of such a state of things arising from purely natural causes becomes evident on a moment's consideration."[3]

There was the lingering thought among the population that Martians would come to visit one day. This idea was very much alive in the last years of the nineteenth century when a former science teacher in the town of Surrey took a walk with his brother, who mused, "Suppose some beings from another planet were to drop out of the sky suddenly and begin laying about them here!"[4]

Herbert George Wells had left London for his health and would take bicycle rides and walks to get inspiration for ideas and work out the plots of his books. He was already a successful writer of scientific romances (as science fiction was then called), including *The Time Machine*, *The Island of Doctor Moreau*, and *The Invisible Man*. Like Ray Bradbury, who would come to fame in the 1960s, H. G. Wells inserted modern science into stories that possessed the great *what-if* and took readers on a ride that amazed and sometimes terrified. When his brother, Frank Wells, mused on Martians visiting the earth, it was a match to the fuse that led to the *War of the Worlds* broadcast. The Wells brothers had been talking about the colonization of Tasmania, where "European settlers there had wiped out the entire indigenous population by trapping some people like animals, giving others poisoned food, and shooting the rest on sight."[5] When Frank mentioned the idea to his brother, he imagined the Martians might want to colonize humans the same way.

Wells spent the rest of the summer researching and writing a book based on the idea of a Martian invasion of Earth in a you-are-there style, complete with maps and magazine articles that Wells had written himself. Wells spent hours bicycling and working out the exact locations for his ballet of death by aliens. He used actual newspapers and real locations, painstakingly plotting locations where the Martians would land and begin the destruction of Earth. The plot was simple: The Martians shoot cylinders with a giant cannon that land on earth, and, from these, the three-legged machines emerge with a death ray and poisonous gas to destroy the humans or harvest them for the blood they need to live. The real locations convinced people that this type of invasion could happen.

The book was a sensation, and the novel's beginning was a natural opening for the broadcast: "We know now that in the early years of the twentieth century this world was being watched closely by intelligences greater than man's."[6]

War of the Worlds was terrifying when it was published in 1898, and it was still terrifying in concept in 1938. A description of a battle with a Martian war machine in the town of Shepperton holds up even today in action and pacing: "It . . . raised itself to its full height again. . . . The six guns . . . fired . . . the last close upon the first, made my heart jump."[7]

So Orson Welles wanted *War of the Worlds* as his next radio play. Howard Koch was tasked with turning the novel into a script. Koch had turned up at John Houseman's office during work on the set of *Danton's Death*. Some of the Mercury financiers had recommended him, and the WPA's Federal Theatre had produced some of his plays. The future scriptwriter of *War of the Worlds* had graduated from Columbia Law School and then decided to become a playwright, creating a short-lived Broadway comedy in 1929, followed by a play, *The Lonely Man*, for the Federal Theatre Project in Chicago in 1937.

The lanky Koch, with his midwestern manners, impressed Houseman. Koch signed with Mercury for six months with the agreement that he owned any radio script he wrote. Howard was paid $75 a week to create the sixty-page radio scripts. Usually Koch would get the book at the beginning of the week and race to turn it into a radio script in six days. He worked around the clock, passing the pages to Welles and Houseman, who would return them with notes, changes, and deletions. The changes went up to the day of the broadcast. Houseman often let Koch use his secretary, Anne Froelich, to type the pages of the penciled script as soon as he finished them. Koch adopted *Hell on Ice* and *Seventeen*, and then he found out his next assignment was H. G. Wells's *War of the Worlds*.

Orson had brought the idea to Houseman's attention: a radio show people would think was real and achieved with breaking news bulletins. It was vintage Welles—shock as he did in Harlem with *Macbeth*, break convention with *Julius Caesar*, outrage with *The Cradle Will Rock*, and pull off the ultimate prank by fooling a nation into believing Martians were really invading. It was all an unheralded, unrated, unsponsored show could do to break out of its box. Orson used the same approach from his plays and radio shows—when in doubt, insult and shock grandly.

The claim that Orson Welles had little to do with the *War of the Worlds* script is untrue. As Frank Brady states in his biography, "Welles maintained complete control and authority, creatively and legally, over the content of all his shows. He alone selected, sometimes after consultation with Houseman and others, the story to be dramatized. Often, he had clear ideas of what approach was to be taken, what scenes were to be developed or deleted, and which characters should be highlighted or excised. This was conveyed, usually by direct discussion, sometimes by memorandum, to whoever was responsible for putting the first draft script together."[8]

Orson brought the idea of the news bulletin show first to Houseman and the director of the broadcasts, Paul Stewart. Houseman was sure Welles hadn't read the book, but it didn't matter. On October 23, while rehearsing *Around the World in Eighty Days*, Welles, Houseman, and Stewart decided to make the Halloween eve show based on H. G. Wells's *War of the Worlds*. Orson agreed it would take place in America and Howard Koch would transform the book into a radio play. With only six days to write the script, Koch had phoned Houseman and said the task was impossible. Later, he wrote in his memoir, "Reading the story, which was set in England and written in a different narrative style, I realized I could use very little but the author's idea of a Martian invasion and his description of their appearance and their machines. In short, I was being asked to write an almost entirely original play in six days."[9]

The book was passed onto Koch with instructions to turn it into a show *that was actually happening* with breaking news bulletins. After trying to find his way through the book for three days, Koch called Houseman and said it was impossible to convert the story into some form that would work for radio. Then Anne Froelich, who was working with Koch, got on the line. "It's all too silly . . . we're going to make fools of ourselves, absolute fools,"[10] she said.

Houseman promised to talk to Welles, but Orson was in the throes of a thirty-six-hour rehearsal on *Danton's Death*. There was no time and really no other book. So, Houseman did what any producer would do when staring at a broadcast only six days away. He told Koch he had spoken to Welles and that he was adamant about doing the H. G. Wells book. He said it was Orson's favorite project. Koch hung up and gloomily stared at his typewriter. He just didn't know how to appeal to a modern American audience who mostly preferred to listen to a wooden-headed dummy named Charlie McCarthy.

The Script

October 24, 1938

HOWARD KOCH STARED OUT FROM HIS MANHATTAN APARTMENT AT Central Park's leafy fall-turning colors. He smoked his tenth cigarette, drank his fourth cup of coffee, and felt the burning in his stomach from the acid-grinding hours of staring at his typewriter. The book that was the cause of all this trouble was right behind him. He hated the Martians with their ray guns and poison gas and their cylinders and their soul-destroying three-legged machines. H. G. Wells was an idiot as far as he was concerned. Orson needed the script in three days, but how do you make something as silly as a Martian invasion appeal to a modern audience? The premise was ridiculous and one that modern audiences would not believe. Howard smoked miserably, feeling the walls of his apartment closing in. He had to get out.

So, on Monday, October 24, Koch drove to see his family in Kensington, just ninety miles from New York. Kensington was a small town in New Jersey where Koch often headed to escape the city, where he might think more clearly. As he drove, he smoked and turned over the central problem in his head. How do you turn an absurd premise from a nineteenth-century book into a radio play that would fit Orson Welles's first-person, singular format? Koch visited with his parents for a while and then left to drive back on Route 9W. The red and yellow fall colors were amazing, and Howard felt a calm descend on him. He was thinking again and suddenly pulled over and stopped his car in front of a one-pump gas station in the middle of nowhere in the middle of New Jersey. Koch stepped out of the car and watched the wind toss paper in front of the lone station. He stared at the station. The dust swirled again, and he listened to the airy lost sound of the country.

Howard leaned against his car and looked down the road. He paused, squinting into the dusky twilight. *Why not?* he thought. *Why not have the Martians invade New Jersey?* He bought a map from the man inside the station and opened it on the hood of his car. Howard picked up the pencil he carried in his top left pocket and dropped it in the center of the map. He blinked and stared at the map, muttering, "Grovers Mill."

There! Right there was where his invasion would take place. Grovers Mill. Right in good old USA. Koch returned to his apartment off Central Park and began pounding out the story of a Martian invasion in America. He would later write in his book, *As Time Goes By,* that the work was "a nightmare of scenes written and rewritten, pages speeding back and forth to the studio, with that Sunday deadline staring me in the face. Once the Martians had landed, I deployed the opposing forces over an ever-widening area, making moves and countermoves between the invaders and defenders. After a while I found myself enjoying the destruction I was wreaking like a drunken general."[1]

Koch devised a script Orson could read out loud with the other actors. Many times, the script sounded awkward or verbose when spoken. So, Welles would gather the actors, and they all would read in a circle, calling out the problems and making changes on the spot until the dialogue had the ring of truth. The bad lines of the script were tossed, and new lines were inserted. Many references that worked in England didn't work in America. "Drains" in England referred to sewers, but for Americans, drains referred to the drain in a sink. So, the line "We'll live under ground, and I've been thinking about the drains" became "I've been thinking about the sewers." When the second script was produced, Orson continued working, "still changing dialogue, shifting scenes, and adding action as he deemed necessary."[2] Then he got together with John Dietz, the sound engineer, and worked out all the sound effects for the script. Next, musical bridges and cues were added, and Welles changed the music to fit the mood he wanted. Then the legal department of CBS suggested changes, or Davidson Taylor, the executive producer for the network, would suggest changes to the script.

Finally, a dress rehearsal with Orson was held for timing and honing the script further. The script had to fit into the sixty-minute time slot with a one-page-per-minute ratio. Most of the *Mercury Theatre on the Air* scripts came in at around sixty pages. Orson would continue changing the script right up to airtime, with the actors, musicians, and sound technicians becoming increasingly stressed. But the last-minute changes, the epiphanies that came to Orson during the time compression of any production, and the chaos he created by pushing everyone to the wall gave his productions a viscerally charged wire ambiance. Everyone was learning their changed lines on the air, and the reactions were genuine as Orson shepherded them through the dangerous sea of his vision. *War of the Worlds* was twice as stressful as his other productions because they had lost so much time on *Lorna Doone*. When Houseman and Welles gave the book to Howard Koch, "Welles gave specific instructions to modernize the language and dialogue to localize the action and to dramatize the story in the form of radio news bulletins."[3] After that, Koch was on his own.

Working closely with Houseman over the phone, Koch finished the script for Orson to read on Wednesday night. Welles didn't read it, but there was a quick rehearsal on Thursday night, with Koch and Houseman making whatever adjustments and changes seemed needed. Then an acetate recording was made and given to Richard Wilson, who carried the disc of the completed broadcast through Manhattan traffic, darting through the trellised October sunshine falling from the skyscrapers. Wilson was just twenty-two, had graduated from Princeton, and had come to New York to be an actor. He had been hired as the youngest member of *Mercury Theatre on the Air*, and part of his job was to deliver the recordings of each week's program to Welles at the St. Regis Hotel. Sometimes Welles might answer the door naked, as he had once before, and say nothing but "thank you" and take the disc from Richard's hands. This practice freed Orson from the rehearsals and allowed him to hear the entire show. He then started dismantling the show and sticking it back together with the proper Wellesian characteristics that were Braille to his listeners. The disc that Orson jammed under his arm had to transition from rehearsal on Thursday to the final broadcast with changes being made right up to airtime.

To make matters worse, Orson was buried in his play, *Danton's Death*, which turned out to be a disaster. Already one actor had broken his leg when he fell through a trapdoor on the stage. On Thursday night, Welles didn't return to his room at the St. Regis until late and found John Houseman and Paul Stewart waiting for him. The film footage of *Too Much Johnson* was all over the room, and they had to sit on the floor and listen to the recording. Welles had not been at the rehearsals, and this was his first chance to see what Koch had pulled off with his script. Houseman later said they all felt the show was dull. Welles could take anything, but he couldn't tolerate a radio show that was boring and uninspired. Houseman said they all agreed the show was terrible and that "its only chance of coming off lay in emphasizing its newscast style—its simultaneous, eyewitness quality."[4]

Koch, Houseman, and Stewart started changing the script immediately, pumping in the breaking news format. It was all or nothing. If people didn't believe the Martians were invading, it was just a dated science-fiction story. "All night we sat up—Howard, Paul, and I, spicing the script with circumstantial allusions and authentic detail,"[5] Houseman later wrote. The script transitioned into a compressed, real-time event, in which the havoc of the Martian invasion was in the first thirty-eight minutes of the show with no station break.

On Friday, the script was sent to Davidson Taylor for his pre-show reading, and he turned it over to legal for approval. The verdict came back quickly: "The script was too believable and . . . its realism would have to be diminished before the show could go on the air. They were also worried that using actual institutions' names could be legally actionable."[6] Thirty changes came back, mainly concerning the names of actual places. The Martian battle cry of "Ulla Ulla Ulla" was stricken, as well as a line that had mobs trampling people (it was deemed too graphic). The names of institutions were changed to avoid liability, with Langley Field becoming Langham Field and the United States Weather Bureau becoming the Government Weather Bureau. More changes came from the cast. Everyone hoped the show wouldn't be as bad as they thought it might be.

Sound and music would be significant factors in the *War of the Worlds* broadcast and would be relied on to bring off the required authenticity. Because the production was a broadcast within a broadcast, with dance music playing between scenes of terror, the dance music needed to be as believable as the sound of the Martians and the soldiers at war. Stewart oversaw production, and Houseman recalled, "He worked for a long time on the crowd scenes, the roar of the cannons in the Watchung Hills, and the sound of New York Harbor as the ships with the last remaining survivors put out to sea."[7] Stewart then had to work with Bernard (Benny) Herrmann, the CBS head of music. Stewart later wrote, "We had such a limited budget for the program that we could not get the dance band from CBS for our unsponsored show on Sunday night; so, we had to use the symphony men, many of whom had worked with Toscanini and the New York Philharmonic. To get Benny to conduct the dance songs I had suggested (including 'Stardust' and 'La Cumparisita') was almost an impossibility. He didn't understand the rhythms at all. I said, 'Benny, it's gotta be like this,' and snapped my fingers—and he got very upset. He handed me the baton and said, 'You conduct it!' I got up on the podium. All the musicians understood Benny's personality, so when I gave the downbeat they played it just the way I wanted it. I said, 'Now that's how you do it!' I handed the baton back to Benny, who was crestfallen. The moment in the broadcast when Herrmann conducts 'Stardust' with the symphony orchestra is one of the most hysterical musical moments in radio."[8]

But Welles was a perfectionist who demanded realism, pushing himself and others to extraordinary lengths. Sound, to Welles, *was* the story, and to that end, when he did *A Tale of Two Cities*, he demanded the correct sound of a human head being severed. "Various solid objects were tried under a cleaver wielded by one of the best sound men in the business: a melon, a pillow, a coconut, and a leg of lamb. Finally, it was discovered that a cabbage gave just the right scrunching resistance."[9] For a battle scene, Welles had hundreds of feet of audio cable strung up on the roof of the building "and had extras firing handguns . . . it was a great idea except for the arrival of squad cars full of irate police who threatened to arrest everyone for illegal possession of firearms."[10]

Orson would also make good use of toilet bowls throughout his career. For *Les Misérables*, Welles needed to duplicate the sounds of Parisian sewers and went to Liederkranz Hall on the north side of Fifty-Eighth Street. Richard Wilson, a *Mercury Theatre on the Air* member, recalled that it was "an ancient turn of the century building with lots of toilets and urinals. . . . So, Orson went to the old building and put a microphone in there to represent the sewers of Paris because all the johns and urinals leaked, dripped, and so forth. Somebody made their way through [used a toilet], and on the program on a coast-to-coast broadcast, we heard this toilet flushing . . . this went out over the national broadcast. Orson, as usual, had his headphones on, and the look on his face was extraordinary, it was incredible."[11] And so, when it came to the sound of the Martian cylinder unscrewing in the pit, sound technician Aurore (Ora) Daigle Nichols and her husband took an empty pickle jar into a nearby bathroom stall, where she slowly unscrewed the lid in the porcelain bowl of the toilet.

Frank Readick, who had been the voice of the Shadow before Orson, was Carl Phillips, the on-the-spot man who would describe the Martians and eventually die on the air. Readick listened to the live recording of the *Hindenburg* disaster to get the right tonal inflection as he was gassed and burned to death. Herbert Morrison's *Hindenburg* reporting was the closest he could get to an event in which radio became part of the story. Howard Smith was the brave bomber pilot who crashed his plane into one of the Martian machines. Bernard Herrmann provided the musical interludes crucial to cutting away from the dance music to the invading Martians. On Saturday, another rehearsal was held with preliminary sound effects, and on Sunday, Welles arrived just after noon to begin the preparations that would lead to the evening broadcast.

Orson had another run-through of the script, with actors pinpointing what worked and what didn't. Dan Seymour, the announcer, was the only member of the cast who did not come from the Mercury Theatre or was not one of Orson's radio friends. "Orson railed at the text, cursing the writers," recalled producer Richard Barr. "The first rehearsal with the cast occasioned many small changes in dialogue, with all hands contributing feedback about tone and characterization, trying to knock all the corniness out of the draft."[12] Kenny Delmar was a former child actor in D. W. Griffith films and would handle three parts, including the interior secretary of the United States. "OK, Kenny, you know what I want,"[13] Welles said with a wink, nudging Delmar's secretary voice closer to his dead-on impersonation of FDR. A full rehearsal was held, with Orson's perfectionism falling on the shoulders of sound engineer John Dietz and special effects engineer Ora Daigle Nichols.

The second full rehearsal that afternoon had the station breaks to get the timing down to sixty minutes, though this target was rarely reached because of Orson's constant changes. "Welles continued to emphasize the importance of inserting a sense of immediacy into the script with news bulletins and eyewitness accounts, devices he argued could be used successfully. Koch and Houseman attempted to make the play more realistic by inserting the names of real places and people whenever possible; they also increased the number of flash bulletins in the script."[14]

At one point, Welles dropped the script and called it "the worst piece of crap I've ever had to do."[15] The other actors broke up in laughter. The most innovative part of the script was also the most problematic. This was the dead-air part of the script when the reporter was cut off by the Martians' heat rays, poison gas, or technical problems. Welles stretched the silences that went back to the music as if the station was reverting to some automatic format beyond the control of humans. Houseman protested, saying they would lose listeners, but Welles stretched out the opening with the dance music, gradually increasing the tension. He thought this was the only way listeners would believe the events were happening when the show's pace sped up and time was compressed. "The broadcast moved listeners swiftly through space, much like *The March of Time*, but without that series' central narrator, the effect was wildly distorting."[16] Welles believed once listeners bought into the broadcast, he could do whatever he wanted. Still, Houseman saw only disaster ahead: "Over my protests, lines were restored that had been cut at earlier rehearsals. . . . I cried there would not be a listener left."[17] Welles ignored him and stretched the interludes like a long, taut violin wire.

The other actors took breaks as the afternoon wore on, but Orson "busily ironed out wrinkles, huddling with Herrmann and the musicians, the sound team, the actors."[18] Sandwiches and milkshakes were ordered for the cast and crew while Orson sipped on the pineapple juice he had before every broadcast. This was when Frank Readick went down to the CBS library, dug out the recording of the *Hindenburg*, and listened to Herbert Morrison's live reporting of the disaster. Howard Koch had written the script; John Houseman, Paul Stewart, and Orson had made changes; but now, early in the Sunday evening, Orson Welles, like every good director, had transformed the *War of the Worlds* into his alone. "However divergent the eyewitness accounts of this radio production, they all agree on their portrait of the single-minded and clearheaded Welles, shaping the evolution and quality of *War of the Worlds* despite the staff's continued opposition and skepticism, thoroughly in command of the show's concepts and details. Every important decision was his to make; he was the producer and the star, and the highest artistic executive."[19]

Orson took what others had created and then changed it in a hundred ways. Some of the changes were major; many were nuanced, but they contributed to the art that was Orson Welles. Orson did this on plays, radio shows, and later film. He sucked in whatever vehicle presented itself and then regurgitated it with his magic. Even Howard Koch, who wrote the script, later admitted that "Orson's actual writing on the radio scripts often took place at the eleventh hour on those crazy Sundays, but while it may have been brief, it was very important. He could do wonders in a few minutes."[20] Anyone can write a script. Anyone can play a part. CBS had given Orson Welles his show, allowing him to star in, write, and produce the show, because he could do what others could not. With just hours to spare, Welles would often cut apart the script with scissors and put it back together in a revolutionary way. The Welles magic was undefinable, and it usually came in the last minutes or even during the broadcast, when the unexpected happened and then the brilliant moment. Looking back at the phenomenon of *War of the Worlds*, John Houseman tried to pinpoint the Welles magic that energized broadcasts and plays; when it wasn't there, the play or broadcast was just mediocre: "Welles is at heart a magician whose particular talent lies not so much in his creative imagination (which is considerable) as in his proven ability to stretch the familiar elements of theatrical productions beyond the normal point of tension. For this reason, his productions require more elaborate preparation and more perfect execution than most. Like all complicated magic tricks, they remain, until the last minute, in a state of precarious balance. When the tricks come off, they give, by virtue of their unusually high intensity, an impression of great brilliance and power; when they fail, when something in their balance goes wrong, or the original structure proves to be unsound, they provoke among their audience a particularly violent reaction of unease and revulsion."[21]

Houseman described the final rehearsal before the broadcast in which Orson stepped in and took control: "Sweating, howling, disheveled and single-handed he wrestled with chaos and time—always conveying an effect of being alone, transduced by his collaborators, surrounded by treachery, ignorance, sloth, indifference, incompetence and—more often than not—downright sabotage."[22]

At 7:58 p.m., after eight hours of rehearsal, Orson Welles gulped down the bottle of pineapple juice, moved his mouth experimentally, cleared his throat, and stepped onto a raised podium with a music stand in front of him. He slipped on his headphones and rolled up his sleeves, loosened the knot of his tie, "and gave announcer Dan Seymour a signal to start the show, precisely as the clock's second hand indicated 8 PM."[23] From here, Orson Welles would control the broadcast like a conductor at the top of his form, pointing, throwing cues, nodding, shaking his head, altering the pacing. Now we are back to that classic picture of Welles in the studio. "The actors and music director Herrmann turned to him. Orson looked at the clock, then at Houseman and others in the control room. The announcer Dan Seymour introduced them to their waiting audience. '*The Columbia Broadcasting System and its affiliated stations present Orson Welles and the* Mercury Theatre on the Air *in* The War of the Worlds *by H. G. Wells.*'"[24]

Orson cued the orchestra for the Mercury Theatre theme music with the strings of Tchaikovsky's *Piano Concerto No. 1 in B Flat Minor* playing out over the airwaves as he stepped close to the microphone. The music began to fade, and then, in his shirtsleeves and suspenders, his pants pulled high, with the headphone wires trailing down from his left ear, Orson Welles lifted his arms and, in that amazing baritone, unleashed the *War of the Worlds*.

II

THE BROADCAST

The Crapperoo

October 30, 1938

PEOPLE LISTENING TO THE RADIO ON THE NIGHT OF OCTOBER 30, 1938, had to do some searching to find an interesting program. Secretary of Agriculture Henry Wallace discussed with General Hugh Johnson and Professor John Lyman what the country should do with farm surpluses. Further down the dial, spooled up for the eight o'clock hour, was Edgar Bergen and the *Charlie McCarthy Show* from 8:00 to 9:00 p.m. Then, at 10:00 p.m., it was boxing with the Welterweight Championship on the line between the champ Henry Armstrong and contender Ceferino Garcia. This show was broadcast live from Madison Square Garden with all the excitement of a large cheering crowd. Some people might have opted for a stroll through the autumn night to the movie theater, where they would find *Too Hot to Handle* with Clark Gable and Myrna Loy or maybe *Young Dr. Kildare* with Lew Ayres and Lionel Barrymore or some lighter fare with Mickey Rooney and Spencer Tracy in *Boys Town*. Supposing radio or movies didn't strike a chord, there was always a stroll down to Broadway to see *Knickerbocker Holiday* with Walter Huston, the Pulitzer Prize–winning *Our Town*, Robert Morley in *Oscar Wilde*, or Ole Olsen and Chic Johnson in *Hellzapoppin'*.

There were options other than Orson Welles's *War of the Worlds* performed by *Mercury Theatre on the Air*. The listing of the broadcast under "Radio Programs" in the newspapers was small and inconsequential. The *Lancaster Sunday News* showed four competing radio shows at

8:00 p.m.: "WEAF—Charlie McCarthy, WOR—Bach Cantata, WJZ—Gill Orchestra, WABC—Play, Nells' 'War of the Worlds,' Orson Welles and Mercury Theatre Players."[1] The listing was so inauspicious that the spelling of the author's name, H. G. Wells, was listed in nationwide papers as "Nells." Orson's *Mercury Theatre on the Air* was just one of many shows on October 30, 1938.

At 7:58 p.m., the strains of Tchaikovsky's *Piano Concerto No. 1 in B Flat Minor* beamed out across the country from New York to Chicago to Los Angeles into Southern Canada as the affiliated CBS stations picked up the feed and lobbed it on across the United States. People were doing dishes, settling in for the night, listening to the radio in slippers with kids on the floor. Some were in bars and restaurants, and some were in cars. Middle-aged people born around the turn of the century had been infants when the Wright brothers flew and children when the *Titanic* sank. Older Americans had grown up with the horse and buggy; some veterans had fought in the Civil War and watched Henry Ford transform the country with the Model T. Veterans of World War I had been following the news from Europe wearily, worried about their sons who would be of draft age and the first to go if the United States was dragged into a new conflict. The sensibility of America was still that of a small town, and radio was still considered a novelty.

The *Mercury Theatre on the Air* opening with classical music signaled the show's serious intent. The other shows, such as the *Chase and Sanborn Hour* with Edgar Bergen and his dummy Charlie McCarthy, shoveled out what Welles called "the crapperoo," but that was what 34 percent of the audience was listening to on this mild evening in October. The Mercury Theatre audience of only 3.6 percent of the six million listeners were traditionally "upper-middle culture taste—well-educated, well-read, and artistically inclined listeners. They were not quite at the forefront of avant-garde high culture, but they rejected the melodramatic thrillers, soap operas, and comedy variety shows most popular with listeners."[2] As one New York listener put it in a letter to Welles, "I want you to put your programs on earlier because I have to battle with my family at eight to be able to listen to you. . . . They like that McCarthy dummy."[3]

The music ended, and Orson came on in that marvelous baritone. Now people were on their own as the broadcast moved into the end of a weather report and then into the Meridian Room of the Hotel Park Plaza in downtown New York, where they were entertained by Ramón Raquello and his orchestra.[4] This was when the first hook was thrown into the sea of the listening audience. A later Gallup poll found "that 60 percent of those who heard the broadcast tuned in after it started."[5] People tuned into the music like many do today. They began channel surfing and landed on the dance music, some using it for background, others because they liked the Spanish strains of Raquello's orchestra. Even though this slow beginning made John Houseman nervous and had one man in the control room refer to the broadcast "as a bore," this introduction was needed to lure the audience in because now the first interruption occurred during a tango number.

"*We interrupt our program of dance music to bring you a special bulletin.*"[6] The report of astronomers seeing explosions on Mars was the first shot across the bow of terror. A teaser, and then the music returned to Bobby Millette playing "Stardust" from the Hotel Martinet in Brooklyn. But this announcement was just the warmup for what was to follow. The panic was already beginning.

"'*Quick, listen! Mars is exploding!*' shouted Lucile McLain, a patient in a tuberculosis sanitarium in Oregon, to the other convalescents resting nearby." In Los Angeles, Mrs. Johanna Wilizenski "called friends and neighbors, as we were told, to listen in for further reports." Edward A. Callahan of Elmhurst, Long Island, wrote Orson Welles later that he and his seventeen-year-old daughter could not decide what to listen to: "We are all lovers of all radio stories. . . . We also love Edgar Bergen. So, we flipped a coin to determine which we would listen to, and the coin decided on Orson Welles."[7]

Callahan and others heard the music interrupted again. Six minutes into the show, reporter Carl Phillips (played by Frank Readick) interviewed Professor Pierson (played by Welles) at the Princeton Observatory. The professor, who had been observing the explosions, was unalarmed. "*You're quite convinced . . . that living intelligence . . . does not exist on Mars?*"[8] Pierson's voice projected the bespectacled professor with a pipe in his mouth. *"I should say the chances against it are a thousand to one."*[9] E. C. Parmenter had just tuned in and, with his family, gathered around the radio in a suburb of Cleveland, Ohio. "This is funny. . . . I haven't got the Mercury Theatre. It's just some astronomer giving a scientific talk."[10] The integrity of the broadcast had just been established, and now Phillips was interrupted by a telegram delivered to the professor, which he read on the air. He described an explosion of "earthquake intensity."[11] Professor Pierson played it down, saying it was probably a meteor strike and had nothing to do with the explosions on Mars. The broadcast swung back to New York for some piano music. It was now twelve minutes into the broadcast. On the other side of the radio dial, Nelson Eddy had begun to croon "Neapolitan Love Song" on the *Charlie McCarthy Show*. The listeners, who were there only for the dummy theatrics, began to turn their dials and landed on the broadcast in progress that had just cut away to describe *"a huge flaming object . . . in the vicinity of a farm in the neighborhood of Grovers Mill."*[12] Twelve percent of the Charlie McCarthy audience left, and Orson Welles's *Mercury Theatre on the Air* program, which had consistently trailed in the ratings, got supercharged up to the six to twelve million listener mark.[13]

Reporter Phillips and Professor Pierson raced to the scene, making it there in eleven minutes to describe the meteorite that had become a cylinder in a pit thirty yards in diameter made of "yellowish-white metal." Then there were the sounds of sirens as police arrived and kept back the crowd that had gathered around the smoking pit. Reporter Phillips complained about a policeman blocking his view, and people listening heard people shouting over each other. A man from Colorado who later wrote to the FCC justified his being taken in by the broadcast at this point: "Imagine tuning into some dance music, and suddenly it is interrupted by a news flash, later by another. This is quite a common occurrence, isn't it? Then, a radio commentator comes on with an interview with a Princeton professor and later an eyewitness account. Isn't that all happening in reality almost every day?"[14]

Then Phillips interviews the farmer who owns the land, Mr. Wilmuth, and the interview is a rambling, awkward bit of radio improvisation:

Wilmuth: Well, I was listenin' to the radio.

Phillips: Closer and louder please.

Wilmuth: Yes, sir—while I was listening to the radio and kinda drowsin', that Professor fellow was talkin' about Mars, so I was half dozin' and half . . .

Phillips: Yes, yes, Mr. Wilmuth. Then what happened?

Wilmuth: As I was sayin', I was listenin' to the radio kinda halfways . . .[15]

Phillips shuts him down and moves on. Now a strange sound is coming from the cylinder. Phillips moves closer to the pit. The cylinder head begins to unscrew, and Professor Pierson comments that it is the cylinder cooling, but Phillips cuts him off and announces the top of the cylinder is coming off. The grinding, scraping sound of the Martian cylinder continues as sound technician Ora Nichols unscrews a mayonnaise jar in a toilet stall down the hall from CBS's Studio One.

Dead Air

October 30, 1938

CIVIL WAR VETERANS WERE LISTENING TO ORSON WELLES'S *WAR OF the Worlds* broadcast, as were formerly enslaved people and others who were old enough to have read about the death of Abraham Lincoln in the newspapers—another event that must have been unbelievable. Often when we think of the 1938 *War of the Worlds* broadcast, we have an urban bias in mind. We see people in cities or suburbs listening to their new radios in apartments or homes. They are generally educated; many would write letters after the broadcast, and these letters would be the reference point for scholars. Conclusions would be made from a sampling of well-educated urban Americans. But the truth is that the broadcast beamed out across America and was relayed by affiliates into the far enclaves of farms; small, isolated towns; coastal cottages; camps, cabins, shacks, and barns. People heard the broadcast in general stores, bars, barbershops, restaurants, diners, barracks, and their cars.

Sound specialist Ora Nichols continued unscrewing the mayonnaise jar in the bathroom stall to simulate the alien cylinder top coming off, followed by a dull thud as it fell, and reporter Carl Phillips (played by Frank Readick) used the inflections of a man slowly descending into horror. Police shouted at the crowd to stay back. Welles specialized in the sound of chaos as the actors in the studio huddled around microphones and called back and forth in different voices. In one of the pictures of the broadcast, we see five actors around the large CBS microphone holding their scripts with Orson in front of his microphone and music stand with his arms raised over his head; to his right, conductor Herrmann is directing a front row of violinists with headphones and a baton. The *War of the Worlds* broadcast was a symphony. It was an orchestra of people working to produce a desired effect, with reporter Phillips throwing an unforgettable image out into America. Readick played the reporter out of breath, talking rapidly, excitedly, describing what he saw in real time and describing a monster with serpent black eyes, saliva dripping from its mouth. He then seemed so distressed that he signed off, "*Hold on, will you please? I'll be back in a minute.*"[1]

Readick had taken the newscast to a new level. He had done his homework well. WLS Chicago reporter Herbert Morrison had had to go off the air to compose himself during the *Hindenburg* crash. Overcome with the horror of the Martians, Phillips excused himself and brought radio into the broadcast as a character. The medium was in the studio as listeners were left with piano music in the Park Plaza Hotel. It was jarring, discombobulating, and very realistic. "I only wish I could forget it,"[2] a woman from Washington wrote later. But listeners were left with the horrible image of the creature's mouth, "*V-shaped with saliva dripping.*"[3]

For thirty seconds, inane piano music played. Some listeners, of course, figured out that the broadcast was a play at this point. "Of course, when the Martians appeared, the horror element became comedy for me in the realization that I had been had,"[4] wrote a man from Connecticut. But at what point did he understand it was a broadcast play? Many who wrote in did it to assure themselves and others they had not really been duped when many others had. Eighty percent of Americans owned radios on the night of October 30, 1938. This is out of a population of 97 million families, and the number of people owning radios was "a greater proportion than have telephones, automobiles, plumbing, electricity, or magazines. The radio was their principal and, in some cases, their only source of information about the wider world. They were accustomed to trusting it."[5]

The Golden Age of Radio had begun in 1930, but its banner year was 1938. On March 13, Edward R. Murrow went on the air with his first live report on the Anschluss in Austria. On April 14, President Franklin D. Roosevelt presented a fireside chat on the economy. On June 24, he presented another fireside chat. On July 11, Orson Welles broadcast his first *Mercury Theatre on the Air* presentation of *Dracula*. On September 12, commentator H. V. Kaltenborn broadcast marathon coverage of the Sudetenland crisis on CBS, where he ate and slept in the studio. On October 30, Orson Welles broadcast H. G. Wells's *War of the Worlds*.

Hearing the description of an alien emerging from the smoking cylinder in the pit scared up to twelve million people who had never been in life-threatening situations. "I knew it was something terrible, and I was frightened," said Mrs. Ferguson, a northern New Jersey housewife. "But I didn't know what it was. I couldn't make myself believe it was the end of the world. I've always heard that when the world would come to an end, it would come so fast nobody would know—so why should God get in touch with this announcer? When they told us what road to take and get up over the hills and the children began to cry, the family decided to go out. We took blankets, and my granddaughter wanted to take the cat and the canary."[6] The listeners who had come over from the *Charlie McCarthy Show* broadcast had no chance. They were tuning into the middle of a developing news broadcast. A man from Arkansas wrote to CBS that "there it was, presented as fact by the Columbian Broadcasting System as News, there being no way for a late tuner, or a tuner otherwise occupied at the beginning of the program, to know that it was drama and not a bona-fide News Bulletin."[7]

Phillips returned to the air, presenting the same chaotic feeling of a broadcast in crisis: "*I'll give you every detail. . . . Two policemen advance with something in their hands. . . . It's a white handkerchief tied to a pole.*"[8]

Logical listeners, at this point, might have smelled the hoax. Three policemen approaching an alien from another planet with a white flag is more like some boys playing war. It made no sense, but the suspension of disbelief had occurred through the broadcast's authenticity, the reporter's emotion, and the speed of events. From this point on, listeners were strapped in for the ride into the haunted house, and Orson was about to deliver his most incredible horrifying thrill.

Sound effects technicians in the CBS studio provided a low sub-sonic hum that grew with increasing intensity while Phillips described what was happening. "*There's a jet of flame . . . it leaps right at the advancing men!*"[9] Now the *Hindenburg* tragedy is front and center as Phillips loses his broadcasting shield and becomes terrified. "*They're turning into flame!*"[10] Now the actors scream and shriek around the parabolic CBS microphone as Phillips loses his composure. The sound of an explosion as he frantically describes the spreading fire: "*It's coming this way. About twenty yards to my right.*"[11]

Listeners all over America heard the crash of the microphone, and then . . . DEAD SILENCE. Reporter Phillips had just been inciner-ated on the air. There was no sound inside CBS's Studio One up in the skyscraper in Manhattan. The musicians watched Orson. The conductor, Herrmann, watched Orson. The actors watched Orson. The control room personnel watched Orson. That image returns: Orson holding up his hands for silence. There are two pictures of this moment. One has Orson with both hands over his head, and the other has him with his left hand up, holding the moment. The second one is the signal to the conductor, the musicians, and the actor to not move, not to speak, but to sit while the sin of radio was committed. *DEAD AIR.* For in the dead air fanning out across America came the terror. People were now their own worst enemies as they conjured up nothing less than the death of civilization.

A Midwesterner, Joseph Hendley, was later interviewed for the investigative Contril report and gave the effect of the broadcast on his entire family: "That Halloween boo sure had our family on its knees before the program was half over. God knows we prayed to HIM last Sunday. It was a lesson in more than one thing to us. My mother went out and looked for Mars. Dad was hard to convince or skeptical or something, but he even got to believing it. Brother Joe as usual got more excited than he could show. Brother George wasn't home. Aunt Grace, a good Catholic, began to pray with Uncle Henry. Lily got sick to her stomach. I don't know what I did exactly, but I know I prayed harder and more earnestly than ever before. Just as soon as we were convinced that this thing was real. How pretty all things on earth seemed, how soon we put our trust in God."[12]

Closer to home in New York, Mrs. Anna Ferrell had just tuned in and heard reporter Phillips's description and then his incineration. "I was crying so hard . . . that my sister woke up and wanted to know what I was crying for; well, she listened."[13]

Orson Welles, for six seconds, held the nation in thrall. As Welles demanded silence, all the way down in Tampa, Florida, pandemonium broke loose. The *Tampa Times* reported, "Hundreds Flee Homes, Others Pray as Attack from Mars Is Described." The article went on to say that Tampans had "badly shattered nervous systems . . . when word flashed through Tampa that a national calamity—maybe the end of the world was taking place."[14]

Meanwhile, after the six-second pause in the CBS studio, Orson dropped his hand and allowed the broadcast to proceed. An announcer came on: *"Due to circumstances beyond our control, we are unable to continue this broadcast from Grovers Mill."*[15] The announcer then quoted a Professor Indellkoffer, who stated that *"the explosions on Mars are undoubtedly nothing more than severe volcanic disturbances on the surface of the planet."*[16] Then, incredibly, the station went back to piano music. The swerving from terror to the banal dance music in a hotel dropped the temperature of the terror thermometer and further disoriented listeners. The announcer then came back on, like a returning nightmare, and said he had just been handed a message from Grovers Mill. *"At least forty people, including six state troopers, lie dead in a field east of the village of Grovers Mill."*[17]

The roller coaster of terror began again. The *War of the Worlds* had been on the air for seventeen minutes, and it was almost 8:20 p.m. on the East Coast. People listening to the news broadcast of Martians landing in a small town called Grover Mills dared not move. They were pacing, kneeling, sitting, standing, but not venturing from the yellow dial on which their very existence depended. Others ran and drove, fleeing from the terror. The *Bergen Evening Record* in New Jersey reported that by "8:15 o'clock, calls started pouring into every radio station throughout the country. As the flawless radio performance gained momentum, the listeners became more and more panicky until, in desperation, they switched off their radios and ran into the streets crying and shouting for help. . . . The Kansas City bureau of the Associated Press received inquiries on the 'meteors' from Los Angeles; Salt Lake City; Beaumont, Texas; and St. Joseph, Mo."[18] The paper reported that "Ramsey police stopped a driver whose car was zigzagging down the road. Apparently, he had been drinking, they thought. The man, white with fear and terror, said he was fleeing with his family to the mountains in New York State. The Orange Mountains in Essex County were thronged with persons trying to escape the gas attack by going to a higher elevation . . . women were seen praying in the streets in many places. Autos packed with fleeing families sped over highways without any destination."[19]

Now it was time for the *Mercury Theatre on the Air* cast and crew to pile on the carnage and the terror. The hook had been set, and anyone listening had bought in on the premise that Martians had landed and were incinerating people. Time didn't matter anymore; there was only panic and anxiety. People had heard a reporter describing horrible aliens emerging from a cylinder. That same reporter was then murdered on the air. Then came six seconds of terrifying dead air. What followed in the broadcast drove people out of their homes and into their cars in their pajamas and slippers, taking pets with them—birds, dogs, and cats—running for subways, trains, and buses, falling down stairs, having heart attacks, leaving businesses, screaming down streets, running into churches, synagogues, contemplating suicide or running literally for the hills. America was now under assault by an alien force from the planet Orson Welles.

A Wave of Mass Hysteria

October 30, 1938

DARKNESS HAD DESCENDED ALONG THE EAST COAST, WITH PORCH lights falling on pumpkins that smiled eerily out into the night. Along the coastline, cottages dotted the shore. In a few short years, these same cottages would be instructed to keep their lights off lest they signal German U-boats. The dishes had been put away and Americans were enjoying their tobacco in the form of cigarettes, cigars, and pipes. Blue smoke rolled out of kitchens into the dens where radios played soft music and children did homework as the week turned over and the world settled down. Dials were turned and tuned when suddenly the night was interrupted by a stentorian voice.

"*I have been requested by the governor of New Jersey to place the counties of Mercer and Middlesex as far west as Princeton and east to Jamesburg under martial law.*"[1]

The people who had missed the first quarter of the *War of the Worlds* broadcast were sucked into the vortex of a news program in progress. Wives sat down by their husbands; children looked up from kitchen tables. The news has the same feel as the bulletins about Adolf Hitler and the Nazis the weeks before—ominous, foreboding, terrifying. The warm dinners recently consumed felt heavy as anxiety pushed in. People tried to glean details as the announcer came back on. "*The strange creatures . . . crawled back into their pit and made no attempt to prevent the firemen from recovering the bodies.*"[2] Creatures? Bodies? People who hadn't heard the

Martians had landed were piecing together an extraordinary story as the announcer cut back to Professor Pierson (played by Orson Welles).

"I can give you no authoritative information—either as to their nature, their origin, or their purpose here on Earth."[3]

The professor rambled on, but people had already jumped up and decided on their own what had happened. Earth was being invaded by aliens who were using a heat ray to incinerate humans. In Riverside, California, the *Riverside Daily* led with a bold front-page headline the next day: "Thousand Flee Homes as Radio Drama Too Realistic." The article reported that "dozens of startled Riversiders rush[ed] to the phone to get details from the Press . . . last night . . . one horrified listener phoned the newspaper office that Trenton, New Jersey had been wiped off the map by a meteor, another insisted a foreign nation had attacked the east coast with airplanes."[4]

At this high-intensity moment, the brilliance of the script is evident in the maneuver that Koch, Welles, and Houseman came up with, taking the drama out of the lap of the reporters and throwing it to the military.

The announcer cuts back in: *"We have received a request from the militia at Trenton to place at their disposal our entire broadcasting facilities."*[5] Now suspension of disbelief is in full swing. Listeners are with the army that somehow materialized in ten minutes in force with eight battalions or seven thousand soldiers surrounding the creatures. Captain Lansing of the signal corps takes over and says confidently, *"The situation is now under complete control."* The army might not have heavy field pieces, but Lansing says they *"are adequately armed with rifles and machine guns."*[6] Captain Lansing reduces the temperature by reassuring the listening audience that the army has everything well in hand.

"The things . . . do not even venture to poke their heads above the pit."[7] The captain then rambles about the troops and how it looks like a real war, and the tension builds again. *"Seven thousand armed men closing in on an old metal tube. . . . It's going higher and higher . . . actually rearing up on a sort of metal framework. . . . Hold on!"*[8]

Then the feed is cut off. The Martian machine has been introduced, and now the *Mercury Theatre on the Air* in CBS's Studio One is lowering the boom on the millions of people listening to their broadcast. For those who switched from the antics of an inane dummy, for those looking for some music, for those who were trying to piece it all together, for those who had been listening all along, the trap is sprung, and the sin of gullibility called to account. A somber announcer comes on: "*The evidence of our eyes leads to the inescapable conclusion that those strange beings . . . are the vanguard of an invading army from the planet Mars.*"[9]

The announcer tells the audience that the Martians have incinerated seven thousand soldiers. It is now 8:26 p.m. Eastern Time; the military has been destroyed, and the Martian machines are loose. Gasoline is poured on the flames as people rush out of their houses and into the streets. The *Journal-Times* of Racine, Wisconsin, announced, "War Refugees Flee from Homes Convinced Devastation Is Near." The newspaper reported that "thousands of persons in every part of the country believed last night that the Eastern United States had been invaded by creatures from the planet Mars. . . . In Newark, NJ, hundreds fled from two city blocks, carrying what possessions they could snatch up in their flight."[10] Time did not exist anymore, as the Martian machines had taken over the eastern half of the United States. People were called in to hear the incredible news; children were called in to listen; wives, mothers, brothers, sons, daughters, uncles, and grandparents all heard the carnage. The announcer described railroad tracks torn up, communication lines destroyed, and trains and highways crowded with fleeing people. "*Police and army reserves are unable to control the mad flight. . . . Martial law prevails throughout New Jersey and eastern Pennsylvania.*"[11]

Archie Burbank, a Newark, New Jersey, filling station operator, had had enough. He and his girlfriend took to the road. "My girlfriend and I stayed in the car for a while just driving. Then, we followed the lead of a friend. All of us ran into a grocery store and asked the man if we could go into the cellar. He said, 'What's the matter? Are you trying to ruin my business?' So, he chased us out. A crowd collected. We rushed to an apartment house and asked the man in the apartment to let us in his cellar. He said, 'I don't have any cellar! Get away!' Then, people started to rush out of the apartment house, all undressed. We got in the car and listened some more."[12]

To people in their cars trying to escape, it was not unlike trying to drive away from a forest fire. As more information came in drivers would head a different way. A woman from New York wrote to the station, "My family were panic stricken . . . my mother, father, brother, sister, nephew, cousin, brother-in-law, and myself were crying and we just didn't know what to do."[13] People rushed from homes and kept their radios on in their cars.

Then Orson had Kenneth Delmar, an actor who had done impersonations of President Roosevelt before, make an announcement as the secretary of the interior. Orson told him with a wink to make it sound presidential. Many people who heard the announcement thought it was FDR, as his voice had become familiar to listeners of his fireside chats. This unofficial presidential announcement sealed the veracity of the broadcast for many people who now fully believed the United States was under attack.

"Citizens of the nation: I shall not try to conceal the gravity of the situation . . ."[14]

Because of FDR's fireside chats, people regarded radio as above the fray and formed a trusted personal bond with the president on the radio. This is why Kenny Delmar's speech was so powerful as he slyly slid into an FDR voice. When Delmar finished his speech, many thought the Germans had invaded. One panicked woman in New Jersey later said, "I kept saying over and over again to everybody I met, 'Don't you know New Jersey is destroyed by the Germans—it's on the radio.'"[15] Some thought the announcer was mistaken: "I knew it was some Germans trying to gas all of us. When the announcer kept calling them people from Mars, I thought he was ignorant and didn't know yet that Hitler had sent them all."[16]

The cadence of Kenny Delmar's speech is remarkably close to the speech President Roosevelt would give three years later to Congress, asking for a declaration of war when the Japanese attacked Pearl Harbor. It is full of Rooseveltian markers: *"A nation united courageous and consecrated to the preservation of human supremacy on Earth."*[17] To people tuning in late and hearing the actor who sounded like FDR, it was the president talking about Adolf Hitler. One listener wrote Orson Welles later, "As we listened, it was some time before Mars, or Martians, was mentioned or we caught such mention."[18] It didn't matter. As the *Roanoke World-News* would later write, "The simulated news bulletins which accompanied a CBS dramatization of H. G. Wells' fantasy, the *War of the Worlds*, became so realistic that they sent a wave of mass hysteria across the continent."[19]

The wave was just beginning.

Go Home and Prepare to Die

October 30, 1938

NOW WE ARE BACK TO THE BEGINNING OF THIS BOOK, WHEN CBS EXEC-utive Davidson Taylor had just picked up the phone in the control room and rushed out of the studio. Orson was busy conducting the final segment of the first half of the broadcast before the station break, at which time *War of the Worlds* would be identified as a radio play. The clock was approaching 8:30 p.m., and the break would occur in ten minutes. Welles then saw Davidson burst back into the control room. Ray Collins was broadcasting live from a New York rooftop, which was the heart of the terror portion of the broadcast. Taylor tried to force his way into the studio and was blocked by John Houseman. The sweating, agitated Taylor told Houseman that "CBS switchboards [are] overwhelmed with calls from frightened listeners. He'd even heard rumors that people were killing themselves because of the broadcast or trying to flee from Martians in droves. They had to announce that it was all fake immediately."[1]

Houseman shut the door on Taylor. Welles watched the confrontation from his podium and saw Davidson staring at him. The broadcast was nearing its denouement, and even though Davidson had heard rumors of "panicked mass flight, injuries, and even suicides,"[2] he was not permitted into the studio. The reality of what was going on in the country was impossible to fathom. The broadcast proceeded as Welles and his actors plowed on toward the station break, unaware of the building wave of terror sweeping over the country.

After hearing the broadcast in Pennsylvania, a young girl would later write, "What are we going to do? What can we do? What difference does it make whether we get killed now or later. I was really hysterical. My two girlfriends and I were crying and holding each other, and everything seemed so unimportant in the face of death. We felt it was terrible we should die so young. I'm always nervous anyway and I guess I was getting everybody even more scared. The boy from downstairs threatened to knock me out if I didn't stop acting so hysterical. We tried another small station which had some program on that confirmed our fears. I was sure the end of the world was coming."[3]

Switchboards all over the country lit up as the American Telephone and Telegraph Company reported an increase of 39 percent in traffic. The role of the telephone in disseminating the *War of the Worlds* broadcast was significant. People were now finding out the country was under attack from other people and not by radio. One woman reported that her "sister called up, and I immediately got scared."[4] Another woman said she "was resting when an excited person phoned and told me to listen to the radio that a big meteor had fallen. I was really worried."[5] These calls from trusted friends spread out across the country as the telephone passed the news that Martians had landed and were murdering humans. Fantasy quickly became facts, and people who didn't hear the broadcast added their spin to the story.

Many people couldn't get through the overloaded switchboards and took to the streets or headed for the closest church. "In Harlem, a black congregation fell to its knees; in Indianapolis, a woman ran screaming into a church where evening service was being held and shouted, 'New York has been destroyed. It's the end of the world. Go home and prepare to die!'"[6] A woman gave birth prematurely, and another fell down a whole flight of stairs. In Newark, New Jersey, all the occupants of a block of flats left their homes with wet towels around their heads as improvised gas masks. In Staten Island, Connie Casamassina was just about to get married. Latecomers to the reception took the microphone from the singing waiter and announced the invasion. "Everyone ran to get their coats. I took the microphone and started to cry—'Please don't spoil my wedding day'—and then my husband started singing hymns, and I decided I was going to dance the Charleston. And I did, for fifteen minutes straight. I did every step there is in the Charleston."[7]

The *Trenton Evening Times* of October 31 reported that "one hysterical man entered a police station with the alarming news that planes were bombing New Jersey. When the officer on duty asked how he knew this, the man replied that he heard it on the radio. He had gone to the roof of his building and said he could see the smoke from the bombs." In the same article, a Boston woman called a switchboard and reported that "the flames of ravaged New Jersey were visible in Massachusetts."[8] People were completing the story on their own, with some claiming they saw poisonous gas approaching. During a thunderstorm in Concrete, Washington, a transformer blew and plunged the town into darkness as people heard New York had just been destroyed by Martians. People ran into the streets in the lightning and rain and believed it was the end of the world. Albert Frank would later recall driving into town, and "here comes this woman out of the house there yelling that the world was coming to an end. She had been watching Orson Welles movie [*sic*] in the house and it was on the radio and scared her."[9]

Mothers and fathers tried to protect their infants and children from the advancing Martians. Mrs. Walters from New England was later interviewed by researcher Cantril for his report on the broadcast. "I kept shivering and shaking. I pulled out suitcases and put them back, started to pack but didn't know what to take. I kept piling clothes on my baby, took all her clothes out, and wrapped her up. Everybody went out of the house except the neighbor upstairs. I ran up and banged on his door. He wrapped two of his children in blankets, and I carried the other, and my husband carried my child. We rushed out. I wanted to take some bread, for I thought that if everything is burning, you can't eat money, but you can eat bread."[10]

Davidson Taylor's story of suicides, deaths, and panic in the streets was hard to verify, but clearly the nation was reeling from the news that Martian machines had murdered thousands of people and were advancing on New York City and other parts of the country. Orson Welles kept his eye on Davidson and Houseman at the studio door and concentrated on getting through the most dramatic part of the broadcast before he would let the world know on the station break that it was all just a radio play.

A scant twenty-one years had passed since the last world war that horrified the nation with the mega-death carnage on an industrialized scale. The nineteenth-century approach to war was still fresh when France and Germany lined up in trenches and began to kill each other with .50-caliber machine guns, high-explosive shells, flamethrowers, and poisonous gas. Gas was the most horrific. Gas canisters would land, and there would be a rush to get on masks, but for those who didn't, the results were gruesome and horrific. Mustard gas, chlorine gas, bromine, phosgene, or tear gas—men drowned in fluid in their lungs or had horrible chemical burns on their skin. Blindness was expected and America was treated to pictures of men holding on to each other in long rows, blinded by a chemical gas attack. Gas conjured up the worst evolution of warfare in the twentieth century, and Welles used it in his broadcast of *War of the Worlds.* Two soldiers discussed getting gassed as they battled the Martian machines.

"Put on the gas mask."

"Still can't see, sir. The smoke's coming nearer."[11]

Listeners were wondering what the smoke was, and before they could catch their breath, the broadcast was handed off to a bomber crew. There was no reality left. Why were people listening to bomber crews, how had the feed been hooked up quickly, and how did they get planes in the air in minutes? It was all of 8:30 p.m. by this time, but it didn't matter. Listeners who came in late made the jump quickly, and listeners who had started with Welles were too far down the rabbit hole. Panic dictates its own logic as the brain is flooded with adrenaline. A fight-or-flight response kicks in, accounting for people jumping into their cars and driving aimlessly. Then Welles took the poisonous gas to its terrifying conclusion.

The commander of army bombing plane V-8-43 from Bayonne, New Jersey, Lieutenant Voght, came on in command of eight bombers. *"Enemy now turns east, crossing Passaic River into the Jersey marshes. . . . Objective is New York City."*[12] For people listening in New York or Newark, the terror was complete as they ran for trains, subways, and jumped in cars.

Listeners then heard a loud buzz. As people leaned in close to their radios, they heard in realtime the death of the bomber commander.

"They're spraying us with flame. . . . No chance to release bombs. Only one thing left . . . drop on them, plane and all . . ."

An explosion erupted on the radio, and then, *"Eight army bombers in engagement with enemy tripod machines over Jersey flats. Engines incapacitated by heat ray. All crashed . . . now discharging heavy black smoke."*

"This is Newark, New Jersey. . . . Poisonous black smoke [is] pouring in from Jersey marshes. Reaches South Street. Gas masks useless. Urge population to move into open spaces . . . automobiles use Routes 7, 23, 24, avoid congested areas."[13]

There was no mistaking it: Martians were using poisonous gas to extinguish humans the way someone might use insecticide on roaches or the way the Germans had used it against the French, British, and Americans in World War I. All people knew was that the Martian killing machines with their heat rays and poisonous gas were coming. Full-blown panic was setting in across the land. Hadley Cantril later interviewed Mrs. Joslin for his study. Her husband was a day laborer living in a large eastern city. "I was frightened. I wanted to pack and take my child in my arms. . . . I ran and called my boarder and started with my child to rush down the stairs, not waiting to catch my hat or anything. When I got to the foot of the stairs, I just couldn't get out; I don't know why. Meantime my husband tried other stations and found them still running. He couldn't smell any gas or see people running, so he called me back and said it was just a play. So, I set down, still ready to go at any minute till I heard Orson Welles say, 'Folks, I hope we ain't alarmed you. This is just a play!' Then I just set!"[14]

Radio again became a character as the announcer stationed himself atop a "broadcasting station" in New York City. It could well be the CBS studios. The announcer started by describing a city fleeing from the invading Martians.

"The bells you hear are ringing to warn the people to evacuate the city. . . . Army wiped out . . . artillery, air force, everything wiped out. . . . We'll stay here to the end."[15]

The entire armed forces had been wiped out in minutes. Time and space had collapsed. It had only been thirty minutes since the Martians crashed to Earth. One Long Island listener later wrote the FCC and said, "You may question my sanity, you may wonder what was the matter with me, a man supposed to be educated and experienced, that I did not realize that such could not possibly be true. . . . My only answer is that I am, or was, a person who believed in the basic honesty of a Press Radio News bulletin, and that I know that never in God's world would any high government official, sane or insane, drunk or sober, ever play such a practical joke."[16]

But the joke continued with the announcer on the roof reporting on the advancing Martian machines in other parts of the United States.

"Three million people have moved out along the roads to the north. Hutchinson River Parkway still kept open for motor traffic. . . . Martian cylinders are falling all over the country. One outside Buffalo, one in Chicago, St. Louis . . ."[17]

Earth was under attack. In small towns in Michigan, people looked out windows to see whether the machines were advancing. A couple from Michigan later wrote to the station: "Here we're both college graduates, both levelheaded and really not silly at all . . . yet tomorrow the whole town will be giving us the laugh."[18] The couple had done something that put them out front and center with the town. They might have burst into the local stores and told people to flee the oncoming Martian fire-spewing, poison gas–pumping machines. They might have jumped into their car, as people all over the country were doing, and drove to get away from the marauding machines. Maybe they called up friends and told them to take shelter. But who could blame them? The radio reporter on the roof was about to die on live radio. Ray Collins, the actor in Studio One, read the lines like a man watching his destruction, anxiety building in his voice.

"Now the first machine reaches the shore. . . . He waits for the others. . . . Now they're lifting their metal hands."[19] Ray is frantic, the radio announcer sacrificing himself for the greater good. *"This is the end now . . . People in the streets see it now. They're running toward the East River . . . thousands of them dropping in like rats. . . . Now the smoke is spreading faster. It's reached*

Times Square.... Now the smoke is crossing Sixth Avenue ... Fifth Avenue ... a hundred yards away ... it's fifty feet ..."[20]

On the radio, people heard the thud of a body falling, the microphone hitting the ground. Then there was the sound of the city in chaos with foghorn whistles and screams. Listeners hearing this sat dumbfounded as a final voice came back on like a ham radio operator. *"2X2L calling CQ ... 2X2L calling CQ ... 2X2L calling CQ ... New York. Isn't there anyone on the air?"*[21] New York had been destroyed. This was the inescapable conclusion. All life had just been exterminated between the heat rays and the poisonous gas. People needed to hear no more. This was when Archie Burbank, the filling station operator, jumped in his car with his girlfriend and started driving. "We got into the car and listened some more. Suddenly the announcer was gassed [and] the station went dead so we tried another station, but nothing would come on. Then, we went to a gas station and filled up our tank in preparation for riding as far as we could. The gas station man didn't know anything about it."[22]

The *Mercury Theatre on the Air* actors had told people they were hopelessly encircled by murdering Martian machines that had decimated the East Coast, and it was just a matter of time before all humanity was wiped out. Miss Delany, an ardent Catholic in a New York suburb, could not leave her radio. "I held a crucifix in my hand and prayed while looking out of my open window for falling meteors. I also wanted to get a faint whiff of the gas so that I would know when to close my window and hermetically seal my room with waterproof cement or anything else I could get hold of. My plan was to stay in the room and hope that I would not suffocate before the gas blew away. When the monsters were wading across the Hudson River and coming into New York, I wanted to run up on my roof to see what they looked like, but I could not leave my radio while it was telling me of their whereabouts."[23]

The broadcast wasn't over, but people didn't stick around. People left their homes and their radios, jumped into cars, and drove to get away from the death machines coming their way. "I could not stop crying," wrote a woman from Ohio. "Every muscle in my body became tense and today I am unable to go to my work, because I feel like I had been beaten all over. My head aches all over too."[24] As people fled, radios were left on in empty houses, apartments, stores, and hotels. In homes all over America, empty rooms were left with radios on, doors left open, windows open, and coffee steaming on the table. And as people fled their homes, a sonorous voice came on: "You are listening to a CBS presentation of Orson Welles and the *Mercury Theatre on the Air* in an original dramatization of the *War of the Worlds* by H. G. Wells. The performance will continue after a brief intermission. This is the Columbia Broadcasting System."[25]

But it was too late. The radios playing in living rooms, kitchens, bedrooms, dens, stores, and bars played to no one as people ran for their lives. Some had already gone to bed only to be awakened to a world gone mad. A mother in a small eastern town was interviewed by Hadley Cantril soon after the broadcast: "Right after we turned in, I had gone out to see my baby when my husband called to me. I ran in and got frightened right away. I ran downstairs to the telephone and called my mother. She hadn't been listening. Then I took the little baby, and my husband wrapped our seven-year-old child, and we rode with friends who live on the street to the tavern where my mother works. By the time we got there, my mother had the radio on, and all of the people in the tavern were excited. I just sat down and cuddled my baby and shook so that I couldn't talk. I was sick in bed for three days after the broadcast."[26]

In CBS's Studio One, Orson Welles had reached the halfway point of the broadcast. Thirty-eight minutes into the radio play, the station break was his first chance to catch his breath. He saw Davidson Taylor pushing past John Houseman and rushing toward him.

The president of CBS, William Paley, smoked a cigarette and sipped his Old Fashioned in his home on Long Island. He enjoyed playing cards at home with his wife Dorothy to unwind. Usually, the radio was on low, but tonight there was just the sound of the logs crackling in the fireplace and the heavy breathing of the golden retriever next to the couch. Paley liked gin rummy, and he was winning when the phone rang. He stood to answer, and his wife heard him say he knew nothing about Martians. He hung up, and then the phone rang again. Paley shook his head and said he knew nothing about an invasion. He started back to the living room but never made it. The phone began to ring incessantly. As fast as he hung up, the phone would ring again. And they all wanted to know about the

Martians. Years later, when asked about the calls, Paley said, "I remember very well I was annoyed by it." Then a call came in from CBS, and a voice on the other end told him, "A terrible thing has happened." Paley later said of that night, "The whole country was bursting open."[27]

While the rush to stop Orson Welles from finishing the *War of the Worlds* broadcast had begun in Studio One, the world outside was in chaos. A mother in a crowded New Jersey tenement later testified:

> I thought it was all up with us. I grabbed my boy and just sat and cried, and then I couldn't stand it anymore when they said they were coming this way, so I turned off the radio and ran into the hall. The woman next door was out there crying, too. Then a man ran up the stairs, and when he saw us, he laughed at us. He laughed at us and said downstairs the people were fooled too and that it was only a joke. . . . We didn't believe him and told him to pray. . . . He said he had called the police and they told him it was a play. So, I went back into the apartment and just kept crying till my husband came home because I was still upset.[28]

Actress Caroline Cantlon would enjoy more fame from the *War of the Worlds* broadcast than she ever would from her acting. When she heard the reporter overcome by poisonous gas after he said New York City was the target of the murdering Martians, she ran into the street from her apartment and fell and broke her arm. The New York *Daily News* would pick up the story and plaster her picture, complete with her arm in a sling, on the front page under the bold black headline "Fake Radio 'War' Stirs Terror Through the U.S."[29] Underneath her picture, in smaller type, were the words "'War' Victim." Papers across the country would pick up the story, and Caroline Cantlon would become one of the enduring images of the broadcast, along with a picture of Welles shot from below with his hands out.

Before all this happened, though, Orson would have to conclude his broadcast. Currently, he was still on the air, wrapping up with his peroration in which he admitted his intent to fool his audience into believing the end of the world had arrived.

"This is Orson Welles, ladies and gentlemen, out of character to assure you that the War of the Worlds has no further significance than as the holiday offering it was intended to be. . . . So goodbye, everybody, and remember, please, the terrible lesson you learned tonight. That grinning globular invader of your living room is an inhabitant of the pumpkin patch, and if your doorbell rings and nobody is there, that was no Martian . . . it's Halloween."[30]

But Welles's voice was tight, and he mishandled the phrase "next best thing," instead saying "best next thing," before he signed off and sat, drenched with sweat. He listened to the announcer, Dan Seymour, sign off for the station, and that's when the door opened, and, like a balloon full of hot air, the control room emptied its cargo of lawyers, executives, and police into the studio. The CBS lawyers began grabbing scripts from the actors; recording discs were either confiscated or destroyed, and any copies of notes on the script, Welles's script, and even Herrmann's compositions for the radio play were taken.

Then Orson Welles and John Houseman were in that locked office, and we are finally back to that moment when Orson Welles was sitting in the unearthly quiet. CBS didn't know what to do with their two outlaws at this point and, after thirty minutes, released them to reporters who assembled in the hallways of CBS. Welles and Houseman had no answers and escaped out a side door. CBS started making statements while Welles caught a taxi to the Mercury Theatre for a dress rehearsal of *Danton's Death*, but he noticed a commotion in Times Square at Forty-Second and Broadway and got out of the cab. Orson stood up out of the cab and looked up at the scrolling Times Square marquee and saw, to his amazement, on the moving news sign, the letters glittering across the dark Manhattan sky: *"Orson Welles Frightens the Nation."*

Meanwhile, newspapers could not get through the overloaded switchboard, so more reporters descended on the CBS building. Newsrooms all over the country were thrown into turmoil trying to get to the bottom of the story that murdering Martians had descended, and the country was in a panic. Radio critic Ben Gross described how the New York *Daily News* was trying to deal with the calls and misinformation: "Phones rang everywhere as confused reporters struggled to get a call into CBS. Photographers dashed out in search of the story—whatever it was. At the blazing switchboard, a telephone operator rapidly assured caller after caller, 'There ain't no men from Mars.'"[31] The *New York World-Telegram* would later report that as far away as Memphis, journalists at the *Press-Scimitar* were swiftly mobilized to tackle the late-breaking story. "The managing editor, city editor, and several reporters sped to the office after receiving wild reports that cities are being bombed."[32]

The telephone was becoming the first source people turned to, and jammed switchboards that were already overloaded were paralyzed. Many news organizations missed the Martian part of the story and settled on the fact meteors had descended. An Associated Press (AP) bulletin described a reported meteor fall. Callers into the newspapers wanted to know whether reports of gas raids were accurate or if the East Coast had been bombed and should they follow the instructions during the broadcast on evacuation. The *New York Times* operators said later, "These callers often sounded agitated, even hysterical—obviously in a state of terror."[33] Many calls were from the police trying to get information, as they were getting deluged with calls. Most papers knew about the radio show, and the story quickly became *the panic* the *War of the Worlds* broadcast set off. This change shifted the news coverage from something from outer space to stories of people's reactions to the broadcast.

The teletypes unwound scrolls of reports of people running into the streets, into churches, and even running for the hills. One famous bulletin concerned a man who came home in Pittsburgh to find his wife sitting at the kitchen table with a vial of poison in front of her. When he asked her what she was doing, she responded, "I'd rather die like this way than like that," referring to the Martians with their heart rays and poison gas. This was picked up by wire services and ended up in newspapers nationwide.

People began to believe they saw what had been reported to them, with one woman in Boston calling the *Boston Globe* and claiming she could see the fires set by the Martians and that she and her neighbors were getting in their cars. Kansas City AP said a man had called in after loading his family into the car with a full gas tank, asking where it was safe. The disinformation and information collided on the night of October 30, 1938, with the news organizations becoming part of the story as they unwittingly spread the panic with their reporting of panic. Reports of hysteria were strung together, and a nationwide picture of the panic was beginning to emerge. A critic for the *Daily News* later wrote, "As the AP, UP, and the Chicago Tribune News Service wires in our office gave evidence, the panic coils had also clutched most of the cities, towns, and hamlets from coast to coast and down south to the Mexican border. . . . The people of the United States had succumbed to an unprecedented mass hysteria."[34]

But before the newspapers could get out their stories, they had to get to the bottom of the story. The reporters who had invaded the CBS building weren't going away, and CBS executives decided to have an impromptu press conference where they could control the narrative and tamp down the crisis. The assumption was that Orson Welles gave no interviews right after the broadcast, but this belief is proved false by the statements in the press.

CBS would have their press conference, but John Houseman would not do. This called for an actor of the highest order, and CBS wanted Orson Welles, the show's star, to be their man out front at the press conference to take place the following morning. For the first time, Orson Welles and John Houseman were starting to understand the impact of their broadcast. By the time they reached the Mercury Theatre for the dress rehearsal of *Danton's Death* that night, the cast was skeptical of Welles's reason for being late. The cast then went to Times Square and saw the confirmation in lights. The rehearsal was eventually canceled, but Welles seemed like a hunted animal to the cast. The star of *Danton's Death*, Joseph Cotten, surmised from Welles's ashen face and the story he told that Welles "was finished, washed up, a dead pigeon, show business would hear no more of him from then on."

Actress Arlene Francis said later that Welles told her he might be arrested any moment. The composer Bernard Herrmann called his soon-to-be-wife Lucille Fletcher to tell her about the broadcast. "He was like a kid, terribly thrilled," she said years later. "He thought Orson was going to be arrested, and I think he wanted to be arrested too."[35] A crowd of press photographers had figured out where Welles was most likely to be and had arrived. Orson walked out onto the stage, and a photographer snapped a picture of him from below with his hands out, imploring the world to believe he was innocent. This picture would later appear in the New York *Daily News* alongside the one of Caroline Cantlon and her broken arm. But hold on. That is not exactly how it happened. This story was reported for years and has appeared in many of Welles's biographies.

The press photographers did arrive, but Welles *cooperated with them.* "Welles spread his hands, widened his eyes, and consented to pose in front of a low light so that his shadow loomed on the wall behind him. 'I had no idea,' he said, looking like a very reliable young man. He said he had hesitated over presenting the show for fear that 'people might be bored or annoyed at hearing a tale so improbable.'"[36] The picture ran on the front page of hundreds of newspapers and would be reprinted and reprinted with the caption "I didn't know what I was doing!" But Orson Welles *knew exactly what he was doing.* He was doing the same thing he had done when he produced a Black *Macbeth* in Harlem, a rogue play in Manhattan, a fascistic rendition of *Julius Caesar.* From Sally Rand's naked ride into the Chicago 1933 World's Fair and onward, the fundamental maxim that there is no such thing as bad publicity has been proven repeatedly, and Orson Welles knew, beginning with his time in Ireland, the power of the press. It had made him into the boy genius, and now his greatest part in the play of Orson Welles was coming up: the role of a contrite boy genius who had inadvertently started a nationwide panic.

There was no dress rehearsal for *Danton's Death* that night, a moribund play that Welles knew was terrible and would have walked away from if he could. But he needed another springboard, as the run of the Mercury Theatre was approaching an endpoint, and he couldn't be the Shadow on radio forever, and who knew what would happen with *Mercury Theatre on the Air* now? Orson needed something to break him out of the pack. He needed to now milk the shock factor of his ride across Radio America. But it could all go wrong. His stunt was a high-risk reward play, and there was a possibility that it might be a career-ending moment. So, the audition for his greatest part would be the next morning at a press conference at CBS, at which he would fight for his professional life in every way possible—win, lose, or draw.

Daily News front page after Orson Welles's *War of the Worlds* radio broadcast, October 31, 1938. PHOTOFEST

Orson Welles being interviewed by reporters the day after his *Mercury Theatre on the Air* broadcast of H. G. Wells's *War of the Worlds*. PHOTOFEST

Orson Welles directing a rehearsal of his *Mercury Theatre on the Air* troupe, such as created panic on the CBS radio broadcast of the *War of the Worlds*, October 30, 1938. CBS Radio / Photofest © CBS Radio

Orson Welles rehearsing *Campbell Playhouse* for CBS Radio in November 1938. This was a few weeks after his October 30 broadcast of the *War of the Worlds*. CBS Radio / Photofest © CBS Radio

Orson Welles's career depended on his press conference performance. Photofest

Orson Welles (rear left), Ray Collins (below, far left), William Alland (far right foreground), and composer Bernard Herrmann (center rear). Welles holding his hands up for six seconds of silence . . . the dead air of the *War of the Worlds*. CBS Radio / Photofest © CBS Radio

George Coulouris, Harry Shannon, Buddy Swan, and Agnes Moorehead in *Citizen Kane* (1941), directed by Orson Welles. RKO Radio Pictures Inc. / Photofest © RKO Radio Pictures Inc.

U. S. BANS FAKE RADIO ALARMS

Orson Welles dominated headlines all over the country in the days after the *War of the Worlds* radio broadcast. Photofest

The Whole Country Was Bursting Open

October 30, 1938

THE ARGUMENT THAT TERROR WAS RESTRICTED TO THE LESS EDUCATED segment of the population began when columnist Dorothy Thompson wrote an article claiming Orson Welles had done the country a favor by showing what gullible illiterates the American people really were. This approach goes along with the current trend to minimize the impact of the broadcast on the country. The thesis that the newspapers inflated the broadcast with an axe to grind against radio is hard to swallow. The *War of the Worlds* broadcast and the resulting panic was a big news story. To see a reporter rubbing his hands over his typewriter saying, "I'm going to get back at this newfangled invention radio that is competing with us," is even more absurd. The country was on the run. The country was terrified. And it was not restricted to the uneducated because the terror found its way into the very heart of Dorothy Thompson's argument: the college campuses.

There are three sources for what happened on the night of October 30, 1938. Hadley Cantril's extensive report published two years after the broadcast, newspapers that cataloged how people reacted to the broadcast, and letters written after the broadcast. The respondents to Cantril's survey in his report tell stories of terror and panic as they heard the broadcast or received the news from others. Many were college students.

I was at a party, somebody was fooling around with the radio, and we heard a voice; the Secretary of the Interior was talking. We thought it was a normal bulletin because of the conditions abroad. Then, the local militia was called, so we decided to listen. It sounded real but not like anything to get panicky about. The riot or whatever it was still a couple of miles away.[1]

These college students didn't question the veracity of the broadcast and assumed it was a news bulletin. The following interview is a college student who believed the Martians had landed and were spraying poison gas. Interestingly, they were regular listeners to *Mercury Theatre* who were duped by Welles's breaking news bulletins.

When the flashes came, I thought they were really interrupting the play. I did not look for other stations because they said it was the only one not destroyed. We looked at the sky but could not see anything. I was not very upset though because we were in as safe a place as possible—high, and the higher you are the safer you are from gas fumes.[2]

Some listeners believed the broadcast was the news of another country's attack. So great was the feeling of imminent war that many ignored the Martians and assumed it was the Germans or Japanese.

I was in my drugstore, and my brother phoned and said, "Turn the radio on. A meteor has just fallen." We did and heard gas was coming up South Street. There were a few customers, and we all began wondering where it could come from. I was worried about the gas . . . when I heard airplanes, I thought another country was attacking us.[3]

The *Hindenburg* disaster was still on people's minds, and many assumed an airship was involved in the attack.

I happened to tune in when the meteor had fallen. I did not know how I finally found out. I never believed it was anyone from Mars. I thought it was some kind of new airship and a new method of attack. I kept translating the unbelievable parts into something I could believe.[4]

Still, others did believe Martians had crashed to earth and were now attacking. Even though the time was compressed, and the army was destroyed in minutes, panic destroyed logic.

When I heard the militia was wiped out, I went downstairs and listened. . . . I didn't realize at first they were hostile. . . . In a short time, I realized that these creatures were attacking. It wasn't beyond a possibility that such things could happen, but it seemed peculiar that the announcer could be right next to it and watching it.[5]

Hadley Cantril's report found that one-fifth of his respondents "reported visions of soldiers attacking with advanced military weapons."[6] The dread of the next war was palpable.

I felt insecure because although we are not in a war, we are so near it. I feel that with new devices on airplanes, it is possible for foreign powers to invade us. I listened to every broadcast during the European crisis.[7]

I felt it might be the Japanese; they are so crafty.[8]

I felt the catastrophe was an attack by the Germans, because Hitler didn't appreciate Roosevelt's telegram.[9]

The announcer said that a meteor had fallen from Mars. . . . It was really an airplane like a Zeppelin that looked like a meteor, and the Germans were attacking us with gas bombs.[10]

A senior in a large eastern college returning from a date heard the broadcast and turned his car around to rescue his girlfriend from the advancing Martians. His account highlights the belief that his life was about to end and the terrifying nihilism of a God who would allow this to happen.

We had heard that Princeton was wiped out and gas was spreading over New Jersey and . . . we figured our friends and families were all dead. . . . I drove right through Newburgh and never even knew I was going through it. I don't know why we weren't killed. . . . The speed was never under 70. . . . I remember also thinking there wasn't any God. . . . I thought the whole human race was going to be wiped out.[11]

This was not a hysterical woman from a Lower East Side tenement running into the street. The people who minimize the Welles broadcast portray the terror as restricted to some eastern cities where it was an urban phenomenon among people who should have known better. But the truth is that while Orson Welles prepared for his news conference the following day, people all over the United States were in a state of panic that spread to college campuses. At a time before the GI Bill, which sent middle-class people to college for the first time, the class of people who could afford to send their children to college in 1938 was among the upper tier of society in education and wealth. Still, these educated students were among the terrified as well.

A thousand miles away from the college student driving at seventy miles an hour to get his girlfriend, in a college in a southwestern state, the students on the West Coast believed the world was at its end. "The girls in the sorority houses and dormitories huddled around their radios, trembling and weeping in each other's arms. They separated themselves from their friends only to take their turn at the telephones to make long-distance calls to their parents, saying goodbye for what they thought might be the last time. This horror was shared by older and more experienced people—instructors and supervisors in the university. Terror-stricken girls, hoping to escape from the Mars invaders, rushed to the basement of the dormitory. Frantic with fear, a fraternity boy threw off dormitory regulations when he sought out his girlfriend and started for home. Another boy rushed into the street to warn the town of the invasion."[12]

During all this, the newspapers tried to drill down and get their headlines straight for the next day. The newsroom lights were on all over the country as reporters, editors, and copy editors worked frantically to out-scoop other papers on the biggest story since the Sudetenland crisis a few weeks before. Monday was a traditionally slow news day, and the *War of the Worlds* story was perfectly positioned for the feeding frenzy, a hot news story passed around and embellished as it goes from reporter to reporter. Orson Welles was not due to hold his news conference until the following day. Like the sinking of the *Titanic*, when papers had to guess what actually happened and many guessed wrong, the *War of the Worlds* broadcast had to be pieced together with incomplete information. The panic became the story. Inadvertently, the newspapers completed the terror and the hoax. Like atomic fission, the newspaper reporters, editors, and finally the articles and headlines banged into each other, producing a much bigger explosion than the broadcast itself. But this is part of the *War of the Worlds* broadcast. The piercing of the third wall of radio where the medium becomes a character was happening with the nation's newspapers, which would be out with bold headlines all over America.

And while these headlines were being formulated, typeset, and printed, Americans were on their own to decipher fact from fiction. The Martians had been unleashed, and the longest night was still ongoing as people grappled with their own terror. Sylvia Holmes, a housewife in Newark, panicked when she heard the broadcast and conflated the broadcast with Germans, the Sudetenland crisis, and the *Hindenburg*.

> I kept saying over and over again to everybody I met, "Don't you know New Jersey is destroyed by the Germans—it's on the radio." I was all excited and I knew that Hitler didn't appreciate President Roosevelt's telegram a couple of weeks ago.... I looked in the icebox and saw some chicken left from Sunday dinner that I was saving for the Monday night dinner. I said to my nephew, "We may as well eat this chicken— we won't be here in the morning."[13]

The uproar continued to build like a hurricane feeding on itself. The panic was so widespread and hysterical that columnist Walter Winchell was forced to comment on the broadcast during his top-rated 9:00 p.m. show. "Mr. and Mrs. America, there's no cause for alarm. America has not fallen; I repeat, America has not fallen."[14] The announcement had the opposite effect on his several million listeners, who then searched for news of the Martian invasion. People driving in cars who heard the broadcast suddenly began speeding and driving recklessly. The Cantril report has many respondents who heard about the *War of the Worlds* while driving and wrote about the effect on their driving. One driver ignored the possibility of getting a ticket: "My girlfriend pointed out to me that I had passed a couple of red lights and I answered, 'What's the difference if I get a ticket, it will be burned anyway.'"

Drivers suddenly didn't care about the risk of an accident: "I made the forty-five miles in thirty-five minutes and didn't even realize it. . . . On Monday, after it was all over, and I started to think of that ride, I was more jittery than when it was happening."[15]

The modern assessment of the *War of the Worlds* broadcast is that no one died because of it. This is not true. This was not the computer age with the digital revolution of scouring the Internet for information. Deaths occurred in 1938 that were never reported in the news. There were reports of heart attacks, and accidents did happen among drivers whom the broadcast had terrorized. And there were suicides. One man's account during a Cantril interview shows how dangerous driving had become.

> I became terribly frightened and got in the car and started for the priest so I could make peace with God before dying. . . . While en route to my destination, a curve loomed up, and traveling at between seventy-five and eighty miles per hour, I knew I couldn't make it, though as I recall, it didn't greatly concern me either. . . . After turning over twice, the car landed upright, and I got out, looked at the car, and thought it didn't matter that it wasn't mine or that it was wrecked as the owner would have no more use for it.[16]

In New York City, two women listening to the program called a movie theater and demanded management page their husbands. The news spread through the theater, sparking a virtual stampede for the exits while another woman went to the Forty-Seventh Street police station, "dragging two children, all carrying extra clothes. She said she was ready to leave the city."[17] At 8:48 p.m., due to the onslaught of calls to "newspapers, sheriff's offices, radio stations questioning whether the invasion was not real,"[18] the Associated Press (AP) sent out a release.

"Note to Editors: Queries to newspapers from radio listeners throughout the United States tonight, regarding a reported meteor fall which killed a number of New Jerseyites, are the result of a studio dramatization."[19]

Operators who handled the switchboards all over the country were deluged with calls. The AT&T operators in New York who worked at a switchboard a half-block long said, "The entire board lit up." Ann Wohik of New York City later recalled, "Our board lit up when they announced the Martians were coming across the George Washington Bridge."[20] In taped interviews, the operators talked about that night. Marian Sultphin from Princeton, New Jersey, recalled, "Some people asked what they looked like. . . . They were crying and screaming, wanting to know if there was a lot of gas . . . if there was a lot of destruction, bodies all around. . . . One man told me people were jumping out of their windows, and they were going to kill their families before the Martians could get them." Another operator said, "The people they believed it, they believed it, I think of the people begging us to connect them to their families, to mothers and fathers, so they could tell them they loved them before the world ended. . . . One lady said they were as far as Chicago now." Another operator said in summary, "Any man that could cause that kind of upheaval from coast to coast . . . has got to be great."[21]

Still, the panic and terror continued through the night. People telling other people about the Martians, the Germans, the broadcast sent out waves of alarm more terrifying than the broadcast.

The *Windsor Star*, a Canadian paper, reported on panic in the United States: "Samuel Tishman, a Riverside Drive resident, declared that he and hundreds of others evacuated their homes in fear that the city was being bombed. He told of going home and receiving a frantic telephone call from a nephew. 'I turned on the radio and heard the broadcast, which corroborated what my nephew had said; I grabbed my hat and a few personal belongings and ran to the elevator. When I got to the street, hundreds were milling around in panic. Most of us ran toward Broadway, and it was not until we stopped taxi drivers who had heard the entire broadcast on their radios that we knew what it was all about.'"[22]

The *Windsor Star* also reported on "excitement from coast to coast. Tulsa, Okla., reported two heart attacks and a stroke resulting from the dramatization. Los Angeles, Dallas, Tex., Kansas City, and Omaha reported hundreds of telephone calls to authorities and newspaper offices. . . . A message from Providence, R.I., said, 'Weeping and hysterical women swamped the switchboard of the *Providence Journal* for details of the massacre and destruction at New York, and officials of the electric company received scores of calls urging them to turn off the lights so that the city would be safe from the enemy.' . . . Minneapolis and St. Paul police switchboards were deluged with calls from frightened people. . . . In East Orange, N.J., a panicky man rushed into police headquarters, pleading for a place to hide from the bombing. Detectives tried vainly to calm him with an explanation that it was only a radio dramatization. 'Don't tell me what it is,' he shouted. 'I heard the voice of President Roosevelt himself telling us all to hide.'" The *Star* went on to say, "Five boys at Brevard (North Carolina) College fainted and panic gripped the campus for a half hour with many students fighting for telephones to inform their parents to come get them."[23]

On Monday morning, the *Free Lance-Star* of Fredericksburg, Virginia, would lead with the headline "End of World Radio Sketch Is Cause of Excitement Here." The paper listed the turmoil in the Southern city of Richmond. "'My aunt has fainted, out stone cold,' complained an irate Richmonder. 'All the babies are bawling, and the place is in an uproar. It was too damned realistic.'" In Norfolk, Virginia, some people traveling came upon "a group gathered outside a Disputanta filling station, 'faces white as sheets.' A state trooper near Richmond said he stopped a running man, shirttail out, who wanted to find 'an armory, any armory.'"[24]

The *Plainfield Courier-News* reported that a man who heard the broadcast in his car ran into a theater and screamed, "'The state is being invaded. The place is going to be blown up.' The theater was evacuated as people rushed home. . . . An Orange County restaurant, where the radio was turned on, lost a lot of money when all the customers fled without paying their checks."[25]

The *Tulsa Tribune* reported that some of the CBS affiliates swamped with calls took matters into their own hands. In Tulsa, Oklahoma, station KTUL was overwhelmed with calls. William C. Gillespie, the station manager, declared, "I have been in the radio business since 1922 and it was the most amazing demonstration of mass hysteria I have ever seen. I hope never to see anything like it again." He said, "Toward the end of the broadcast . . . the Tulsa station broke in on its own accord to announce that the drama was not based on fact because of the number of calls being received."[26]

While people roamed the countryside; drove crazily; called police, newspapers, and CBS for any information, and the newspapers worked feverishly rearranging front pages against deadlines, Orson Welles had a sleepless night. He called the headmaster of the Todd School for Boys, Roger Hill, along with other friends, confidants, and colleagues, veering from fear to triumph and checking on news reports of the broadcast. Roger Hill would later write in an unpublished memoir that Welles called him that night and was "stuttering, trembling, in search of something stable to hang onto in a world that was reeling around him."[27]

Orson talked with his wife Virginia, who initially endorsed the show's realism. He called his lawyer, Arnold Weissberger, and tried to determine his liability. Weissberger told him that his CBS contract assigned legal responsibility for the broadcasts to the network, which had vetted the script; the reported accidents and fatalities were in a gray area concerning his liability. Orson couldn't be sure whether he might be sued into oblivion by listeners who reporters had claimed had been injured, had heart attacks, and even died because of the broadcast. Lawyers for CBS had been woken up and put to work limiting liability for the network. At some point, Orson met with Henry Sember, the *Mercury* publicist, and a representative from the network to work out a strategy to limit legal liability and to get control of public relations. The crisis was too big for just a press release. There had to be a press conference at the CBS building in the morning. That would be their best shot to take control of the narrative. All Orson Welles could now do was wait through the wee hours of the morning to see what the damage would be. It was a long night for the boy wonder of twenty-three.

Terrorist in Action

October 31, 1938

THE BLEARY-EYED AUTHOR OF THE PLAY VERSION OF *WAR OF THE Worlds*, Howard Koch, woke up the next morning, unaware that Orson Welles had been hiding from reporters and with no idea of the effect the broadcast had on the nation. He had been exhausted from the six-day writing marathon and had fallen into a deep, dreamless sleep after listening to the broadcast. John Houseman had tried to contact him, but Koch either never got the call or didn't pick up the phone. He was walking along Seventy-Second Street to get a haircut on his day off when he began to hear strange comments about an invasion and then a panic. Howard assumed something had happened overseas, or maybe Hitler had finally started the war that was sure to come.

It wasn't until Koch reached his barber and asked what all the commotion was about that he got the shock of his life. The barber, without a word, handed him the New York *Daily News*, and Koch's face turned bright red as he took in the headline: "Fake 'War' on Radio Spreads Panic Over U.S." Beneath it: "A radio dramatization of H. G. Wells' *War of the Worlds*—which thousands of people misunderstood as a news broadcast of a current catastrophe in New Jersey—created almost unbelievable scenes of terror in New York, New Jersey, the South and as far west as San Francisco between 8 and 9 o'clock last night."[1]

Across town, Orson Welles emerged onto the street in the early dawn of October 31 and bought a copy of the *New York Times*. His heart was in his throat as he stared at the center of the front page: "Radio Listeners in Panic, Taking War Drama as Fact." Orson stood on the street corner, his eyes devouring the article. "A wave of mass hysteria seized thousands of radio listeners throughout the nation between 8:15 and 9:30 o'clock last night when a broadcast of a dramatization of H. G. Wells's fantasy, 'The War of the Worlds,' led thousands to believe that an interplanetary conflict had started with invading Martians spreading wide death and destruction in New Jersey and New York. The broadcast, which disrupted households, interrupted religious services, created traffic jams, and clogged communication systems, was made by Orson Welles, who, as the radio character 'the Shadow,' used to give 'the creeps' to countless child listeners. This time, at least a score of adults required medical treatment for shock and hysteria."[2]

Welles read on as the article described how "in a single block at Heddon Terrace and Hawthorne Avenue, more than twenty families rushed out of their houses with wet handkerchiefs and towels over their faces to flee from what they believed was a gas raid."[3] Orson held the paper down and looked for the other major newspaper, the New York *Daily News.* Surely this one would not be as bad as the *New York Times.* As Welles walked to another newsstand and saw the *Daily News,* he had much the same reaction as Howard Koch. Below the massive black headline screaming about the "Fake War" was the picture the photographers had snapped the night before at the *Danton's Death* rehearsal with Orson holding his hands down and looking up to the ceiling. He was wearing a striped double-breasted suit coat and tie with a handkerchief in his left pocket. Under the picture in bold type were the words "I Didn't Know."[4] But even worse, to the left of the picture of Welles was the photo of Caroline Cantlon, the actress who had fallen and broken her arm. She was sitting on a bed looking at the headline under the picture that read, "'War' Victim."

Welles sat down in shock, reading the article: "Thousands of listeners rushed from their homes in New York and New Jersey, many with towels across their faces to protect themselves from the 'gas.' . . . Simultaneously thousands more in states that stretched west to California and south to the Gulf of Mexico rushed to their telephones to inquire of newspapers, the police, switchboard operators. . . . Occupants of Park Avenue apartment houses flocked to the street. . . . In Harlem excited crowds shouted that President Roosevelt's voice had warned them to 'pack up and move north because the machines are coming from Mars.'"[5]

The paper then listed the bulletins from the Associated Press (AP) in bold scrolling headlines and gave a national roundup of the impact of the broadcast.

Woman Tries Suicide: Pittsburgh.—A man returned home in the midst of the broadcast and found his wife, a bottle of poison in her hand, screaming: "I'd rather die this way than like that!"

Man Wants to Fight Mars: San Francisco.—An offer to volunteer in stopping an invasion from Mars came among hundreds of telephone inquiries to police and newspapers tonight during the radio dramatization of H. G. Wells's story. One excited man called Oakland police and shouted: "My God! Where can I volunteer my services? We've got to stop this awful thing!"

Church Lets Out: Indianapolis.—A woman ran into a church screaming: "New York destroyed; it's the end of the world. You might as well go home to die. I just heard it on the radio." Services were dismissed immediately.

College Boys Faint: Brevard, N.C.—Five Brevard College students fainted, and panic gripped the campus for a half hour, with many students fighting for telephones to inform their parents to come and get them.

It's a Massacre: Providence, R.I.—Weeping and hysterical women swamped the switchboard of the *Providence Journal* for details of the "massacre." The electric company received scores of calls urging it to turn off all lights so that the city would be safe from the "enemy."

She Sees "the Fire": Boston.—One woman declared she could "see the fire" and told the *Boston Globe* she and many others in her neighborhood were "getting out of here."

Where Is It Safe?: Kansas City.—One telephone informant said he had loaded all his children into his car, had filled it with gasoline, and was going somewhere. "Where is it safe?" he wanted to know.

Prayers in Richmond: Richmond, Va.—The *Times-Dispatch* reported some of its telephone calls came from persons who said they were praying.

Atlanta's "Monsters": Atlanta.—Listeners throughout the Southeast called newspapers reporting that "a planet struck in New Jersey, with monsters and almost everything and anywhere from 40 to 7,000 people were killed."

Carolina Weeps: Fayetteville, NC.—Persons with relatives in New Jersey went to a newspaper office in tears, seeking information.

Minneapolis Scared: Minneapolis.—Police switchboards were swamped with calls from frightened people.[6]

Orson felt the morning chill and began to shake, snapping the paper shut; he then opened it again, scanning the long interior article that described "hundreds of physicians and nurses were among the callers. Many of them said they were prepared to rush at once into the devastated area to aid in caring for their victims."[7] Motorists were turned away from the devastated areas as two members of the geology faculty from Princeton University "equipped with flashlights and hammers started for Grovers Mills."[8] At the same time, scores of students were ordered home by their parents. A hysterical girl phoned the Princeton Press Club from Grovers Mill and screamed, "You can't imagine the horror of it! . . . It's hell!"[9] Another man came into the club and said he saw the meteor strike the earth and "witnessed animals jumping from the alien body."[10] In Watchung, New Jersey, an excited policeman on desk duty who had been "notified by horrified citizens that a meteor struck somewhere nearby sent squad cars out to look for [the] injured."[11]

Newark police received a call about a gas explosion at 145 Hedden Terrace and "raced to the scene to find that more than thirty people, occupants of the house, were on the street holding their clothes and bedding."[12] Residents Louis Celowitz and his wife Esther had been the Paul Reveres of the broadcast. "We got nervous," said Celowitz, "and notified everyone in the house."[13] They told those in the building that six hundred people had been killed by gas. The tenants rushed out, taking with them whatever they could grab. In Irvington, New Jersey, people "shouted warnings to each other in the streets. 'Drive like hell into the country; we are being bombed by enemies.' Motorcycle police, astounded by the sudden bursts of speed by motorists, rushed to call boxes to inquire from headquarters about the supposed raids."[14] In the Sacred Heart Church in Elizabeth, priests were astounded by "an influx of panicky persons who rushed inside, fell on their knees and began to pray."[15]

Orson Welles closed the paper and began to walk toward CBS. Many would later claim he hadn't read the newspapers before he met the reporters. This is not true. Welles couldn't have missed the papers on the streets and in people's hands as he made his way through midtown Manhattan. And he wanted to see the effect of his broadcast. But he couldn't have known the scope of his Martian invasion or that, in Chicago, the *Herald-Examiner* led with a half-page headline that read, "Radio Fake Scares Nation," with the subsequent article following up with "Hundreds of Chicagoans were deceived and besieged newspaper offices, police headquarters."[16]

Welles couldn't know about the bus ride described in the *Asheville Citizen*, in which a bus en route from Charlotte to Asheville on Sunday night was stopped by a frantic man, "sobbing and praying," who told the driver and passengers the country was under attack. Passenger Joe Hollingsworth provided details on the wildest ride he would ever take: "That trip from Mooresboro to Forest City . . . was the most horrible experience of my life. The bus driver was scared about as badly as I was and if you must know the truth I was really scared." He described how the frightened bus driver "stepped on it," and that was when the wild ride began. "[Passengers] in the back of the bus carried on like they were at a funeral." The passengers held on as the bus skidded around corners. "Hollingsworth said it was the opinion of most of the passengers that the United States had been invaded by a foreign power. . . . We just thought that Germany was already caught up with and that she had decided to come on over and finish up right now."[17]

As Orson made his way across the city, he didn't know about the people in Chicago who ran out of restaurants without paying for their meals or the man who jumped out of a hospital bed in Macon, Georgia, after surgery and tore his stitches open. Or the residents of Concrete, Washington, who had fled into the foothills of the Cascade Mountains and had to be found the next day by search parties and convinced to return to their homes. Or Sam Tishman of Manhattan, who grabbed a few belongings after his nephew phoned him and ran for the elevator. "When I got to the street, there were hundreds of people milling around in panic."[18] Or the man from Brooklyn who demanded a gas mask and, when told it was just a play, responded, "What do you mean it's just a play . . . we can hear the firing all the way here, *and I want a gas mask. I'm a taxpayer!*"[19] Or the man from the Bronx who stood on the roof of his home and shouted down to neighbors a description of the flames and gas of the war.

Orson had no way of knowing about the bartender in Montgomery, Alabama, who after hearing the broadcast and then a loud plane passing overhead, shouted, "Fire me if you please, but I'm going home to my wife and kids,"[20] as he ran out of the building with his apron on. He hadn't heard about the Providence, Rhode Island, woman who "fainted at the wheel of her automobile on North Main Street and was involved in a minor collision."[21] Or the crying boy who ran down the road in Roanoke, Virginia, and was picked up by M. C. Richards of the Chesapeake and Potomac Telephone Company. The boy then "begged them to take him home so he could die with his family." Richards took him to his family, stating, "He wanted to do a good deed before they died."[22] Then there was the man who went into the Wadsworth Avenue police station in New Jersey and said he heard planes had bombed Jersey and "were headed for Times Square."[23]

Orson would have been astounded to read the article in the *Asheville Times* about what happened at Clemson College when a quiet Sunday night was turned into full-blown panic. The headline read, "Sturdy Cadets Grow Faint at Radio 'Attack,'" with the following story: "Impromptu prayer meetings were held throughout the barracks. One freshman knelt beside his bed and began his confessions aloud. One cadet was playing poker when the broadcast started; when it ended, he was praying. Some students fled the buildings and rushed to the highway seeking rides they knew not where. Gossip said two had not yet returned. One boy headed for the Seneca River, asserting he would jump in if the enemy's heat rays became too intense. A freshman couldn't stand the idea of being wiped out while he had as much as eleven dollars. He rushed to the barracks store and succeeded in spending five dollars. Cadet Frank Perna, of 51st Street, New York City was following the reported invasion on a map; he fainted dead away when the announcer described the crumbling of buildings on 50th and 51st streets."[24]

Orson would eventually become aware of the story of George Bates, an unskilled laborer in Massachusetts who spent his last money in his savings account trying to escape. He later wrote to Welles, "I thought the best thing to do was to go away, so I took 3.25 out of my savings and bought a ticket. After I had gone 60 miles, I heard it was a play. Now, I don't have any money left for the shoes I was saving up for. Would you please have someone send me a pair of black shoes, size 9-B?"[25] Sarah Jacob of Illinois, a regular listener to the *Mercury Theatre*, later told Hadley Cantril in an interview, "They should have announced it was a play. We listened to the whole thing, and they never did. I was very much afraid. When it was over, we ran to the doctor to see if he could help us get away. Everybody was out in the street, and somebody told my husband it was just a play."[26]

The *Philadelphia Inquirer* blanketed the top of the front page with bold black letters: "Radio Drama Causes Panic." The subtext read, "Play Portrays Men of Mars Invading NJ. Thousands in Nation Flee Homes After Fake News Bulletins Tell of Destruction." The paper went on to say that the 151-station broadcast by CBS had resulted "in many neighborhoods of Philadelphia families packing their belongings and preparing to leave their homes. One small hotel proprietor said every person in the hotel hastily left. In less than an hour, more than 4,000 telephone calls poured into the Philadelphia Electrical Bureau . . . and into the office of the *Inquirer* came more than 1,000 calls. . . . One woman appeared at

City Hall asking for protection."[27] The article went on to say the local station WCAU received more than "4,000 calls" and had to interrupt programming to tell peoplethat "monsters were not actually invading the world." The article described the panic that ensued, with a man racing into a police station in Hillside, New Jersey, asking for a gas mask and panting out "a tale of terrible people spraying liquid gas all over the Jersey meadows." Another woman stopped motorcycle patrolman Lawrence Treger and "asked where she should go to escape the attack." Another terrified motorist asked the patrolman the way to Route 24 and screamed, "All creation's busted loose. I'm getting out of Jersey!" Fifty people left Colligan's Inn in Stockton and headed to Grovers Mill to see the incredible damage. The paper reported "fifteen people were treated for shock in one Newark hospital," and Samuel Tishman of Riverside Drive "declared he and hundreds of others evacuated their homes fearing the city was being bombed and later denounced the broadcast as 'the most asinine stunt I ever heard of.'"[28] Kansas City hospitals reported two heart attacks.

Orson certainly was not aware and would have scarcely believed that across the Atlantic Ocean in England, the *Derby Evening Telegraph*, a forerunner of tabloids, announced in a bold black headline that paraded across the top of the paper that "Welles Novel Broadcast Panics U.S. Listeners." Then, just below that, there was a subhead that read, "Thought 'War of Worlds' Was World's End . . . Real Names of Towns Used."[29] Orson Welles had gone from a relatively unknown radio personality to a world-famous one.

Orson would not have wanted to know about the *Knoxville News-Sentinel*'s informative headline "Fictional Broadcast of Rocket Attack on New Jersey by Men from Mars Creates National Panic as Listeners Think End of World Has Arrived." Beneath the headline was a photo of Orson in a tuxedo with the caption "'Terrorist' in Action."[30]

A quick rundown of the major newspapers in the country shows how widespread the panic had become overnight. The *New York Times* led with "Radio Listeners in Panic, Taking War Drama as Fact."[31] United Press International (UPI) shot out "'War of the Worlds' Radio Broadcast Causes Panic" over the wires.[32] The *Boston Daily Globe* blasted out,

"Radio Play Terrifies Nation."[33] The *San Francisco Chronicle* declared, "Panic Sweeps U.S. as Radio Stages Mars Raid."[34] The *New York Post* proclaimed, "Radio War Panic Brings Inquiry, U.S. to Scan Broadcast Stations."[35] *Sarnoff Collection* kept the terror going with "Martians Attack!"[36] The *Tampa Tribune* blared, "Realistic Radio Play of Attack from Mars Causes Stir Over U.S."[37]

On October 31, 1938, people all over America woke to the most incredible headlines. Many have eschewed the coverage of the *War of the Worlds*, but that takes away the most important resource for knowing precisely what happened—the note-taking, gum-chewing, fedora-wearing, hustling, flat-footed reporters of 1938 were no more in cahoots to produce a sensational story than anyone else in the media. At a time when switchboards were still local and people used mail and telegrams to communicate, there was simply no way for a grand conspiracy of print journalists to hype a specific story. Besides, they didn't have to. The story was sensational, and the reporters in the early hours after the crisis had deadlines to meet and were expected to report the news as it happened.

The most significant evidence that the panic was nationwide is the newspapers. The crackling Monday papers told an incredible story over coffee, cigarettes, and kitchen tables; on buses and subways; in cars, bars, restaurants, and beauty parlors. Small papers also led with bold black headlines. The *Amarillo Globe-Times* told Texans in a bold headline, "Thousands Flee Homes, Pray, or Faint, as Fictitious Radio Program Relates Invasion by Martian Hordes."[38] "Hysteria Sweeps Nation,"[39] the *Daily Times* of Davenport, Iowa, screamed. Other papers ominously warned of consequences for those responsible. The *St. Louis Star-Times* led with "U.S. Probes Radio Invasion Scare."[40]

UPI reported on Concrete, Washington, where the power to the town went out during the broadcast. "The citizens of this little mountain town claimed today that they took the real brunt of the invasion of the earth by the men of Mars, which was released last night as a radio dramatization. Just as an announcer was choked off by poisonous gas in what he had just said might be 'the last broadcast ever made,' the lights in Concrete failed. Many who were tuned into the program became panic-stricken. They called friends on the telephone until all the lines were clogged. They shouted from house to house. The more they talked, the more excited they became. Others who had not listened in on the program became alarmed. Hysteria swept over the more excitable of the 3,000 residents. One man from his home grabbed a small child by the arm and headed into the adjacent pine forest. Others prepared hastily to flee into the hills, believing the invasion had already reached across the continent from New York."[41]

The government lost no time determining whether radio itself had gotten out of control. The *Roanoke World News* announced, "'Mars War' Broadcast Terrifies Thousands; Federal Inquiry Begun."[42] The article then described the local carnage the broadcast had caused: "Telephone calls flooded the news office, police and fire stations, and telegraph offices, long distance calls to New Jersey increased. . . . Youths left a home near Villamount to visit a girl. About 10 minutes until 9, they rushed back, gasping, 'New York has been destroyed, and the Hudson River is a puddle of mud!' The boys had stopped in a store to buy cigarettes and found everyone crying. . . . 'I hope nothing like this ever happens again,' one man quoted another as saying. 'He said that he was scared and told his wife everything about it himself, and he was still hearing about it this morning.'"[43]

At some point, Orson gave the AP a statement that ran on October 31. This was before the news conference at CBS. Whether Welles managed to get it out or CBS put it out that morning or possibly the night before is unknown. He was probably interviewed by CBS the night before, and a statement was released to the AP in the morning.

Orson Welles, on behalf of the *Mercury Theatre on the Air*, is deeply regretful to learn that the H. G. Wells fantasy *War of the Worlds*, which was designed as entertainment, has caused some apprehension among Columbia's network listeners. Far from expecting the radio audience to take the program as fact rather than a fictional presentation, we feared that the classic H. G. Wells story, which has served as inspiration for so many moving pictures, radio series, and even comic strips, might appear too old fashioned for modern consumption. We can only suppose that the special nature of radio, often heard in fragments or parts disconnected from the whole, has led to this misunderstanding.[44]

Contrition would be Orson Welles's only ally going into the press conference of his life.

The Long Night

October 31, 1938

HORTENSE HILL KNEW SOMETHING WAS WRONG WHEN THE HEAD OF the Todd School in Woodstock, Illinois, Roger (Skipper) Hill, got into bed that night. Orson Welles had been their unofficial son ever since he came to the Todd School, and now Roger was taking on the role of father again, talking Orson off the ledge in the middle of the night in New York City. Hortense listened while her husband explained that Orson might have really done it this time. The boy genius who came out of nowhere and created Shakespearean plays and then led a summer play festival at the school with theater owners from Ireland, where he had made his debut, might have found his level of incompetence and could quite possibly go to jail. Roger Hill always wondered what would happen to Orson if he banged up against that hard edge of America, which is supreme indifference to the artist. Hill knew how people like Orson walked the line of danger by not recognizing the world, and then, when they did, it was too late. He told Hortense there was to be a news conference that would determine Orson's fate one way or another.

The lawsuits coming into CBS were rumored to be in the millions. A man called CBS and promised to sue "for every cent you've got."[1] The Federal Communications Commission (FCC) got wind of a $50,000 suit in the works but had not decided what action to take against Orson Welles and CBS. The letters coming in to CBS and Welles did not mince words. A man from Rhode Island wrote, "I think you are nothing but an impossible sawed-off nincompoop who should be barred for life from radio, and I shall work towards that end. . . . I only wish I could get my hands on you for five minutes."[2] Another man from New Jersey wrote ominously, "Your days of fame are just about over Mr. Orson Welles. . . . Perhaps hundreds of people who listened to your program either died or at this very moment are suffering a nervous breakdown. And to think the blame will be placed on you."[3] Several people suggested that Welles leave the country. Add to this the death threats and bomb threats CBS had received on the night of the broadcast, along with the rumors of death, suicide, and heart attacks, and the future for Orson looked bleak. He had gone too far. He knew this now, but it was too late.

The *Buffalo Evening News* carried a story headlined "Inquiry Follows Broadcast of H. G. Wells War Drama." The article read, "The Federal Communications commission started an investigation of the broadcast after the program resulted in many calls to police and newspapers."[4] There would be an investigation by the FCC and there might be financial as well as restrictive penalties. The *Tampa Tribune* quoted Senator Clyde Herring of Iowa, who said he planned to introduce in Congress a bill "controlling just such abuses as we heard over the radio tonight. . . . Radio has no more right to present programs like that than someone has in knocking on your door and screaming."[5] Orson Welles's broadcast had impacted even Washington, DC.

The rats all began jumping ship immediately. H. G. Wells, author of the novel *War of the Worlds*, claimed he never gave permission for anyone, least of all CBS, to rewrite his book and demanded a public apology.[6] Then demand for his book skyrocketed. When Dell released a new copy of *War of the Worlds*, the blurb across the front read, "When They Told It on the Radio . . . It Terrified the Nation." But that wasn't going to help Orson Welles, and the consensus was that the broadcast had ruined him. Welles himself would later say, "If I had planned to wreck my career, I couldn't have gone about it any better."[7] He understood the high stakes for the interview.

The famous interview of Orson Welles by the gaggle of reporters on the morning of October 31, 1938, has been viewed a million times by historians, journalists, and other people curious as to what really happened on that Halloween eve. Orson had arrived at CBS, unshaven. He had been instructed to read a statement created by CBS lawyers and executives. The executives, including William Paley, had decided to control the narrative, which meant taking the loose-fitting-shirt-and-suspenders-wearing Welles from the broadcast and putting him a crisp new suit and telling him he was going to be contrite and apologetic. Watching the interview is like watching a movie from the noir 1930s or 1940s. The reporters were smoking pipes, cigarettes, scribbling on pads in shorthand while photographers snapped pictures, replaced bulbs in their cameras, and then began snapping again with the slightly musical chink. There was an ashtray in front of Orson, fedoras were all pulled low, and everyone was in a suit, including Orson, though his looked large on him.

Orson Welles—who had bluffed his way onto the Irish stage; bluffed his way into American theater; bluffed his way through the New Deal theatrical scene with bold projects like an anti-Fascist *Julius Caesar*, a Black *Macbeth*, and *The Cradle Will Rock*; and then bluffed his way into *The Shadow*, *March of Time*, and *Mercury Theatre on the Air*—was now auditioning for his greatest role. And he had a supporting cast behind him. At first glance, it looks like Orson is literally surrounded by reporters. But behind him are eight men in dark suits, glasses, mustaches, without pads or cameras. They are the CBS executives. During the interview, one of the men began distributing a statement. Then, while Welles was taking questions, a CBS executive leaned over and attempted to read a reporter's pad while he was taking notes. This was a high-drama act, and the repercussions for CBS and Welles were mighty.

For his part, Orson had a light beard and looked tired, but at twenty-three he looked surprisingly fresh and spoke remarkably well for the situation. At this point, Orson's job, his career, maybe his freedom was at stake in this very high-profile interview that would go out on the newsreels. The interview opened with Welles sitting down and leaning forward with photographers snapping pictures and swiftly putting the spent bulbs in their coat pockets. The four photographers quickly took their pictures and left.

Scholars have pointed to the press conference as Welles's first reaction to the broadcast, but Orson had given an interview that appeared in the *Philadelphia Inquirer* on October 31, dated October 30. This must have been when the reporters stormed the Mercury Theatre and found Welles on stage. The article appeared under the headline "Reaction of Public to Radio Drama Amazes Welles."

The article read, "Advised of the furor his radio dramatization of H. G. Wells's *War of the Worlds* had created, Orson Welles, playwright, said, 'We've been putting on all sorts of things from the most realistic situations to the wildest fantasy and nobody ever bothered to get serious about them before. We just can't understand why this would have had such an amazing reaction. . . . It started off with music and then I made a speech, supposedly in 1939, saying that as I looked back, I never dreamed such things existed as had actually come before my sight.'" Welles then explained the show's progression and gave himself cover by saying, "Things seemed to be in a bad way all right, but just then we broke in for station announcements and disclosed once again it was all a huge make-believe."[8]

But this article was lost in the news juggernaut, and for most Americans the first glimpse they received of Orson Welles was the news conference at CBS. Still, it would seem Orson gave another interview before the newsreel interview. On November 1, the *Allentown Morning Call* led with the headline "U.S. Considers Greater Control of Radio After Spook Play."[9]

"I'm really quite shocked," Welles said. His hair was awry, and he said he had no sleep the previous night, although he attributed this state more to the fact he was in rehearsal for a new play than his concern over the scare he gave the country. He denied that he had any notion that people would accept his highly dramatized version of H. G. Wells's famous novel, *War of the Worlds*, as fact instead of fiction.

Then, in the smoke and the lights and the murmuring voices, Orson was staring at the camera like the changeling he always saw himself as. He was red-eyed and holding another statement that had been shoved into his hands by CBS executives. The boy wonder who had wowed the world was now in the cold. When he read the prepared statement, his voice was slightly high-pitched and adenoidal. Gone was the booming baritone, replaced by the voice of a bewildered young man. The statement would appear in papers all over the country. Orson then read off the four reasons people should not have believed the broadcast was real:

> Despite my deep regret over any misapprehension which our broadcast last night created among listeners, I am even the more bewildered over this misunderstanding in the light of an analysis of the broadcast itself. It seems to me that there are four factors which should have in any event maintained the illusion of fiction in the broadcast. The first was the broadcast was performed as if occurring in the future and as if it were then related by a survivor of a past occurrence. The date of the fanciful invasion of this planet by Martians was clearly given as 1939 and was so announced at the onset of the broadcast.
>
> The second element was the fact that the broadcast took place at our regular weekly Mercury Theatre period and had been so announced in all the papers. For seventeen consecutive weeks we had been broadcasting radio drama. Sixteen of those seventeen broadcasts have been fiction and have been presented as such. Only one in the series was a true story, the broadcast of Hell on Ice by Commander Ellsberg and was identified as a true story within the framework of radio drama.
>
> The third element was the fact that at the very outset of the broadcast and twice during its enactment listeners were told that this was a play and that it was an adaptation of an old novel by H. G Wells. Furthermore, at the conclusion a detailed statement to this effect was made.
>
> The fourth factor seems to me to have been the most pertinent of all. That is the familiarity of the fable, within the idiom of Mars and Martians. For many decades "The Man from Mars" has been almost a synonym for fantasy. . . . This fantasy, as such, has been used in radio programs many times. In these broadcasts, conflict between citizens of Mars and other planets has been a familiarly accepted fairy tale. The same make-believe is familiar to newspaper readers through a comic strip that uses the same devices.

The questions began. The men behind the camera nodded for several retakes. Welles stared at the camera and then spoke: "You want me to speak now? I'm sorry. Okay. Of course, we are deeply shocked and deeply regretful about the results of last night's broadcast. The date of the broadcast was 1939. It came rather as a great surprise to us that a story, a fine H. G. Wells classic fantasy, a classic, the original for some, many adventure stories and comic strips and novels about a mythical invasion by monsters from the planet Mars should have had so profound an effect on radio listeners. . . . Okay, that's enough."[10]

Orson was staring at the camera like a boy. Film, the very medium that would propel him in a few short years to worldwide fame, was determining his fate as an actor, director, and artist. He had turned back into a twenty-three-year-old and was imploring the viewers to be on his side. The CBS executives behind him were hustling to get out more copies of the statement. They were grim-faced men who stared at Orson as if he were an animal in the zoo. They stared at the reporters as if they were suspected criminals. The questions begin with Orson responding to the first few and feigning ignorance. His voice was strangely high and adenoidal. Gone was the Orson Welles voice. The question about the psychological impact of the broadcast elicited two lies from Orson.

"I simply don't know. I can't imagine—you must realize that when I left the broadcast last night, I went into a dress rehearsal for a play that is opening in two days and have had almost no sleep and know less about this than you do. . . . I haven't read the papers."[11]

Orson had read the papers and had cancelled the dress rehearsal for *Danton's Death*. But he was playing the part of the bewildered schoolboy innocent of any malicious intent who didn't understand what had happened.

"When were you aware something was wrong?" reporters shouted.

"When it was over," Orson answered.

A man in a dark fedora leaned in. "Were you aware of terror, when you were in this role, aware of terror throughout the nation?"

Orson shook his head, one hand on top of the other on his creased suit pants with the microphones piled up in front of him.

"Oh no, of course not . . . we did *Dracula* . . . one doesn't believe in the radio audience much, you don't know whether they are listening or not; you have no idea how many people are listening or what they are thinking. I had every hope that, uh, that the people would be excited, as they would be in a melodrama. . . . You don't play down the melodramatic effect of a melodrama."

"Did you feel people listening in on this program would know there is no such thing as Martians?"

One CBS executive was behind Orson's shoulder. A reporter scribbling behind Orson turned with a pencil in his mouth.

"Well, it would seem to me unlikely that, uh, this tale of an invasion from Mars would find ready acceptance. I was frankly terribly shocked to find that it did."

Another reporter asked, "Are you from Mars yourself?"

Welles smiled and responded, "No."

Everyone laughed, including a CBS executive who was so close to the reporters that he was reading some of the notes. Welles should have taken heart here. The press was not totally against him; in fact, they seemed to be going out of their way to be respectful.

"Mr. Welles, why did you use local towns?"

"Well, H. G. Wells used local towns addressing an English audience; I was addressing an American audience."

"Did you take unfair advantage of the public by using a method for the conveyance of authentic news?"

The newsreel photographer yelled for the reporter to speak louder. And then there is an obvious retake in the film where the new scene is spliced in. This happens several times where people are placed strategically and Welles himself is directed to look at the camera several times. These points suggest that the interview was staged. How did all those CBS executives end up in a perfect uniform circle, perfectly dressed like executives in a movie, and why were the questions so tame? The reporters were dressed like Humphrey Bogart, smoking pipes, legs crossed. It is as if it was the perfect noir news interview. This is a Universal Newsreel that CBS set up. The questions were all softballs really. The questions stuck to the four points CBS released in their statement. The original release sheet for the newsreel film reads, "Radio Play Terrifies Nation . . . Thousands of radio listeners throughout the U.S. are frightened into mass hysteria by dramatization of H. G. Wells' old thriller 'The War of the Worlds,' as staged by Orson Welles, young actor-manager."[12]

So, Welles played his part in this short film set up as a public relations play by CBS. "I don't believe that I have," he said, replying to the question about taking advantage of the radio audience. "It is not a method original with me. It is used by many radio programs. I am terribly shocked by the effect it has had."

"Do you think there ought to be a law against such enactments as we had last night?"

"I don't know what the legislation would be. . . . Radio is new, and we are learning about the effect it has on people."

"Do you think this will curb the use of bulletins on the radio?"

"I simply don't know. . . . Radio executives and an organized public will decide these things for us . . . I am the accused."

The accused? Yes, he was. But he was also the man behind the scenes orchestrating his own interview. Watching the video again, it is obvious the interview is staged. It is orchestrated and dictated by the newsreel camera crew who direct Welles with several takes, with Orson asking whether he should speak. CBS saw the ratings of *Mercury Theatre on the Air* go through the roof. They saw the value of the publicity and made decisions in the early morning hours of October 31, 1938, setting up the interview, releasing the statement, and coordinating with Universal for the newsreel. And getting the reporters.

Orson Welles played his part in the interview—contrite, bewildered, helpful. But the fix was in, and at the end of the interview Welles motioned to John Houseman with a thumbs-up. Howard Koch saw this gesture and later wrote about it. Koch realized it was all a charade and this convinced him more than anything else that Orson Welles had orchestrated the hoax and knew exactly what he was doing.

Of course he did. The magician always pushes the envelope, and Welles's art was one of constant experimentation that either blew up in his hand or furthered his career. So far, each experiment had furthered his career and had pushed him along, but the chaos, the tearing down of walls, the breaking of boundaries, was where Orson Welles lived. The last-minute changes, the going off script, and the pushing of people, sets, and technology to the breaking point to produce something no one had ever seen before were all part of his process. So why shouldn't the press conference of the greatest hoax in radio history be another hoax? That is pure Orson Welles.

CBS wasn't taking any chances and issued its own apology to the nation: "Naturally it was neither Columbia's nor the Mercury Theatre's intention to mislead anyone, and when it became evident that a part of the audience had been disturbed by the performance, five announcements were read over the network in the evening to reassure those listeners. In order that this may not happen again, the program department hereafter will not use the technique of a simulated news broadcast within a dramatization when the circumstances of the broadcast could cause immediate alarm to numbers of listeners."[13]

Author H. G. Wells reiterated to the press his outrage that his material had been changed. His spokesman in New York, Jacques Chambrun, released a statement: "In the name of Mr. H. G. Wells, I granted the Columbia Broadcasting System the right to dramatize Mr. H. G. Wells's novel *The War of the Worlds* for one performance over the radio. It was not explained to me that this dramatization would be made with a liberty that amounts to a complete rewriting of *The War of the Worlds* and renders it into an entirely different story. Mr. Wells and I consider that by doing so, the Columbia Broadcasting System should make a full retraction. Mr. H. G. Wells is deeply concerned that any work of his should be used in a way, and with a totally unwarranted liberty, to cause deep distress and alarm throughout the United States."[14]

Nothing came of the statement, and the matter was quietly dropped. Newspapers took up the broadcast and raged about "the terror that Welles had perpetrated on the listening audience, calling for self-regulation or even further governmental restrictions."[15] The *Washington Post* ran a full-page editorial suggesting censorship. Not only had Orson Welles potentially dealt a death blow to his own career, but many also wondered whether he had hurt the new medium of radio.

Orson would have felt better had he read another article released by United Press International (UPI). "Officials of the Columbia Broadcasting System reported today they were receiving a deluge of telephone calls concerning the 'War of the Worlds' broadcast. They added that 'five out of six' requested that the feature be repeated. CBS officials admitted they were considering the requests."[16] Another release from UPI dated the same day gave people their answer: "Columbia Broadcasting System officials here said today that, requests or no requests, the 'War of the Worlds' program would not be repeated."[17]

CBS had had enough of the *War of the Worlds*, but the FCC wanted the broadcast repeated and ominously requested the script. FCC Commissioner Frank R. McNinch announced he would investigate at once while Senator Herring prepared a bill for Congress. The *Asheville Times* led with an article titled "Herring Will Demand U.S. Radio Control," in which they explained that the senator had prepared a bill that "would give the Federal Communications Commission authority to pass on every radio program before its presentation. 'The main purpose of the bill is to prevent the unnecessary frightening of children by such programs,' he said.... 'The program last night was a good demonstration of the very thing I've been striking at.'"[18]

Ironically, Orson Welles's decision to push the boundaries of radio had brought in the very real possibility of censorship. Welles and radio were not out of the woods yet. And there were still people who believed America was under attack by Martians. In Asheville, North Carolina, radio station WWNC reported that calls were coming in from the campus of the Asheville Normal and Teachers College at 10:15 the next morning and the students wanted to know after the mass hysteria of the night before that reigned on campus, "Is it true that space ships from Mars have landed in New Jersey and are blowing up everything in the state. And has the United States appealed to Europe for aid in driving out the invaders?"[19]

People all over America couldn't be sure Martians were not still roving the countryside after the night of terror, and this concern prompted the Associated Press on October 31 to release a story quoting Harvard astronomers regarding the possibility of life on Mars. The *Asheville Times* led with "No Men on Mars, Harvard Savants Assure Nation," with the article reading, "The Harvard astronomical observatory, responding to a request for an opinion on the possibility of life on Mars, today issued a statement saying there was no evidence that the higher forms of life, as known on earth, exist on Mars.... Communication or transmission of projectiles from any planet was material for fancy and fiction and not for science."[20]

Benedict Arnold and John Wilkes Booth

November 1, 1938

THE MAN WHO HAD CAUSED ALL THE TURMOIL LEFT CBS OUT A SIDE door after the interview with John Houseman and went back to the Mercury Theatre. An employee eating a Mars bar was fired on the spot in the theater. Welles dug into the dress rehearsal for the show that night, but his strange calamities were not over yet. An electrician keeled over after being at the switchboard for seven hours. A couple of student journalists from the *Daily Princetonian* caught up with him, amazed to find Orson Welles agreeable to an interview, and scooped one of the first interviews after the staged newsreel press conference. Welles was still playing the contrite young man who had inadvertently overstepped the bounds. It was not at all clear which way the winds were going to blow. Welles still half expected to be arrested, served with papers, and/or fired from CBS. One or all three were possible in the hours after the press conference on October 31. Lawsuits against CBS had risen to almost one million dollars.

Welles later said of this period, "I was a combination Benedict Arnold and John Wilkes Booth."[1]

Welles gave the Princeton students a circumspect interview designed to further paint the mosaic of his contrition: "When you cause pain, you can't laugh about it. Ordinarily I might be indignant with people for their gullibility, but as the unwitting agent of the suffering, I feel a little like one accused of murder."[2] At this point, an unnamed Mercury actor burst into the room in full costume, overflowing with excitement. "Look at the Boston papers," he told Welles. "You throw sevens all the time. Anyone else would be thrown off the air for a performance like that and you get out."[3]

That night during the performance of *Danton's Death*, Welles was clearly distracted. The play was cursed with one actor breaking his leg on the set, and now Orson was on stage and couldn't remember his lines. Bill Alland was at the prompt desk in the wings and threw one line after another at him. "Welles stumbled and stumbled. I threw a line at him then another. Finally, he came into the wings and spat at me, saying, 'You sonofabitch. I didn't ask you to do that.'"[4] Then he went back onstage and finished the play.

Danton's Death did not do well. The reviews centered on Orson more than the play. The *Brooklyn Eagle-Examiner* ran the headline "Orson Welles Does Buchner's 'Danton's Death' Over into a Little Thing of His Own, Enjoying Life as a Boy Prodigy." Arthur Pollock's article centered on Welles and dismissed the play by saying basically Orson could fix anything: "Don't worry. When Master Welles gets to be an old man of twenty-eight or twenty-nine he will have given up the idea that the theatre is his own particular playroom and he'll settle down to work. All this Danton business is just animal crackers. Boy prodigies do not always disappear altogether."[5]

But for all the fame *War of the Worlds* generated for Orson, it did nothing for *Danton's Death*. The box office receipts suffered, and the play was a flop. Orson's heart was no longer in it. The play was shut down on November 19 with a production cost of $50,000 when only $10,000 had been budgeted. Fourteen days later, Welles and Houseman announced that they were leasing the Mercury Theatre and talked about co-producing future shows, but the Mercury Theatre era was over. *Mercury Theatre on the Air* was it now, and no one was sure whether that was going to continue. Virginia and Orson escaped with baby Christopher and left for the Todd School campus in Woodstock, Illinois. Welles was exhausted and depressed.

The belief that Orson had gone too far was predominant, and many thought his show would be yanked off the air. The Federal

Communications Commission (FCC) had requested a copy of the script from CBS, and everyone was waiting for the other shoe to drop. The sixty-five-year-old commissioner of the FCC, Frank McNinch, had pressure on him to do something. Letter writers implored the commission to penalize Welles and CBS, or they were "just a bunch of spineless swivel chair holders,"[6] as one man from Tennessee wrote. The FCC was torn by the desire to control but not censor. FCC Commissioner George Henry Payne would like nothing more than to sanction CBS and have Orson Welles thrown off the air. He had long railed against programs "that produced terrorism and nightmares among children." Senator Clyde C. Herring of Des Moines Iowa was quoted as saying, "Some of the bedtime stories that put children to sleep but involve murder and violence are an outrage and should be stopped."[7]

The broadcast set off a general attack on the morality of radio. The *St. Louis Star-Times* quoted Reverend Don Frank Fenn of Baltimore as saying, "Many of the radio programs now designed for children are utterly unsuitable and indeed quite detrimental to the proper development of mind and spirit of the children who listen to them."[8] Commissioner Payne believed that programs and radio stations should adhere to certain standards, and the price for violating those standards was to revoke the license of the station. One commissioner of the FCC told reporters that *War of the Worlds* should win the booby prize of the year but stopped short of saying the show should be taken off the air.

Still, Commissioner McNinch kept his own counsel, though many feared his reformer zeal. While many letters encouraged the FCC to take Welles off the air, there were others who were of the opposite view. "If, because of your drama of Sunday, The Mercury Air Theatre [*sic*] is discontinued or molded into the nauseating familiar pattern of the radio theaters,"[9] wrote one couple, "there will be a good radio for sale cheap at our house."[10] A thirteen-year-old boy in Chicago wrote a letter on behalf of his classmates: "How sorry we are that the people didn't like your play *War of the Worlds* . . . and what ever happens because of your radio play you will know that a dozen children will stick by you."[11] Many of these listeners saw Welles's show as one of the few intelligent ones on the air: "Nine-tenths of the other dramatic programs are plain saw-dust;

they devitalize the existing intelligence of the unwary listener . . . we need quality."[12] Others echoed in alarm that they would be stuck with the dummy Charlie McCarthy. A listener from Utica, New York, asked, "Must we always listen to swing and low-class comedians? Can't we have a little drama, realistically done, for a change."[13] One man who wrote to the FCC, thinking Welles would have to tone down his program, asked the chairman not to "humor the whims of the stupid."[14]

Orson would later receive letters spiked with vitriol over the broadcast. A letter from A. G. Kennedy, a judge from South Carolina, is emblematic of the rage many listeners felt after the broadcast:

> Your radio performance Sunday evening was a clear demonstration of your inhuman instincts, bestial sensuality and fiendish joy in causing distress and suffering. Your savage ancestors of which you are a degenerate offspring exalted in torturing their enemies . . . doubtless reveled in fiendish delight in you causing death to some and great terror, anguish and suffering to thousands of helpless and unoffending victims of your hellish designs. Your contemptible cowardly and cruel undertaking conceived by a demon and executed by a cowardly cur is doubtless in keeping with your sense of humor. When you are faced with the enormity of your heinous crime and are liable for prosecution for your atrocious conduct and that you are morally guilty of murder if not legally guilty, then you fawn and whimper like a cringing cowardly entrapped wolf when apprehended. . . . I would not insult a female dog by calling you a son of such an animal . . . your conduct was beneath the social standing . . . of a bastard of a fatherless whore . . . your consummate act of asninity never again appear on the stage or on the radio. . . . I hope suit will be brought against you individually, the Company which you represent and also the Columbia Broadcasting Company . . . I also propose to use the radio in appealing to the American people to boycott the Columbia Broadcasting System.[15]

America was in a culture war with the emergence of radio, not unlike the culture war that erupted with the emergence of television. The *Tulsa Tribune* led with "Fictional Invasion from Mars Panics Listeners, Brings Down Wrath on Radio."[16] The *Fort Collins Express-Courier* let

Coloradans know what happened with thick black three-inch type across the front page: "FCC Will Probe Panic Broadcast." The paper went on to describe the panic in the nation and then the panic in Denver. "If the Martians had landed in Jersey Sunday night, Assistant Fire Chief Raymond G. Gifford of the Denver fire department had the situation well in hand. Frantic neighbors who heard parts of the broadcast of an H. G. Wells novel approached Gifford and shouted: 'The World is coming to an end. Warriors from Mars just landed in New Jersey. They're killing everybody. They've got terrible poison gas, it's spreading west.' . . . The assistant chief listened, rushed to the telephone, called department headquarters and ordered all the gas masks available rounded up."[17]

Then, in a small boxed article next to the larger *War of the Worlds* coverage, there was an ominous report covering the death of Nick Gallegos, twenty-eight, of Trinidad, "who was injured when his roadster overturned Sunday night."[18] The paper draws no connection between this accident and the *War of the Worlds* panic, but in light of the frantic driving due to the terror of those trying to escape the murdering Martians, it is not a small jump to make that this freak accident, the overturned roadster, happened on the very night the nation experienced a warlike event of mass panic. This accident raises the question: How many unreported accidents and deaths could be attributed to the broadcast?

Many papers focused on the controversy between a low-brow culture of radio and a high-brow culture of theater, books, and art. World War I had determined not only that many American males were too malnourished for service in the armed forces but also that many were illiterate. The sound bite that emerged was that the average American had the mental capacity of a thirteen-year-old. Sponsors of radio glommed on to this statistic, and the famous adage "You will never go broke underestimating the intelligence of the American public" was born. Radio, because of ease of accessibility and large audiences, became a petri dish of appealing to the lowest common denominator.

The *War of the Worlds* broadcast was touted as a means of proving that Americans were essentially gullible morons. The *Chicago Tribune*, in an editorial following the broadcast, put it this way: "By and large the radio audience isn't very bright. Perhaps it would be more tactful to say that some members of the radio audience are a trifle retarded mentally and that many a program is prepared for their consumption. Newspapers, books, magazines, the stage and even the movies strain the fat boys' power of understanding and appreciation, but they can generally find something on the air which is within their comprehension."[19] Alexander Wolcott sent a telegram that Welles kept for the rest of his life. It read in part, "This only goes to prove, my beamish boy, that the intelligent people were all listening to a dummy and all the dummies were listening to you."[20]

The dust had not yet settled, but Orson, who, along with John Houseman, had started Mercury Theatre essentially to promote themselves and their careers, had achieved the one-in-a-million hit reserved for the very few. Even if Orson ended up in jail (which was not a real possibility) or was broke from the lawsuits despite his lawyer having stricken an indemnification clause from his contract with CBS, he had become a household name overnight. The young man who had blindly pushed his way through Manhattan show business in an ambulance racing from one exploit to another, never sure of his next gig or where it would all lead, had gained the fame he sought. Even when Orson had appeared on the cover of *Time* magazine, few knew him beyond the Broadway community of New York and those who listened to *The Shadow*. But the *War of the Worlds* broadcast dominated headlines of almost every paper in America and around the world.

For the first time, his name became grist for editorialists, political commentators, humorists, and even sports reporters, who now compared the odds in horse races to the odds of Martians landing in New Jersey. Orson was well known on Broadway, but the *War of the Worlds* broadcast brought him worldwide fame. Some might call the broadcast an innocent mistake, but there was nothing innocent about Orson Welles. Still, his only chance was to play the innocent who had blundered and was now remorseful.

That was how Orson wanted the press to see him: a well-intentioned young man who never thought people would believe that Martians were actually attacking America. The close-up of Orson in the newsreel when he looks into the camera and his large brown eyes bleed with sincerity and a pleading *"forgive me"* look tells the whole story. Orson Welles was an actor. He was a magician. He was certainly lying when he declared, "I had no idea that I had suddenly become a national event."[21] His very art was pushing limits and then seeing what happened. Orson knew a stick of dynamite is better than a firecracker and, like the precocious child, Orson Welles had yet to be denied. The impact on media in 1938 cannot be denied now or then. As "the *New York Herald Tribune* blared on its front page, 'Not since the Spanish fleet, sailed to bombard the New England coast in 1898, has so much hysteria, panic, and sudden conversion to religion been reported to the press of the United States as when radio listeners heard about an invasion from Mars.'"[22]

Editorials attacking Welles called for him to be thrown off the air. An editorial in the Camden, New Jersey, *Courier-Post* claimed that the FCC did not believe that Orson was as innocent as he pretended. "We do not condone the broadcast. We think the intention in the minds of Mr. Orson Welles and his *Mercury Theater [on] the Air* was not to frighten anybody but only to produce a 'socko' dramatic effect. We think the methods used were unscrupulous and irresponsible. The program was conceived in a kind of gleeful, 'We'll panic 'em!' spirit which ought to have been checked by somebody in the Columbia organization. We think everybody ought to be called on the carpet by the Federal Communications Commission and that a warning should be issued against such wild man stuff in the future."[23]

Death threats came in and one man vowed to kill Welles on the opening night of *Danton's Death*. Other editorial writers saw it a different way. An editorial in the *Pittsburgh Press* sounded what would become a familiar theme—the ignorance of the American public. "What a furor followed! What fear and trepidation! What anxiety! What weeping and wailing and gnashing of teeth! Screaming! Shouting! Shaking of fists! Yea, even panic! It is almost unbelievable and certainly disgusting that such should be the reward for so excellent and perfect a production. . . . One word tells the story, one word explains the shameful action . . . one word—ignorance!"[24]

On October 31, the far reaches of the country were still reporting in with stories of local panic. In Lincoln, Nebraska, the *Lincoln Star* reported that a local "national guard officer here got so excited over the blowing up of the east coast on a Sunday night radio broadcast he called another officer. They talked about calling out the guard unit before they learned the program was fictitious." The paper reported on the reaction in sororities at the University of Nebraska, stating that "panic swept through sorority row on the University of Nebraska campus Sunday evening after the men from Mars began turning on their heat rays. One coed tried to get her parents in Fremont on the long-distance phone so she could tell them goodbye."[25]

More news was coming in and the night of terror across the United States was becoming more evident. The Associated Press sent out the following at 8:45 p.m. "Note to Editors: Queries to newspapers from radio listeners throughout the United States tonight regarding a reported meteor fall which killed a number of New Jerseyites are the result of a studio dramatization."[26] On October 31, the *Bergen Evening Record* painted a picture of pandemonium the night before: "During the height of the excitement a Hackensack mother rushed to find her daughter so they could die together. She fainted in the street. Bergenfield families rushed children and relatives into cars to flee the men from Mars allegedly destroying the world. . . . Patrolman Gerard Scrivens of Bergenfield reported a caravan of no less than 20 persons at police headquarters demanding the right direction to evade the approaching gases. Scrivens said it was almost impossible to convince them it was just a radio program."[27]

So while Orson hid with his wife and child in the small town of Woodstock, Illinois, the reverberations of the *War of the Worlds* broadcast continued across the country. These seismic tremors would lead to his greatest opportunity and triumph.

Durn Fools

November 1, 1938

GROVERS MILL, NEW JERSEY, HAD BECOME THE EPICENTER OF THE fictional invasion and, for days and weeks following the broadcast, was overrun with people looking for the Martian landing site. On November 1, the *Seattle Star* ran the headline "Curious Crowds Flock to Farm Around Which Radio's 'Scare' Program Revolved." The article went on to say, "Visiting motorists were still driving by the old Wilson farm today to see the spot where monsters from Mars didn't land their rocket ship to begin the onslaught against the earth Sunday night."[1] Grovers Mill had been invaded by journalists, police, state police, and photographers looking for Martians or a story. The village of two hundred that was four miles east of Princeton had become the epicenter of the *War of the Worlds*, and the Wilson farm had been singled out as the place where the Martians were most likely to have landed. Tenant families occupied the farm where James Anderson and his wife had been listening to the *Charlie McCarthy Show* when Mrs. Anderson switched to the *Mercury Theatre* and heard the bulletin stating a large meteor had fallen in her barnyard. She woke her husband from bed, who went out on the porch and looked around.

"Durn fools,"[2] he muttered and went back to bed.

But many others did not go back to bed. Another panicked local resident wanted to get away to reach his wife's family in Pennsylvania but forgot to open the garage door. After he drove through the door, he looked at his wife and said, "Well, we won't be needing it anymore."[3] Another man drank a bottle of whiskey after hearing the broadcast, "threw his dog over a kennel fence to keep him safe, then drove to his brother's house and woke him up, taking him on a wild drunken ride until they heard it was all a play."[4] Neighbors blasted the local water tower with buckshot, thinking it was the Martian machines. Catherine Shrope-Mok, who lived across the street, later said, "You'd think they would know better since they saw it every day."[5]

Sixty-three-year-old William Dock heard the bulletin about the Martians crawling out of their cylinder rocket ship and laying waste. He grabbed his shotgun and went looking for the aliens. Phillip Wassun of Cranberry, New Jersey, five miles east of Grovers Mill, passed "a carload of national guardsman in the road. They asked him the way to the scene of destruction, having heard on the radio that they had been ordered out to fight. 'They were all dressed up to kill,' he said. 'I couldn't convince them it must be a fake, and two hours later, I saw them still riding around looking for whatever it was supposed to be.'"[6]

California's *Modesto Bee* led with the headline "Nationwide Terrorism Created by Radio War Drama Starts Inquiry," with a second headline, "CBS Will Not Rebroadcast Play."[7] As in other states, five out of six callers to the Columbia Broadcasting System in Washington, DC, asked to have the program repeated. The *Daily News* stated on the first day of November, "U.S. Says 'No' to All Future 'Wars' on Air."[8] The Federal Communications Commission (FCC), which had started an investigation, also forbade any war broadcasts. "The nation heard its first and last radio report of an imaginary air attack last night. Banned henceforth is the vivid news bulletin and official report technique used in the *Mercury Theatre on the Air* broadcast to describe an assault on New Jersey by fantastic monsters from Mars."[9]

When Bill Dock of Grovers Mill heard the report of Martians, he grabbed his double-barreled shotgun and headed out into the night to find the Martians. Or so the story goes. There were many stories of farmers out with shotguns that night, looking for aliens to blast into eternity. It is an *American Gothic* image: the farmer defending his homeland against invaders. That image went all over the world when, the day after the broadcast, a photographer from the *Daily News* in New York had Bill

Dock pose in a warehouse with his shotgun. In the famous photo, Bill Dock is in droopy farm attire with turned-up shoes and a pipe in his mouth. He holds his shotgun at waist level. It is cartoonish and conjures up a hundred cartoons in which the farmer is blasting foxes in the hen house. *Life* magazine would include the photo two weeks later in a spread on science fiction stories that included King Kong, Flash Gordon, and Boris Karloff in *Frankenstein*. Bill Dock's photo became part of the legend that had farmers blasting the local water tower they had mistaken for Martian machines. Dock would die seven years later, resenting that the press had made a joke of him, but the picture would continue to circulate and appear fifty years later in DC Comics.

But, of course, Dock became the defining image of the broadcast because he defined the ethos of the frontier man defending his home against invaders. Even though the image of Bill Dock is slightly comic, with his hunched back and glasses and pipe while holding his shotgun, at least he took action. One Michigan woman wrote, "Where are our true Americans that were invaded by Indians in covered wagons and stood up and took it like men? No place to run for protection then. But these molly-coddled jitterbugs show what they're made of. Just a bunch of crybabies."[10] Some believed that the reaction to the *War of the Worlds* broadcast showed that Americans had grown soft in the twentieth century and that the actual fighting spirit belonged to the men of the century before. *Buffalo Bill's Wild West* show had made money on the proposition that modern Americans suffered from *neurasthenia* (nervous disease) and that real men were meant to be out laboring under God's light, not cooped up in office buildings in Manhattan. To many, the broadcast showed that soft Americans of the modern twentieth century lacked the spine of their forefathers.

In terms of fighting men, the broadcast even impacted the armed forces of the United States. The article in the *Daily News* reported, "The next radio broadcast describing an invasion of the United States will really mean war. . . . Today the Federal Communications Commission, the Army, and the Navy united to avert a repetition of the coast-to-coast panic created among the thousands who listened to the vivid dramatization. . . . Chiefs of the national defense, who for months have been laboring over the problem of the part radio shall play in the event of a sudden attack on the United States, deplored the 'false alarm.'"[11]

Orson Welles's broadcast had reached the highest levels of government that forbade dramatized news, which had been a staple of radio. The fact that the leaders of the armed forces had taken note and supported a fundamental change to broadcasting rules shows the government recognized that millions of Americans believed the country was under attack. The threat of radio regulation loomed large in the days following the broadcast. The *Eau Claire Leader-Telegram* announced, "Rigid Radio Regulation Likely to Follow Weird Horror Play Broadcast." The article stated that "urgent demands for federal investigation multiplied tonight in the wake of the ultra-realistic radio drama that spread mass hysteria among listeners across the nation with its news broadcast fantasy of octopus-like monsters invading the United States." Welles was quoted as saying he was "just stunned" and that "everything seems like a dream."[12]

Leaving his play *Danton's Death* behind, Welles, Virginia, and baby Christopher continued their monthlong retreat at the Todd School campus in Woodstock. Orson had returned to the only home he would ever really have and the only parents who would survive into his adult years, Roger and Hortense Hill. He could recharge and fly back to New York for his radio show as long as it lasted.

Mercury Theatre on the Air was in danger at CBS, and the press still wanted Welles's head. Orson must have heard the drumbeats. The *New York Herald Tribune* stated, "Terrifying radio personages as 'The Shadow' have frightened children out of their wits, but this time it was the adults who met the hobgoblins. . . . The whole performance was monstrous and cruel."[13] The *New York Sun* believed "the horribly convincing story of disaster"[14] was totally believable and singled out people who wanted to fight the Martians. The *New York Times* declared, "Radio ought to act promptly to prevent a repetition of the wave of panic in which it inundated the nation Sunday night. . . . What began as entertainment might have ended in disaster. . . . Radio is new, but it has adult responsibilities."[15] The *Detroit Free Press* went for the jugular: "The broadcast was a piece of inexcusable and unforgivable stupidity. . . . That sort of childish smart-aleckism isn't at all humorous, and if the participants do not find themselves responsible for several deaths, they will be lucky."[16] The *Detroit News* called for regulation. "The results were not at all funny. Such a panic as ensued could have had tragic consequences. . . . The lesson calls for stricter regulations to govern the presentation of drama capable of being misunderstood as fact."[17] *The Boston Post* partially blamed the listeners, saying that "people half listening to radio announcements was probably responsible for the alarm which the broadcast caused. . . . There is no question that the panic which the . . . broadcast inspired will sharply curb radio broadcasts . . . in terms of the public this should be done."[18]

Censorship, criminal proceedings, a destroyed career in show business—all were on the table as the calendar turned to November 2, 1938. Orson Welles was in a dark place in his cabin at the Todd School, and many thought he was finished in radio and theater. The current of public opinion was not going his way, but then an editorial by popular columnist Dorothy Thompson appeared and was read by millions. "This blue-eyed tornado," as one journalist called her, had been kicked out of Germany for lampooning Adolf Hitler as "the little man." Her radio broadcasts in the United States would reach six million listeners, and her weekly column "On the Record," in the *New York Herald Tribune*, with its "gutsy and fresh" style, was more popular than Eleanor Roosevelt's column.[19]

Titled "Mr. Welles and Mass Delusion," Dorothy's column went against the grain of papers that were calling for regulation and restriction and asking for Welles to be fired. Thompson started off by saying, "Mr. Welles and the *Mercury Theatre on the Air* have made one of the most fascinating and important demonstrations of all time. They have proved that a few effective voices, accompanied by sound effects, can so convince masses of people of a totally unreasonable, completely fantastic proposition as to create a nationwide panic."[20] Then she swung in and diverted all the blame from Orson Welles: "They have cast a brilliant and cruel light upon the failure of popular education. They have shown up the incredible stupidity, lack of nerve and ignorance of thousands. They have proved how easy it is to start a mass delusion. They have uncovered the primal fears lying under the thinnest surface of the so-called civilized man."[21] Thompson declared poor education was to blame for people believing Martians had invaded the United States, and, more than that, it was the fault of the American people for being so dumb. Dorothy Thompson, as part of the cultural elite of her time, had made the judgment that the mass of people in America were just plain ignorant.

"And far from blaming Mr. Orson Welles, he ought to be given a Congressional medal and a national prize. . . . For Mr. Orson Welles and his theatre have made a greater contribution to an understanding of Hitlerism, Mussolinism, Stalinism. . . . They have thrown more light on recent events in Europe leading to the Munich Pact than everything that has been said on the subject by all the journalists and commentators."[22] Then Thompson dismissed the entire broadcast: "Nothing whatever about the dramatization of 'War of the Worlds' was in the least credible, no matter at what point the hearer might have tuned in. The entire verisimilitude was in the names of a few specific places. . . . A twist of the dial would have established for anybody that the national catastrophe was not being noted on any other station. A second of logic would have dispelled any terror." Next, she pointed out that the "time element was obviously lunatic. . . . Listeners were told that 'within three hours three million people have moved out of New York'—an obvious impossibility."[23] Finally, she exonerated Orson Welles: "And, of course, it was not even a planned hoax. Nobody was more surprised at the result than Mr. Welles. The public was told at the beginning, at the end, and during the course of the drama that it was a drama."[24]

Orson could not have planned it better. A massive influencer like Dorothy Thompson pinned the panic on the stupidity and ignorance of the American public and stated that Orson was just doing his job and had never intended to scare people. The Wizard of Oz had just jumped back behind the curtain, and the magic show was intact. It was a game changer. Orson had done America a favor with his broadcast by showing how vulnerable Americans were to the wiles of dictators.

Orson must have shut the door to his cottage and shouted to the heavens. Peck's bad boy had been redeemed. There was some pushback to Dorothy Thompson's editorial, with one man saying she had failed to consider that intelligent people who tuned into the broadcast in the middle of the performance were duped. The New Jersey man pointed out that he was told by a relative to tune into the broadcast and then heard the governor of New Jersey had instituted martial law. Then a policeman came to the door and told him to evacuate. He maintained that any listener, intelligent or not, would have believed the broadcast to be true and that Thompson had "overlooked the obvious negligence in permitting the use of the precise designation of public officials and the use of an existing locale and to pay an unqualified tribute to Mr. Welles in providing us with this clinical demonstration of mass hysteria is taking an untenable position capable of incalculable harm."[25]

Thompson did note the countless real locations, which convinced many that the broadcast was genuine: the towns of Grovers Mill, Princeton, and Trenton in New Jersey, as well as Plainsboro, Allentown, Morristown, the Watchung Mountains, Bayonne, the Hutchinson River Parkway, Newark, the Palisades, Times Square, Fifth Avenue, the Pulaski Skyway, and the Holland Tunnel. Many who wrote in later pointed to these landmarks as convincing them the broadcast of the Martian invasion was genuine. "When he said, 'Ladies and gentlemen, do not use route number 23' that made me sure," one listener wrote. Another wrote, "I was most inclined to believe the broadcast when they mentioned places like South Street and Pulaski Highway."[26]

Thompson had also pointed out that people could have easily checked other radio stations or the newspaper listings. In the Cantril report, a sampling was taken of listeners, and it was found that half checked other stations and were reassured, but there was another group who checked the information and still believed the report was real. This circumstance pointed to the power of suggestion overcoming logic and that hearing the drama became self-fulfilling. Hadley Cantril's report of interviews about what people did after listening to the broadcast argues against Thompson's thesis that only stupid people believed the program. These were middle-class people reacting in predictable ways to information coming over the radio. In these interviews, the effect on children is predictably terrifying. In the first interview, children had been home alone when they heard the broadcast.

"I was alone with my two younger brothers. My parents had gone to a party in Newark. When they mentioned, 'citizens of Newark come to the open spaces,' I got scared. I called my mother to find out what to do, and there was no answer. I found out later that they had gone to an empty apartment so that they could dance. Nobody was left at the place I phoned. My only thought was the flames had overcome my parents."[27]

Many people were home with their children and had to determine how to protect them from the approaching danger.

"I was listening with my son—I had tuned in a little after eight. At the beginning, it was not here so I was not scared. But when the gas came nearer, the boy started crying. I was terribly upset. I looked out the window where we can see the airport, but I did not see anything. But then the announcer said, 'Everybody go up on [the] roofs' . . . so I took my boy and rushed upstairs."[28]

A girl working on her homework heard the broadcast and joined another girl upstairs, where she felt "she was going crazy and kept on saying, 'What can we do, what difference does it make whether we die sooner or later?' We were holding each other. Everything seemed unimportant in the face of death. I was afraid to die, [I] just kept on listening."[29]

In an apartment building, one woman rushed down the stairs yelling at people to turn on their radio. "I was very scared, and everybody in the room was scared stiff, too. . . . If I had a little bottle of whiskey, I would have had a drink and said, 'Let it go.'"[30]

The panic spread through people calling others and telling them about the broadcast. Families spread the news, trying to bring loved ones together one last time: "We called my brother, who had gone out. He said he would be right down and drive away with us. . . . I felt, why can the children not be with us, if we are going to die. Then I called to my husband, 'Dan why don't you get dressed? You don't want to die in your working clothes.' My husband said we were here for God's glory and honor, and it was for Him to decide when we should drive."[31]

On the night of October 30, 1938, people did not believe the world was under attack because they were ignorant, uneducated, or stupid. They believed an oracle of authority had just told them through the brilliant stagecraft of Orson Welles that the world was under attack from invading Martians. Smart, rich, poor, illiterate—it did not matter.

Professors from Princeton charged over to Grovers Mill to investigate while college students nationwide fled and people in Harlem ran into the streets. So where does this thesis of Dorothy Thompson and others come from that the general public is ignorant? There was something much darker in Thompson's assessment of "the incredible stupidity, lack of nerve and ignorance of thousands."[32] Eugenics was making the rounds as a popular race theory of the 1930s. Promulgated by Herbert Spencer under the banner of Social Darwinism, the theory held that certain races and ethnicities are superior to others and have more chance for survival and will hold the power in society. This idea evolved into the popular movement of eugenics, which called for the sterilization of those with diminished intelligence, who were considered slow, or mentally handicapped. People who would be considered on the autism spectrum today underwent sterilization in the 1930s in the United States. Indeed, a program of sterilization was in full swing in Hitler's Germany. The theories of eugenics led to an assessment of large groups of people as racially inferior or mentally slow. This view, of course, would reach its apotheosis with the Nazis. Still, this wholesale condemnation of the masses as uneducated, stupid, or slow was part of a larger trend that condemned segments of the population while singling out the superior intellectual capabilities of the highly educated upper classes. Friedrich Nietzsche and the Nazis would knock it all down to the Übermensch or Superman.

Dorothy Thompson's thesis that Americans could fall for someone like Adolf Hitler was embedded in her editorial, but the upside was she had disarmed Orson Welles's detractors. Orson should have been dancing a jig. Thompson had just taken his national prank and elevated it to an exercise in demonstrating the dangers of mass hysteria in totalitarianism. If Orson had hired Thompson as his PR person, he could not have done better. "That historic hour on the air was an act of unconscious genius, performed by the very innocence of intelligence."[33] Thompson stated unequivocally that Orson Welles was innocent of any attempt to deceive. Then she took on his critics: "The deceived were furious and, of course, demanded that the state protect them, demonstrating they were incapable of relying on their own judgment."[34] This comment was directed toward the FCC. She then declared no political body must ever have a monopoly on the radio, that "universal education is failing to train reason and logic,"[35] and that "the power of mass suggestion is the most potent force today, and . . . the political demagogue is more powerful than all the economic forces."[36] She had just turned Welles's broadcast into a civics lesson on the dangers of autocrats in the modern age. She concluded by saying, "If people can be frightened out of their wits by mythical men from Mars, they can be frightened into fanaticism by the fear of Reds . . . or of Jews, or of starvation, or of an outside enemy."[37] She lauded Orson for doing everyone a favor by doing the politicians one better: "He made the scare to end scares, the menace to end menaces, the unreason to end unreason, the perfect demonstration that the danger is not from Mars, but from the theatrical demagogue."[38]

In Dorothy Thompson's view, Orson, with his broadcast, had warned the world of the danger of a man like Adolf Hitler. He had proved that radio could be misused with dangerous consequences, and, thank God, he showed us what morons Americans really are so we could start educating the young—not only a brilliant man but also a patriot. In short, Orson Welles was off the hook. For all the bluster and hand-wringing after the broadcast, the official government reaction came to very little. The FCC met on November 1 and still had not listened to the *War of the Worlds* broadcast; it discussed only routine matters. The recordings had not yet been delivered from CBS, but the *New York Times* speculated, "There were fairly definite indications that no action would be taken beyond a possible statement of regret that the program was staged in too realistic a manner."[39] The *Washington Post* quoted commissioners off the record saying they were powerless to do more than issue a stern reprimand to CBS. No one could argue that *War of the Worlds* had "obscene, indecent, or profane language. Everything else fell into a very gray area where the FCC hesitated to venture."[40] As Commissioner Frank McNinch explained, "There is censorship now with the responsibility on the stations themselves. To put such responsibility on the commission, no, I would be opposed to that."[41]

On November 7, there was a meeting to discuss the *War of The Worlds* broadcast with the heads of NBC, CBS, and the Mutual Broadcasting System. Commissioner McNinch suggested that "news terms like 'flash' and 'bulletin' should be kept out of fictional programs to avoid general alarm."[42] The networks readily agreed, and there was a more general discussion of program standards, but this was all in the realm of suggestions. The meeting lasted three hours and "marked the federal government's only direct response to the *War of the Worlds* broadcast."[43]

On December 6, 1938, an article appeared in the New York *Daily News* titled "FCC Won't Punish CBS on Welles Play." The article went on to say, "The Federal Communications Commission bowed to public opinion again today and announced that it will not attempt to censor the Columbia Broadcasting System and member stations which carried Orson Welles' famous 'War of the Worlds' broadcast."[44] The big news was the abandonment of dramatized news stories like the format of *March of Time*. "CBS had agreed not to use the technique of an imitation news broadcast within a dramatization—a technique that frightened radio listeners from coast to coast when Orson Welles employed it to describe a fictional invasion from Mars."[45]

Orson Welles's *War of the Worlds* broadcast had such an impact on America that the very way news was delivered at the time was stopped forever. In a way, Orson took the dramatization of news to its logical conclusion, showed its flaws at the very core, and paved the way for news journalism. After the broadcast of October 30, 1938, the reenactments of news stories essentially stopped. The *March of Time* went off the air in 1939. RCA president David Sarnoff called radio stations voluntarily changing their content as "self-regulation . . . the American answer to an American problem."

Orson Welles had walked up to the cliff's edge but didn't fall into the pit of failure and obscurity. As one listener wrote him from Pennsylvania, "What might have been a catastrophe will probably turn out to be the best publicity for you."[46] Another listener eerily predicted Orson would be besieged with Hollywood offers. Still, others did not share admiration of Orson's ability to deceive. He still received death threats. There would be attacks on Orson Welles, but in the future. For now, the boy wonder had survived his assault on America, and the future was his. The pearl of Hollywood was glimmering just over the horizon.

Campbell's on the Air

December 9, 1938

"I AM HERE TO INTRODUCE THE WHITE HOPE OF THE AMERICAN STAGE as the director and star of the *Campbell Playhouse*—he writes his own radio scripts and directs them and makes them live and breathe with the warmth of his genius. . . . He has been selected by Campbell's as the ideal man to conduct *The Campbell Playhouse*. And so tonight Orson Welles makes his bow as the outstanding program director of the air and I have the very great pleasure of presenting him now, Mr. Orson Welles!"[1]

Like the phoenix rising from the ashes, Orson Welles went from potentially being fired by CBS and never working in show business again to touring large vats of bubbling soup in Camden, New Jersey, with Campbell Soup executives. John Houseman later wrote, "Orson and I, in our most conservative suits and stiff collars, . . . spent several hours with the president of Campbell Soups and his leading executives. Dutifully, we made our tour of the plant and saw hecatombs of dead chickens and huge bubbling vats of tomatoes and peas. At noon, in the executive dining room, we smacked our lips over the thin, briny liquid of which we were about to become the champions."[2] The deal was done, and *Mercury Theatre on the Air* became the *Campbell Playhouse*. The show would stay with CBS but move to Fridays with a prime-time slot of 9:00 p.m. Orson and Houseman would still control the show, but the new sponsors wanted "to orientate the radio show toward popular plays and novels with guest stars from Broadway and Hollywood. Orson lapped it up, telling the Campbell

Soup executives, 'This is a great big chance for me and a great big challenge. With my faith in the radio and your display of confidence in me, by becoming the sponsor, we can possibly create something important. Let's hope nobody is mistaken.'"[3]

Mercury Theatre on the Air could not secure a sponsor before the *War of the Worlds* broadcast. "The sponsor had turned us down the week before because we tended to too much violence and sensationalism," Welles remarked wryly later. "They picked us up the week after the *War of the Worlds*. Thanks to the Martians, we got ourselves a sponsor, and suddenly, we were a big commercial program."[4]

Now Orson would make $1,500 weekly and have the backing of a major sponsor. The *War of the Worlds* had launched him into the stratosphere as he led off with *Rebecca* on December 9, starring Margaret Sullivan. The *New York Times* said the *Campbell Playhouse* was off to "a good start . . . if marred by too many commercials."[5] It was no longer Orson Welles's baby, but he didn't seem to care. He was making money hand over fist and having a great time doing it. The only thing that could be better would be if Hollywood came knocking.

In 1937, David Selznick offered Welles a chance to head the story department at Selznick Studios, but Orson wanted total control. He didn't have to wait long. George Schaefer of RKO Studios offered Orson a one-in-a-million contract on the strength of the *War of the Worlds* broadcast and Welles's fast rise in theater and radio. By August 1939, Welles had signed a contract with RKO for two films. He would receive $100,000 for the first one along with 20 percent of the profits. For the second one, he'd receive $125,000 and 25 percent of the profits.

The coverage in the *Vancouver Sun* was typical of the press coverage he received regarding his continuing good fortune: "Orson Welles Given Free Hand in Movies: Wonderboy of 24 Enters on New Career with Bounding Spirits and Ferocious Energy."[6] Next to the headline was a picture of Orson lying on a couch with a full beard and smoking a pipe while perusing a book, presumably for his next movie. He had the look of a man who had climbed a mountain and was contemplating retirement. Orson Welles was regarded by the press as a genius. "No one person, it would seem, could travel as extensively as he has done, could become involved in as many disparate experiences. . . . This brings us reluctantly to an explanation . . . the word *genius* has a suggestion of gravity, which does not describe the ebullient gentleman. . . . He has everything his own way these days. RKO has given him carte blanche to write, direct, and act in two pictures."[7]

But there were small dark clouds on Orson's very blue horizon. The Hollywood establishment was outraged at the unprecedented contract given to the twenty-four-year-old Welles. Dark stories began to be circulated about the boy wonder. "There is nothing about the town that can be blamed on Hollywood and not the contract. . . . I've been a movie fan all my life," Orson insisted, addressing rumors of "his whimsies, his temperament, his thunderous anger and sullen silences."[8]

Still, the article painted Welles in a positive light as a father who "likes to sit around home barefoot in bathing shorts and a robe, to sleep in pajama pants of his own designing, to smoke 85 cent cigars, to have meat flown out from New York for his personal consumption, to call any maid in his household 'Ingrid' and any chauffeur or taxi driver, 'Alfalfa Bill.'"[9] Orson Welles had made it, and to the press, he could do no wrong.

Orson continued his radio show, flying weekly back to New York while developing his films. RKO could veto any budget that exceeded $500,000 for the two films. The press didn't know that his marriage to Virginia had come apart thanks to continued adultery with actresses and dancers; once he went west to Hollywood, that would mark the end. His old relationships were disintegrating as new ones began, and his relationship with John Houseman ended in a fiery exchange. Orson had long had a love-hate relationship with Houseman, chafing under his control but needing it all the same. The Hollywood deal with RKO had no room for John Houseman, and, like the son feeling his independence, Orson kicked off the last shackles of the older man's control at a staff meeting at Chasen's restaurant in Beverly Hills.

Orson was not in a good mood that night. He had just received notification from RKO that no more salaries would be paid until a final script was approved and a firm shooting date was set. Orson had been struggling with ideas and scripts. He originally became interested in Joseph Conrad's *Heart of Darkness* but abandoned the idea; now approval and a shooting date were far out of reach. He had brought New York actors from the Mercury Theatre and had no money to pay them. Orson was still carrying outstanding personal debt from the Mercury Theatre and living high with apartments, cars, servants, hotels, and an estranged wife and child to support, but he said if RKO would not pay the actors, then he would. John Houseman told him they did not have the money to pay the actors, and Orson became livid and accused Houseman of mismanaging his money. "You're a crook, and they know it! Everybody knows it!"

As Houseman rose from the table, Orson threw flaming dish heaters at his producing partner and friend. "It missed me by a yard and landed at the foot of a drawn window curtain behind me. Another flaming object flew by me as I moved toward the door, which had opened and in which I could see Dave Chasen [the owner of the restaurant], frozen with horror, staring at the flames that were beginning to lick at his curtains. . . . Behind me, I could hear Orson on the landing yelling, 'Crook!' and 'Thief!'"[10]

Their relationship was terminally damaged, but it was fitting that the two men who had produced a story about a fiery meteor streaking to Earth and then mechanical Martians emerging with heat ray guns to incinerate humans should part with fiery meteors flying overhead. It was the perfect ending for the *War of the Worlds*.

Hadley Cantril, meanwhile, had been compiling his book *The Invasion from Mars* and sent Welles a copy to endorse. Orson sent back a letter that said he would be happy to provide a blurb, but the book "in its present form contains an error so grave and in my opinion so detrimental to my own reputation that I cannot in all fairness speak well of it until some reparation is made."[11] Howard Koch had been listed as the author of the *War of the Worlds* screenplay, and Welles protested, saying the script had been "a collaboration of the best sort."[12] Cantril explained that Koch had provided proof he was the author. Orson promised legal action if the book were published with Howard Koch listed as the author. The book was published, and Orson the Magician was not listed as the author. Orson Welles would never receive one cent of royalties from the *War of the Worlds* broadcast bearing his name.

After he tried to light John Houseman on fire, Welles began lighting up Hollywood with his opinions, which made him few friends. On December 5, 1939, the *Kansas City Star* published an article listing Orson's riffs on actors and actresses. It did not bode well for his future working relationships, but Orson was riding high. "'There is no great actress of the screen.' The speaker is Orson Welles . . . whom you may remember for a certain realistic broadcast of a Martian invasion. . . . 'I timidly suggest that Bette Davis could be termed a great actress. . . . She's good but not great in a sense that Helen Hayes is great. Garbo . . . falls below the standard set by the men, with Spencer Tracy at the head of the procession. Rooney is the George M. Cohan of the future. He can do everything. . . . Katharine Hepburn is an amateur who is talented, but even though she tries to be a professional . . . she embarrasses me when I watch her perform.'"[13]

These quotes are cringeworthy today, but Orson Welles was doing what he always did. He tore down the establishment, the art, the play, the broadcast, the film, and then put it back together in a radical new way. The difference was Hollywood is a community with a long memory, and they would eventually make the boy wonder pay for his impertinence. Eventually, Orson would marry Hollywood royalty, the movie star Rita Hayworth, and end up in court in 1944 in a custody battle over child support with his former wife, Virginia. The papers would list his income at $10,000 a month, but his net was only $2,000. Welles posted a loss of $65,000 for the year because of theatrical investments. Virginia and Christopher, the wife and child he would rarely see, received $133 per month and requested $350 and a $100,000 trust fund to be set up. Orson Welles testified that he was financially unable to do so. It would be the theme of the rest of his life.

War of the Worlds

June 1944

IN JUNE 1944, ORSON WAS ON A GRUELING TOUR OF PATRIOTIC PRO-
grams that had him traveling from Texas to California and finally to
Illinois. He was tired, and his business manager, Jackson Leighter, suggested they stop in Kansas City and rest for the night. What happened
next was something Welles would never forget: "The moment Orson
entered the hotel lobby, a man rushed up and began to pound him mercilessly with his fists, screaming, 'I'm going to kill you, I'm going to kill
you! I promised I'd kill you if I saw you!' So unexpected was this sudden violence that for a long moment, the people in the lobby watched
incredulously."[1] Leighter eventually pulled the man away, and a bruised
and confused Welles was bundled into an elevator. A story then emerged
that surely haunted Welles. The man's wife, after listening to the *War
of the Worlds* broadcast, had committed suicide that fateful October 30,
1938. The man had vowed to murder Orson if he ever saw him. Leighter,
after hearing his reason for attacking Welles, dropped the charges.

If the story were apocryphal, it is doubtful Orson Welles's business
manager would have dropped the charges. It is likely that Leighter found
the man's story to be true and quickly realized that a story of that sort
could destroy a career. Better to let the man go and move on than add
to the casualties of the *War of the Worlds*. The claim that no one was seriously injured or died from Orson Welles's broadcast was in the interests
of CBS and Orson Welles. But people *were* hurt, and some died. Orson

had weaponized radio on that warm October night and perfected his prosecution of suspension of disbelief. The suspension of disbelief is the secret to any great fiction, any great hoax, novel, short story, or film. Welles perfected his technique on that Halloween eve, and everything else that followed would be derivative. A great artist doesn't know what he is doing until he does it. The fact that leaders in Hollywood opened up their checkbooks and RKO gave Welles an open mandate to make whatever he wanted shows their understanding that the Svengali who was able to fool the world could be harnessed on film. So, beyond the broadcast nomenclature of how it happened, *War of the Worlds*, in a very real way, was Welles's first movie. It was a horror movie, for sure, but it also was a box office smash.

Some have said Orson was as surprised as anyone else that his broadcast caused mass panic in the United States. But you cannot suddenly detangle a Sunday school boy from the man who had stormed Irish theater at sixteen; put on a Black *Macbeth* in Harlem; and defied the government by putting on a radical play, *The Cradle Will Rock*, which forced the closure of his theater, causing his entire cast and spectators to then walk to another theater where they performed the play from the audience. The man then landed in the middle of radio after starting his own theater company, and all with the touch of precocious genius that marks the great actor, conman, visionary. The very genius of Welles was the fine art of deception he had been experimenting with his entire life. To say that his greatest deception was a gaffe, an unintended consequence, is to deny who Orson Welles was. His genius was creating combustion in everything he did, from the day he was born with that sonorous voice to the day he died with a typewriter propped on his stomach. He was the boy forever lighting the firecrackers and then sitting back and watching them explode.

Over the years, Orson Welles let the truth leak out bit by bit. At one point, he stated his intentions of that night in 1938 plainly, saying, "I had conceived the idea of doing a radio broadcast in such a manner that a crisis would actually seem to be happening . . . and would be broadcast in such a dramatized form as to appear to be a real event taking place at that time, rather than a mere radio play."[2] It doesn't get any clearer than that, and yet people are loath to say Orson knew what he was doing. Would anyone really try to fool a nation and have people break their legs, have heart attacks, run for the hills, get sick, attempt and succeed in suicide? Yes. Orson Welles would, if he found a better way to convey a story, play, or movie. Art was everything to the boy who, at sixteen, found himself doing Shakespeare on the stage in Ireland.

In a BBC interview twenty years later, Orson told the interviewer, "In fact, we weren't as innocent as we said we were. . . . We were fed up [with] the way everything on this magic box was believed . . . our broadcast was an assault on that magic box."[3] As if we didn't suspect it. Welles's expression in his media interviews was that of a mischievous boy gleefully relating his prank. In another interview, Orson was shown the picture of himself with the caption "I had no idea this would happen." Welles laughed and said, "I was lying my head off; I knew exactly what I was doing and what would happen."[4]

Of course he knew what he was doing, but the revisionism of our time views everything from the lens of 2024. The academic thesis is that many people did not really panic and that the whole event was overblown. One just has to research the October 31, 1938, newspapers to see that this is not true. After Welles died in 1985, Howard Koch admitted that he thought Welles knew what would happen from his realistic broadcast. This was confirmed after the newsreel interview when Welles finished and stood up, and Koch "witnessed Welles and Houseman exchange a congratulatory gesture. 'It spoke volumes,' Koch said."[5] Koch's script contains the final smoking gun as to Welles's intentions—Orson's peroration that justified his scaring his listeners to death: "The *War of the Worlds* has no further significance than as the holiday offering it was intended to be. . . . And remember, please, for the next day or so, the terrible lesson you learned tonight."[6] The "terrible lesson" is one of gullibility. Orson warns his listeners, "Don't believe everything you hear."

More evidence is the fact Orson didn't even inquire why the police had entered the control booth and why John Houseman refused to let them enter the studio. It all makes sense that they anticipated the explosion, and that was why Houseman blocked CBS producer Davidson Taylor from interrupting the broadcast as well. They knew what was coming. Orson and Houseman had to know they would cause panic not only among the population but also in the halls of CBS. Stopping the broadcast would foil their plans, which hinged on the bet that the benefit would ultimately outweigh the harm.

Orson Welles, the enormous man who would end up hawking wine in the 1970s, is very hard to square with that dynamic young man who had it all by the age of twenty-four. The man on the television talk shows with an enormous cigar had produced one of the great films of cinema, *Citizen Kane*, but would, for all time, be asked about the *War of the Worlds*. Orson would oblige and drop tidbits and slyly hold back and then drop some more breadcrumbs. And it didn't matter how many movies he made or played in or how many plays he produced; the gum that stuck to the shoe of Orson Welles was when he went up to the CBS studio on October 30, 1938, and attacked the United States with mechanical Martians, heat rays, and poison gas. Welles would distance himself from the broadcast for a time, and then, as project after project fell through, he embraced it.

Orson Welles was not unlike an actor forever tagged with the role played in a series on television. He was the George Reeves of *Superman* who could not shake his role for the rest of his career. Orson Welles was tagged as being the man from Mars. Fame is better than obscurity, and while Welles may not have chosen to have a broadcast about Martians stuck to his name for all time, it did beat oblivion. Still, for a renowned Shakespearean actor, it was maddening to be remembered more for fooling a nation than for creating a great work of art like *Citizen Kane*. The problem with great works of art is that most people don't understand them or like them. Movie audiences who watched *Citizen Kane* did not enjoy the film. Some appreciated *Citizen Kane* as art, but it was not entertaining and was a box office failure. Meanwhile, *War of the Worlds* led to sponsorship, worldwide fame, and the amazing Hollywood contract that produced *Citizen Kane*. Thus, the engine of Welles's great success is more interesting than the result. Every artist experiments each time a new book, play, movie, or radio show is produced. If the artist is any good, that experimentation leads to new epiphanies and new ways of looking at things. Orson Welles was a living petri dish of experimentation.

Like the builders of the atomic bomb, Orson knew fission would occur; he just didn't know where it would lead. And there was a good chance he could blow himself up right along with the *War of the Worlds*. Downplaying the effect the broadcast had on America is the height of our modern arrogance. Like the books we eviscerate, the history we blot out, the *War of the Worlds* has been subject to the hubris of our digital mind that is loath to believe a nation could be duped into believing Martians were murdering people with heat rays and poison gas. That is not plausible. We count listeners and ignore the thousands of newspapers, eyewitness accounts, interviews, the mood of the country, and the innocence of people born at the tail end of the nineteenth century. If we want to know what will happen in America if aliens ever land in our country, then look no further than the night of October 30, 1938. Of all the books, studies, and articles on Orson Welles's grand moment, few have pointed to the broadcast as the only chance we have to see how humans would react if aliens did land. In the conclusion of Hadley Cantril's report on the broadcast, he points to the real source of the dark, unreasoning fear and mass panic and terror caused by the *War of the Worlds* broadcast:

> The invasion of the Martians was a direct threat to life, to other lives that one loved, as well as to all other cherished values. The Martians were practically destroying everything. The situation was, then, indeed a serious affair. Frustration resulted when no directed behavior seemed possible. One was faced with the alternative of resigning oneself and all of one's values to complete annihilation or of making a desperate effort to escape from the field of danger or of appealing to some higher power or stronger person whom one vaguely thought could destroy the oncoming enemy.[7]

A feeling of a gradual loss of control over modern life is another reason the broadcast struck a nerve. "Since the depression of 1929, a number of people have begun to wonder whether or not they will ever regain any sense of economic security. . . . The felt threats of fascism, communism, prolonged unemployment, among millions of Americans . . . create an environment which the average individual is completely unable to interpret."[8] More than anything else, people had no critical ability to evaluate emerging technologies. They took as fact anything that came over the radio. We are facing this same challenge with artificial intelligence, but in 1938 this was a new concept.

Cantril then points out that the panic was complete because no one organized to fight the Martians. People's actions on that Halloween eve were panic-induced and meant to alleviate the feeling of panic, not solve the problem. This situation made the panic all that more complete: "If one assumed that destruction was inevitable, then certain limited behavior was possible; one could cry, make peace with one's maker, gather loved ones around, and perish. If one attempted to escape, one could run to the house of friends, speed away in a car or train, or hide in some gas-proof, bomb-proof out of the way shelter. . . . One could appeal to God or seek protection from those who had protected one in the past. Objectively, none of these modes of behavior was a direct attack on the problem at hand; nothing was done to remove the cause of the crisis."[9]

Hadley Cantril then goes on with a thesis that the broadcast was in its own category. That total destruction at the hands of aliens was so nihilistic, so soul shattering, that people reacted to the immolation of their very being—much like a soldier at the time of dying. Cantril tries to make sense of what people did when confronted with this annihilation by aliens. This is the only known study of what humans would do when confronted with a hostile alien culture based on an actual event of people believing Martians were murdering humans.

For Cantril, what Orson Welles did was actualize the fantasy of the H. G. Wells novel and turn it into the great what-if experiment that all art depends on. His experiment was played out in real time on an American population using a new medium that had the populace already on edge from world events, and this approach cemented the authenticity of the Martians invading and destroying human civilization. This moment on October 30, 1938, was opened up, allowing us to peer into the deep recesses of human psyches under enormous pressure. In summary, Cantril finds humans unable to cope with the thought that the human race could be extinguished by creatures from another world because such an idea challenges the very order of our psychological makeup.

In short, the extreme behavior evoked by the broadcast was due to the enormous felt ego-involvement the situation created and to the complete inability of the individual to alleviate or control the consequences of the invasion. The coming of the Martians did not present a situation where the individual could preserve one value if he sacrificed another. It was not a matter of saving one's country by giving one's life, of helping to usher in a new religion by self-denial, of risking the thief's bullet to save the family silver. In this situation, the individual stood to lose all his values at once. Nothing could be done to save any of them. Panic was inescapable.[10]

We are saturated with UFO sightings, tales of alien abduction, and government cover-ups. If aliens did land, we hope we would not have heart attacks; break our arms; flip our cars over; contemplate suicide; commit suicide; run out of hospitals; run into the streets; head for the mountains; run into churches screaming that the world has ended; huddle with our children; run out of bars; abandon our jobs; grab shotguns and roam the countryside; call the police; notify the papers; cover our faces with wet cloths and stand in the streets; abandon theaters; abandon apartment buildings; drive crazily; take our clothes and children and run for the nearest train, car, bus, anything to get away from the oncoming terror. Young, old, educated, white-collar, blue-collar, Black, White—it didn't matter; across the board, people believed that something terrible had happened on the night of October 30, 1938, and police, newspapers, and radios backed it up, and for one brief moment in time in the United States, it did seem like the end of the world had come.

You can always tell a genius by the confederacy of dunces that surround him. There is a picture of Orson Welles getting out of a taxi in a bow tie with a cigarette holder in his mouth, looking up at the camera. Behind him is the marquee announcing *Citizen Kane*, and then over it, in letters just as big, the sign read "Orson Welles." It is the final arc of Welles's wheel of fame that culminated in his broadcast of *War of the Worlds*, which finally produced the movie that would pin his fame forever in Hollywood, *Citizen Kane*. That movie would be held up in posterity as the greatest film ever made, but it would cost RKO $150,000 as a loss and, because of the parody of William Randolph Hearst, derail the

Welles fame train forever. The experimentation that pushed Orson along met its match in *Citizen Kane*. It's too bad that Orson did not get some comeuppance for his fake broadcast. Instead, he was slingshot into the Hollywood heavens, which marked his apotheosis, and then his long spiral downward came in which *Citizen Kane* was the high point of the arc and everything else was the tearing down of that monument the boy genius had built.

And that's what makes *War of the Worlds* so fascinating. It really was the moment when the illusion was brought to its full realization. If art is the suspension of disbelief, then *War of the Worlds* was the high-water mark. Roll the film of *Citizen Kane* backward again to that opening scene in which young Kane (or young Orson) is playing in the snow with his sled with the *Rosebud* moniker, and his mother, played by Agnes Moorehead, is staring out the window as she contemplates losing her son forever. The awful hurt of the child losing their parents is felt in Orson's art all along the way as the boy losing his mother. The twenty-three-year-old staring at the newsreel camera professing his innocence is a study in hurt. And so the experiments begin. From the beginning, the prodigy moves through life, transmuting reality into art and, each time, furthering his craft until he stumbles onto his greatest play with an audience of millions who are enthralled, overwhelmed, terrified, and the result is an ovation from the cosmos—well done! And now do it again, and, of course, Orson hits the wall with his greatest movie, and the boy genius is left at the end . . . alone.

It was really our only bombing. America was never bombed on its mainland during World War II. Prior to 2001, we had never suffered the effect of an attack. So, in a terrestrial sense, we get the only real glimpse of what could have happened had the Nazis bombed America. It is not surprising how many people thought the Martians were the Germans. World War II certainly marked the end of our isolation or our innocence in America, and Welles's broadcast, coming a week after the Munich crisis, was the first shot across the bow. Martians. Germans. Terror. Hadley Cantril concluded that it was the threat of war and the Nazis that accounted in part for the mass hysteria that the *War of the Worlds* broadcast provoked.

Here, the largest single category of response, except that of a Martian invasion, was the belief that the catastrophe actually was an act of war or some foreign attack. Over a fourth of the people who were disturbed or frightened by the broadcast gave such answers. Further expression of the fear of war is revealed in the images that listeners had of the actual invaders as Martians, giants, or creatures of human form; almost one-fifth of them reported that they had visions of soldiers attacking with advanced military weapons.[11]

If all passes and art alone endures, then that scratchy broadcast on YouTube is Orson Welles's legacy. The man who had to try to make money any way he could at the end would later gladly hawk his *War of the Worlds* wares. It was the detritus of the young man who jumped out of the ambulance and rushed up to the studio. Having just finished the dress rehearsal, he then put on his headphones and stepped up on the podium with his music stand and his script and the giant CBS microphone in front of him. He finished his pineapple juice as he looked at the clock and then at the conductor, the actors, the control room. He wiped his brow, took a breath, and raised his arms over his head as the "On the Air" sign flashed. He cued the announcer to start the play. Then, at that fateful, precise moment in time, he raised his hand and stopped the action and, for six seconds, held the world in thrall.

Epilogue

ORSON WELLES WOULD NEVER ESCAPE *WAR OF THE WORLDS*. WHEN HE went on Jack Benny's show on March 24, 1940, he was greeted by announcer Phil Harris, "Hi, Orson! Still scaring people?" Orson would sue for the right of authorship several times to claim that he deserved credit, if not royalties, from Howard Koch. Both times, he would be ruled against. The week after *Citizen Kane* finished filming on October 28, 1940, Orson Welles went to radio station KTSA in San Antonio, Texas, and met H. G. Wells. The two met for an on-air interview on the second anniversary of the *War of the Worlds*. "Are you sure there was such a panic in America, or wasn't it your Halloween fun?" asked the graying, short man with a mustache. Orson responded, "I think that's the nicest thing that a man from England could possibly say about the men from Mars."[1] The two men were jocular, but interviewer Charles C. Shaw probed for more of a reaction from H. G. Wells. "Well, there was some excitement caused . . . I can't really belittle the amount that was caused, but I think that people got over it very quickly, don't you?"[2]

"What kind of excitement?" Orson responded. "Mr. H. G. Wells wants to know if the excitement wasn't the same kind of excitement we extract from a practical joke in which somebody puts a sheet over their head and says boo! I don't think anybody believes that that individual is a ghost, but we do scream and yell and rush down the hall and that's just about what happened."[3]

Welles could afford to be flip about the broadcast. CBS had settled lawsuits but not for significant sums. His opus, *Citizen Kane*, was released on May 1, 1941. The opening newsreel sequence used all the techniques Orson had brought to radio, "a shaky handheld camera, a mismatched soundtrack, intentionally scratched-up film—that are the visual equivalents of the use of dead air and overlapping dialogue that worked so well in *War of the Worlds*."[4] But this time, Welles did not get away with his tricks.

His parody of William Randolph Hearst in *Citizen Kane* cost him newspaper coverage, and many theaters declined to show the movie. Reviews were stellar, but the audiences didn't know what to make of the film, and RKO lost $150,000. The movie was nominated for nine Academy Awards but won only an Oscar for Best Screenplay. Orson had offended Hollywood elite William Randolph Hearst and then lost more on his next film, *The Magnificent Ambersons*. Welles followed with a documentary about Pan-American culture, *It's All True*. Orson went way over budget, a man died on the set, and when he returned to America, RKO could not make anything out of the film and ultimately shelved it. The combined losses from the three Welles films exceeded one million dollars.

After his divorce from Virginia, Orson remarried twice, first to movie star Rita Hayworth and later to Countess Paola Mori di Gerfalco. He fathered three daughters. From here on, for the rest of his life, Orson Welles would be running after investors for his projects, rarely finding funding. He would eventually direct four movies that all lost money: *The Lady from Shanghai*, *Macbeth*, *Othello*, and *Touch of Evil*. After being named the greatest movie of all time, *Citizen Kane* left Orson with the *War of the Worlds* broadcast as his greater claim to fame.

Over time Orson came to accept the tag as the Martian man and took interviews that wanted to know whether he had really intended to scare the nation. In 1955, he did a television series for the BBC called *Orson Welles' Sketch Book* and, in the final episode, addressed the *War of the Worlds* broadcast: "People, you know, do suspect what they read in the newspapers and what people tell them, but when the radio came, and I suppose now television, anything that came through that new machine was believed. So in a way, our broadcast was an assault on the credibility of that machine; we wanted people to understand that they shouldn't take any opinion predigested and they shouldn't swallow everything that came through the tap, whether it was radio or not."[5]

It was a very intellectual rationalization for a twenty-three-year-old wanting to push the limits of everything, including radio, and wanting to see whether radio could scare the hell out of people. One has to wonder if, twenty years later, Welles had lost touch with that young auteur or if he was just playing to an audience. He had failed to mention that his method of producing his plays and radio shows was to push the boundaries of everything to the breaking point. He wanted people to believe his broadcast. He wanted a big reaction, and he got one.

Orson Welles's broadcast would inspire a television series in 1988 and a 1975 made-for-TV movie, *The Night That Panicked America*. A 1957 docudrama, *The Night America Trembled*, did not have Orson in the film. They had contacted him, but Orson believed they needed his permission and wanted to write and direct the movie. Koch had given them permission, and when Welles held out, they struck his name from the script. Orson sued the network for $375,000, claiming damages for unauthorized use of his broadcast. His lawyers said he came up with the fake news idea for *War of the Worlds* and should be listed as coauthor. The court disagreed, and the royalties all went to Howard Koch.

Over time, Orson Welles struggled financially while John Houseman pursued an acting career. At seventy-one, Houseman played Charles Kingsfield in 1973 in *The Paper Chase* and received an Oscar. Welles and Houseman met for a reunion on *The Merv Griffin Show* and hugged, but Orson still resented Houseman, probably more so for his late fame and financial stability, accusing Houseman of being envious.

Howard Koch would remain a footnote to the *War of the Worlds*, even though he would go on to win an Oscar for Best Adapted Screenplay for *Casablanca*. To most people, Orson Welles was the man who wrote and performed the *War of the Worlds*. On the night of the broadcast, Orson had announcer Dan Seymour omit Howard Koch's name, even though the script gave him credit as the author of *War of the Worlds*. Arch Oboler, a fellow writer with Welles, would later say, "I didn't particularly like Orson; he is a great actor and a fine director, but he didn't know how to give credit to the people around him who did the work. . . . He simply did not admit that in a cooperative business, the entertainment business, that anybody does anything, including sweep the floor, but Orson

Welles."[6] John Houseman would later sum up the dispute between Orson and John Mankiewicz, the scriptwriter of *Citizen Kane*, by saying, "*Citizen Kane* is Welles's film. The dramatic genius that animates it and the creative personality with which it is imbued is wholly and undeniably Orson's, just as in another medium, the *War of the Worlds* owed its final impact to his miraculous touch. But he did not write either of them."[7]

Howard Koch would visit Grovers Mill in 1988 on the fiftieth anniversary of the broadcast. A time capsule was buried on a farm and was not to be opened until October 30, 2038.

The *War of the Worlds* broadcast would be replayed in movies and documentaries, spoofed in cartoons, and become a pop culture staple, lampooned later on *The Simpsons*. Historian Daniel Hopsicker would suggest the 1938 broadcast was a planned experiment by the Rockefeller Foundation to determine what would happen if aliens did land. On a more intriguing note, Captain Edward J. Ruppelt, who headed the US Air Force investigation into UFOs called Project Blue Book, wrote of his experiences in 1956 in the *Report on Unidentified Flying Objects*: "The UFO files are full of references to the near mass panic of October 30, 1938, when Orson Welles presented his now famous *War of the Worlds* broadcast."[8] The government noted the impact an alien landing might have on the population. In this way, Orson Welles inadvertently contributed to the US government's policies on UFOs.

Years passed, and in the end Orson would be reduced to trying to find financing for unfinished films and working the talk show circuit for grocery money, which inevitably centered on the broadcast. On the *Dean Martin Show* in 1970, when asked about the broadcast, Orson quipped, "Now it's been pointed out that various flying saucerscares all over the world have taken place since the broadcast . . . everyone doesn't laugh anymore. But most people do. And there's a theory that is my doing. That my job was to soften you up . . . ladies and gentlemen, go on laughing. You'll be happier that way. Stay happy as long as you can."[9] Many came to know the bearded, cigar-smoking, rotund man hawking Paul Masson wine on television—"We sell no wine before its time"—having no idea of his connection to a broadcast forty years before. On the *Today Show* in 1978, he was asked, "Did you get a laugh out of it, Orson?" Welles paused and then nodded. "Huge, huge, yes, a huge laugh. I never thought it was anything but funny."[10]

Hollywood had turned its back on Orson after 1957 with his last appearance in *Touch of Evil*. Orson embraced his Martian fame and tried to cash in on it any way he could. That a radio play should overshadow his great talent might be tragic if it were not a piece of broadcasting history. There are few traces of Orson left. His adopted hometown of Woodstock, Illinois, has only one dormitory left from the Todd School for Boys, where Orson found his voice and would return time and again as the only place he could call home with Roger and Hortense Hill. The Woodstock Opera House seems to carry the ghost of Orson as the location where he launched many of his plays. The old town square still has the ambiance of the nineteenth century before it gives it all over as just another footstool of Chicago fifty miles to the east.

But, walking around the town square of Woodstock, one turns into a nondescript alley, and suddenly there is Orson. He is painted bigger than life on a cement wall in a mural next to an equally big picture of Bill Murray for the movie *Groundhog Day*, which was shot in Woodstock. But the center of the mural is really a study of how history views Orson Welles. There is Orson with a giant microphone, and across the top of the mural are the words "War of the Worlds." It is all bigger than life and dominates the cement wall. And then, lower and to the right, in smaller letters, is *Citizen Kane*. One can see the artist feeling the obligation to list the movie, but the real star, the real guiding light of Orson Welles's life, was the night of October 30, 1938, when he broke with convention for all time and joined others who dared to do what some might only think about doing.

Orson Welles died on October 10, 1985, with unfinished, unfunded projects, including a film version of *The Cradle Will Rock*, a Hollywood satire *The Other Side of the Wind*, and *King Lear*. In announcing his death, the *Los Angeles Times* picked up an Associated Press release. It led with "Orson Welles, the Hollywood boy wonder who by the age of 26 had terrified the nation with a radio tale of a Martian invasion and created the classic film 'Citizen Kane' was found dead today in his Hollywood residence, apparently of natural causes. He was 70."[11] United Press

International (UPI), as quoted by the *Los Angeles Times*, summed up his life briefly: "Orson Welles, who created the film classic 'Citizen Kane' and a radio tale about a Martian invasion that terrified millions of listeners, died today of an apparent heart attack. . . . Welles panicked America in 1938 with his *Mercury Theatre on the Air* radio adaptation of H. G. Wells's 'War of the Worlds.' Listeners believed the Nation really was being invaded by Martians."[12]

His hometown newspaper of Kenosha, Wisconsin, printed the UPI release at the bottom of the front page. The boy wonder, who was front-page news in 1938 in papers worldwide and had conquered the medium of radio and then film by age twenty-six, still warranted front-page announcements of his death. John Houseman would die three years later. On Halloween.

NOTES

THE MAGICIAN

1. Joe Posnanski, *The Life and Afterlife of Harry Houdini* (New York: Avid Reader Press, Simon and Schuster, 2002), 184.

2. Hadley Cantril, *The Invasion from Mars: A Study in the Psychology of Panic* (New York: Taylor and Francis, 2017), 25.

3. "Fake Radio 'War' Stirs Terror through U.S.," *Daily News* (New York), October 31, 1938, 1.

4. "US Probes Invasion Broadcast . . . Radio Play Causes Wide Panic," *New York Post*, October 31, 1938, 1.

5. "Radio Fake Scares Nation," *Herald-Examiner* (Chicago), October 31, 1938, 1.

6. John Gosling, *Waging the War of the Worlds* (Jefferson, NC: McFarland, 2009), 59.

7. Gosling, *Waging the War*, 59.

8. "A Wave of Hysteria," *New York Times*, October 31, 1938, 1.

9. Brad Schwartz, *Broadcast Hysteria: Orson Welles's War of the Worlds* (New York: Farrar, Straus and Giroux, 2015), 87.

10. Gail Jarrow, *Spooked! How a Radio Broadcast and* The War of the Worlds *Sparked the 1938 Invasion of America* (New York: Astra, 2018), 71.

11. Gosling, *Waging the War*, 65.

PROLOGUE

1. Brad Schwartz, *Broadcast Hysteria: Orson Welles's War of the Worlds* (New York: Farrar, Straus and Giroux, 2015), 95.

2. Richard J. Hand and Mary Traynor, *The Radio Drama Handbook: Audio Drama in Context and Practice* (New York: Bloomsbury, 2011), 27.

3. Mark W. Estrin, *Orson Welles: Interviews* (Jackson: University Press of Mississippi, 2002), 16.

4. David Crespy, *Richard Barr: The Playwright's Producer* (Carbondale: Southern Illinois University Press, 2013), 16.

5. Schwartz, *Broadcast Hysteria*, 96.

6. John Gosling, *Waging the War of the Worlds* (Jefferson, NC: McFarland, 2009), 46.

7. Vincent Terrace, *Radio Program Openings and Closings, 1931–1972* (Jefferson, NC: McFarland, 2015), 162.

8. Schwartz, *Broadcast Hysteria*, 97.

9. James Patrick Chaplin, *Rumor, Fear and the Madness of Crowds* (Mineola, NY: Dover, 2105), 97.

10. Gosling, *Waging the War*, 50.

11. Gosling, *Waging the War*, 50.

12. Gosling, *Waging the War*, 50.

13. Simon Callow, *Orson Welles, Volume 1: The Road to Xanadu* (New York: Penguin, 1997), 404.

CHAPTER 1

1. John Flynn, *War of the Worlds: From Wells to Spielberg* (Owings Mills, MD: Galactic Books, 2005), 37.

2. Jim Harmon, *The Great Radio Heroes* (Jefferson, NC: McFarland, 2001), 66.

3. Neil Henry, *American Carnival: Journalism Under Siege in an Age of New Media* (Berkeley: University of California Press, 2007), 129.

4. Michael K. Robinson, *A New Treatise on a Small Blue Planet* (Cambridge: Vanguard Press, 2007), 63.

5. John Gosling, *Waging the War of the Worlds* (Jefferson, NC: McFarland, 2009), 50.

6. Gosling, *Waging the War*, 202.

7. Gosling, *Waging the War*.

8. Gosling, *Waging the War*.

9. Gosling, *Waging the War*.

10. Gosling, *Waging the War*, 205.

11. *Seattle Daily Times*, "US Launches Inquiry into Radio Panic," October 31, 1938.

12. *Hartford Courant*, "Radio Scare Here Spreads Fear, Anger," October 31, 1938.

13. *Hartford Courant*, "Radio Scare."

14. *Hartford Courant*, "Radio Scare."

15. *Washington Post*, "Army Reacts to Broadcast," October 31, 1938.

16. *Newark Evening News*, "Too Real Radio Drama Gives Nation a Bad Case of War Jitters," October 31, 1938.

17. Gosling, *Waging the War*, 206.

18. Gosling, *Waging the War*, 209.

19. Gosling, *Waging the War*.

20. Gosling, *Waging the War*, 210.

21. Estelle Paultz, letter to Orson Welles, October 31, 1938, University of Michigan, Box 24, folder 1.

22. Paultz, letter to Orson Welles.

23. *Trentonian*, "Radio Show Stops Hospital Work," October 31, 1938.

24. Howard Koch, *The Panic Broadcast: Portrait of an Event* (Boston, MA: Little, Brown, 1970), 89.

25. Mark Estrin, *Orson Welles: Interviews* (Jackson: University Press of Mississippi, 2002), 11.

26. Estrin, *Orson Welles: Interviews*, 11.

27. Alex Lubertozzi and Brian Holmsten, *The Complete War of the Worlds* (Naperville, IL: Sourcebooks, Inc., 2001), 10.

28. Lubertozzi and Holmsten, *The Complete War*.

29. Lubertozzi and Holmsten, *The Complete War*.

30. Koch, *The Panic Broadcast*, 20.

31. *Washington Post*, "Church Services Interrupted by Panicked Parishioners," October 31, 1938.

32. Paultz, letter to Orson Welles.

33. Hadley Cantril, *The Invasion from Mars* (Princeton, NJ: Princeton University Press, 1940).

34. Paultz, letter to Orson Welles.

35. Paultz, letter to Orson Welles.

36. Paultz, letter to Orson Welles.

37. Paultz, letter to Orson Welles.

38. Gosling, *Waging the War*, 211.

39. Brad Schwartz, *Broadcast Hysteria: Orson Welles's War of the Worlds* (New York: Farrar, Straus and Giroux, 2015), 6.

CHAPTER 2

1. Frank Brady, *Citizen Welles: A Biography of Orson Welles* (Lexington: University Press of Kentucky, 2023), 76.

2. Brady, *Citizen Welles*, 77.

3. Brady, *Citizen Welles*.

4. Mark W. Estrin, *Orson Welles: Interviews* (Jackson: University Press of Mississippi, 2002), 114.

5. Estrin, *Orson Welles*.

6. Estrin, *Orson Welles*.

7. Estrin, *Orson Welles*.

8. Estrin, *Orson Welles*.

9. Estrin, *Orson Welles*.

10. Matthew Asprey Gear, *At the End of the Street in the Shadow: Orson Welles and the City* (New York: Columbia University Press, 2016).

11. John Houseman, *Unfinished Business: Memoirs, 1902–1988* (New York: Applause Theatre & Cinema Books, 1989).

12. David Thomson, *Rosebud: The Story of Orson Welles* (Boston, MA: Little, Brown and Co., 1996), 89.

13. Thomson, *Rosebud*, 74.

14. Thomson, *Rosebud*, 86.

CHAPTER 3

1. Mark Jenkins, *Rosebud: The Lives of Orson Welles* (Saint Davids, Wales: Infested Waters, 2004), 11.

2. Barbara Leaming, *Orson Welles: A Biography* (New York: Limelight Editions, 2004), 8.

3. Patrick McGilligan, *Young Orson: The Years of Luck and Genius* (New York: Harper Perennial, 2015).

4. Leaming, *Orson Welles: A Biography*, 5.

5. Leaming, *Orson Welles: A Biography*, 5.

6. Leaming, *Orson Welles: A Biography*, 17.

7. Leaming, *Orson Welles: A Biography*, 17.

8. Simon Callow, *Orson Welles, Volume 1: The Road to Xanadu* (New York: Penguin Books, 1997).

9. Todd Tarbox, *Orson Welles and Roger Hill: A Friendship in Three Acts* (Duncan, OK: BearManor Media, 2013).

10. Callow, *Orson Welles*.

11. Tarbox, *Orson Welles and Roger Hill*.

12. Callow, *Orson Welles*.

13. Callow, *Orson Welles*, 38.

14. Leaming, *Orson Welles: A Biography*, 37.

15. Callow, *Orson Welles*, 52.

16. Callow, *Orson Welles*, 60.

17. Leaming, *Orson Welles: A Biography*, 38.

18. Frank Brady, *Citizen Welles: A Biography of Orson Welles* (Lexington: University Press of Kentucky, 2023), 18.

19. Callow, *Orson Welles*, 74.

20. David Thomson, *Rosebud: The Story of Orson Welles* (New York: Knopf, 1997), 185.

21. Callow, *Orson Welles*, 81.

22. Brady, *Citizen Welles: A Biography*, 28.

23. Brady, *Citizen Welles: A Biography*, 28.

24. Callow, *Orson Welles*, 86.

25. Brady, *Citizen Welles: A Biography*, 30.

26. Brady, *Citizen Welles: A Biography*, 36.

27. Callow, *Orson Welles*, 87.

28. Thomson, *Rosebud: The Story*, 8.

CHAPTER 4

1. David Thomson, *Rosebud: The Story of Orson Welles* (New York: Knopf, 1997), 37.

2. Simon Callow, *Orson Welles, Volume 1: The Road to Xanadu* (New York: Penguin Books, 1997), 88.

3. Callow, *Orson Welles*, 93.

4. Callow, *Orson Welles*, 94.

5. Callow, *Orson Welles*, 94.

6. Callow, *Orson Welles*, 95.

7. Callow, *Orson Welles*, 96.

8. Frank Brady, *Citizen Welles: A Biography of Orson Welles* (Lexington: University Press of Kentucky, 2023), 32.

9. Thomson, *Rosebud*.

10. Micheál MacLiammoir, *All for Hecuba: An Irish Theatrical Biography* (Berkeley: University of California Press, 2011), 133.

11. Callow, *Orson Welles*, 99.

12. Callow, *Orson Welles*, 99.

13. Thomson, *Rosebud*, 40.

14. Callow, *Orson Welles*, 108.

CHAPTER 5

1. John Houseman, *Unfinished Business: Memoirs, 1902–1988* (New York: Applause Theatre & Cinema Books, 1989), 72.

2. John Houseman, *Run-through: A Memoir* (New York: Simon and Schuster, 1980), 143.

3. Simon Callow, *Orson Welles, Volume 1: The Road to Xanadu* (New York: Penguin Books, 1997), 197.

4. David Thomson, *Rosebud: The Story of Orson Welles* (New York: Knopf, 1997), 52.

5. Callow, *Orson Welles, Volume 1*, 197.

6. Callow, *Orson Welles, Volume 1*, 200.

7. Todd Tarbox, *Orson Welles and Roger Hill: A Friendship in Three Acts* (Duncan, OK: BearManor Media, 2013), 55.

8. Frank Brady, *Citizen Welles: A Biography of Orson Welles* (Lexington: University Press of Kentucky, 2023), 80.

9. Brady, *Citizen Welles*.

10. Callow, *Orson Welles, Volume 1*, 204.

11. Brady, *Citizen Welles*, 81.

12. Brady, *Citizen Welles*, 81.

13. Brady, *Citizen Welles*, 81.

14. Brady, *Citizen Welles*, 82.

15. Brady, *Citizen Welles*, 82.

16. Brady, *Citizen Welles*, 82.

17. Brady, *Citizen Welles*, 82.

18. Brady, *Citizen Welles*, 82.

19. Brady, *Citizen Welles*, 82.

20. Brady, *Citizen Welles*, 83.

21. Brady, *Citizen Welles*, 84.

22. Marguerite H. Rippy, *Orson Welles and the Unfinished RKO Projects* (Carbondale: Southern Illinois University Press, 2009), 78.

23. Rippy, *Orson Welles and the Unfinished RKO Projects*.

24. Brady, *Citizen Welles*, 113.

25. Brady, *Citizen Welles*, 113.

26. Brady, *Citizen Welles*, 115.

27. Brady, *Citizen Welles*, 115.

28. Brady, *Citizen Welles*, 115.

29. Brady, *Citizen Welles*, 115.

30. Brady, *Citizen Welles*, 115.

31. Brady, *Citizen Welles*, 117.

32. Brady, *Citizen Welles*, 117.

33. Brady, *Citizen Welles*, 117.

34. Brady, *Citizen Welles*, 117.

35. Brady, *Citizen Welles*, 85.

36. Brady, *Citizen Welles*, 88.

37. Brady, *Citizen Welles*, 87.

38. Thomson, *Rosebud*, 60.

39. Thomson, *Rosebud*, 60.

40. Brady, *Citizen Welles*, 91.

41. Brady, *Citizen Welles*, 92.

42. Brady, *Citizen Welles*, 93.

43. Barbara Leaming, *Orson Welles: A Biography* (New York: Limelight Editions, 2004), 103.

44. Callow, *Orson Welles, Volume 1*, 234.

45. Richard France, *Orson Welles on Shakespeare: The W.P.A. and Mercury Theatre Playscripts* (New York: Taylor & Francis, 2013), 15.

46. Robert Burns Mantle, "WPA 'Macbeth' in Fancy Dress: Negro Theatre Creates Something of a Sensation in Harlem," *Daily News* (New York), April 15, 1936.

47. Robert Burns Mantle, "Theme of Two Productions: Negro 'Macbeth,' Ghosts, Futuristic Fantasy Provide Spooky Fare," *Chicago Tribune*, April 26, 1936.

48. Mantle, "Theme of Two Productions."

49. Brady, *Citizen Welles*, 108.

CHAPTER 6

1. Simon Callow, *Orson Welles, Volume 1: The Road to Xanadu* (New York: Penguin Books, 1997), 290.

2. Callow, *Orson Welles*, 290.

3. Callow, *Orson Welles*, 293.

4. Callow, *Orson Welles*, 296.

5. Frank Brady, *Citizen Welles: A Biography of Orson Welles* (Lexington: University Press of Kentucky, 2023), 127.

6. Brady, *Citizen Welles*, 127.

7. Brady, *Citizen Welles*, 128.

8. Brady, *Citizen Welles*, 128.

9. Robert Burns Mantle, "'Cradle Will Rock' Given Stage Room by New Mercury Theatre," *Daily News* (NY), December 7, 1937.

10. Brady, *Citizen Welles*, 133.

11. Brady, *Citizen Welles*, 134.

12. Brady, *Citizen Welles*, 135.

13. Brady, *Citizen Welles*, 135.

14. Brady, *Citizen Welles*, 136.

15. Brady, *Citizen Welles*, 137.

16. David Thomson, *Rosebud: The Story of Orson Welles* (New York: Knopf, 1997), 86.

17. Robert Burns Mantle, "'Julius Caesar' in Overcoats Mercury's First Experiment," *Daily News* (NY), November 12, 1937.

18. "All Hail Julius Caesar," *Vancouver Citizen*, December 8, 1937.

19. Robert Sawyer, *Shakespeare Between the World Wars: The Anglo-American Sphere* (New York: Palgrave Macmillan, 2019), 172.

20. Brady, *Citizen Welles*, 151.

21. "The Theatre: Marvelous Boy," *Time*, May 9, 1938.

22. "The Brightest Moon Over Broadway," *Time*, May 9, 1938.

23. Todd London, *An Ideal Theater: Founding Visions for a New American Art* (New York: Theatre Communications Group, 2013), 215.

24. Brady, *Citizen Welles*, 151.

25. Brady, *Citizen Welles*, 151.

26. Brady, *Citizen Welles*, 151.

27. Brady, *Citizen Welles*, 151.

CHAPTER 7

1. Chris Welles Feder, *In My Father's Shadow: A Daughter Remembers Orson Welles* (Chapel Hill, NC: Algonquin Books, 2009), 52.

2. Feder, *In My Father's Shadow*, 52.

3. Barbara Leaming, *Orson Welles: A Biography* (New York: Limelight Editions, 2004), 153.

4. Simon Callow, *Orson Welles, Volume 1: The Road to Xanadu* (New York: Penguin Books, 1997), 373.

5. Christopher Sterling, *The Concise of Encyclopedia of American Radio* (New York: Routledge, 2010), 454.

6. Jonathan Rosenbaum, *Discovering Orson Welles* (Berkeley: University of California Press, 2007), 32.

7. John Houseman, *Unfinished Business: Memoirs, 1902–1988* (New York: Applause Theatre & Cinema Books, 1989), 181.

8. Frank Brady, *Citizen Welles: A Biography of Orson Welles* (Lexington: University Press of Kentucky, 2023).

9. Brady, *Citizen Welles*.

10. Brady, *Citizen Welles*.

11. Callow, *Orson Welles*, 376.

12. Callow, *Orson Welles*, 376.

13. Callow, *Orson Welles*, 377.

14. Callow, *Orson Welles*, 379.

15. David Thomson, *Rosebud: The Story of Orson Welles* (New York: Knopf, 1997), 99.

16. Thomson, *Rosebud*, 99.

17. Brady, *Citizen Welles*.

18. Brady, *Citizen Welles*, 162.

19. Brady, *Citizen Welles*, 165.

20. Brady, *Citizen Welles*, 165.

21. Brady, *Citizen Welles*, 165.

22. Callow, *Orson Welles*, 387.

23. Callow, *Orson Welles*, 387.

24. Joseph Kaye, "Prodigy of New York Stage Bites Hand That Is Feeding Him during Course of Talk Before Group of Educators—Orson Welles Asserts Movies Have It All Over Stage—Plans Ambitious Season for Mercury," *Cincinnati Enquirer*, August 7, 1938, 1.

25. Kaye, "Prodigy."

26. Kaye, "Prodigy."

27. Kaye, "Prodigy."

28. Kaye, "Prodigy."

29. Feder, *In My Father's Shadow.*

30. Leaming, *Orson Welles*, 122.

31. "Mercury Theatre with Orson Welles Now at Stony Creek," *Hartford Courant* (Connecticut), August 18, 1938, 10.

32. Callow, *Orson Welles*, 375.

CHAPTER 8

1. Associated Press, "Hitler Boosts Price of Peace," *Bergen Evening Record* (Hackensack, NJ), September 22, 1938.

2. Associated Press, "133 Known Dead in Hurricane, Damage in Millions; Property Loss Here Over 300,000; Relief Speeded," *Bergen Evening Record* (Hackensack, NJ), September 22, 1938.

3. Associated Press, "Sudetenland or War, Says Hitler," *The Mercury* (Pottstown, PA), September 27, 1938.

4. Tim Kisha, *A Newscast for the Masses* (Detroit, MI: Wayne State University Press, 2009), 9.

5. Bernie Higgins, "Battle for the Airwaves: Radio and the 1938 Munich Crisis," interview with author David Vaughan, Radio Prague International, September 29, 2008, https://english.radio.cz/battle-airwaves-radio-and-1938-munich-crisis-8591724.

6. Higgins, interview.

7. Higgins, interview.

8. Webb Miller, "World Doubts Europe Peace Is Permanent: England Continues to Arm in Spite of Hitler's Recent Statements," *Hammond Times* (Munster, IN), October 6, 1938, 5.

9. Franklin D. Roosevelt, *My Own Story: From Private and Public Papers* (New York: Routledge, 2017), 305.

10. "U.S. Lines Ready to Bring Home All Americans," *Burlington* (VT) *Daily News*, September 28, 1938, 5.

11. Frank Brady, *Citizen Welles: A Biography of Orson Welles* (Lexington: University Press of Kentucky, 2023), 183.

12. Robert Torricelli and Andrew Carroll, *In Our Own Words: Extraordinary Speeches of the American Century* (New York: Kodansha America, 2000), 111.

13. Torricelli and Carroll, *In Our Own Words*, 111.

14. Torricelli and Carroll, *In Our Own Words*, 111.

15. Michael McCarthy, *The Hidden Hindenburg: The Untold Story of the Tragedy, the Nazi Secrets, and the Quest to Rule the Skies* (Lanham, MD: Lyons Press, 2020), 99. Footage of the disaster, complete with Morrison's commentary, can be found online at https://www.youtube.com/watch?v=A7Ly1Oh-xvs.

16. Alexander Rose, *Empires of the Sky: Zeppelins, Airplanes, and Two Men's Epic Duel to Rule the World* (New York: Random House, 2020), 442.

17. Ray Poindexter, *Golden Throats and Silver Tongues: The Radio Announcers* (Conway, AR: River Road Press, 1978), 151.

18. Torricelli and Carroll, *In Our Own Words*, 111.

19. Torricelli and Carroll, *In Our Own Words*, 111.

CHAPTER 9

1. Frank Brady, *Citizen Welles: A Biography of Orson Welles* (Lexington: University Press of Kentucky, 2023), 180.

2. Brady, *Citizen Welles*, 180.

3. *Atlantic Monthly*, "Martian Canals," vol. 76 (New York: John Ballister Collection, 1895), 112.

4. Patrick Parrinder, *Learning from Other Worlds: Estrangement, Cognition, and the Politics of Science Fiction and Utopia* (Durham, NC: Duke University Press, 2001), 142.

5. Brad Schwartz, *Broadcast Hysteria: Orson Welles's War of the Worlds* (New York: Farrar, Straus and Giroux, 2015), 47.

6. Erik Barnouw, *The Golden Web: A History of Broadcasting in the United States, 1933–1953* (Oxford: Oxford University Press, 1968), 86.

7. Alex Lubertozzi and Brian Holmsten, *The Complete War of the Worlds* (Naperville, IL: Sourcebooks, Inc., 2001), 157.

8. Brady, *Citizen Welles*, 180.

9. Howard Koch, *As Time Goes By* (New York: Harcourt Brace, 1979), 3.

10. David Colbert, *Eyewitness to America: 500 Years of American History in the Words of Those Who Saw It Happen* (New York: Knopf, 1998), 452.

CHAPTER 10

1. Howard Koch, *As Time Goes By* (New York: Harcourt Brace, 1979), 4.

2. Frank Brady, *Citizen Welles: A Biography of Orson Welles* (Lexington: University Press of Kentucky, 2023), 181.

3. Brady, *Citizen Welles*, 181.

4. Bill Kovarik, *Revolutions in Communication: Media History from Gutenberg to the Digital Age* (New York: Bloomsbury Academic, 2015), 224.

5. John Houseman, *Unfinished Business: Memoirs, 1902–1988* (New York: Applause Theatre & Cinema Books, 1989), 192.

6. Brady, *Citizen Welles*.

7. Houseman, *Unfinished Business*, 192.

8. Steven C. Smith, *A Heart at Fire's Center: The Life and Music of Bernard Herrmann* (Berkeley: University of California Press, 2002), 66.

9. Houseman, *Unfinished Business*, 180.

10. Houseman, *Unfinished Business*, 180.

11. Houseman, *Unfinished Business*, 180.

12. David Crespy, *Richard Barr: The Playwright's Producer* (Carbondale, IL: Southern Illinois University Press, 2013), 16.

13. Brady, *Citizen Welles.*

14. Brady, *Citizen Welles*, 184.

15. Brad Schwartz, *Broadcast Hysteria: Orson Welles's War of the Worlds* (New York: Farrar, Straus and Giroux, 2015), 62.

16. Schwartz, *Broadcast Hysteria*, 63.

17. Houseman, *Unfinished Business*, 198.

18. Houseman, *Unfinished Business*, 198.

19. Warren Buckland, *Who Wrote Citizen Kane? Statistical Analysis of Disputed Co-Authorship* (Cham, Switzerland: Springer Nature, 2023), 14.

20. Koch, *As Time Goes By.*

21. James Naremore, *The Magic World of Orson Welles* (Chicago: University of Illinois Press, 2015), 45.

22. David Thomson, *Rosebud: The Story of Orson Welles* (New York: Knopf, 1997), 111.

23. Brady, *Citizen Welles*, 186.

24. Brady, *Citizen Welles*, 186.

CHAPTER 11

1. "Radio Programs," *Lancaster Sunday News*, October 30, 1938, 17.

2. Brad Schwartz, *Broadcast Hysteria: Orson Welles's War of the Worlds* (New York: Farrar, Straus and Giroux, 2015), 66.

3. Schwartz, *Broadcast Hysteria*, 67.

4. Schwartz, *Broadcast Hysteria*, 67.

5. Schwartz, *Broadcast Hysteria*, 70.

6. Ezra A. Bowen, *This Fabulous Century: 1930–1940* (New York: Time-Life Books, 1969), 35.

7. Schwartz, *Broadcast Hysteria*, 71.

8. Alex Lubertozzi and Brian Holmsten, *The Complete War of the Worlds* (Naperville, IL: Sourcebooks, Inc., 2001), 36.

9. Lubertozzi and Holmsten, *The Complete War*, 36.

10. Schwartz, *Broadcast Hysteria*, 72.

11. John L. Flynn, *War of the Worlds: From Wells to Spielberg* (Owings Mills, MD: Galactic Books, 2005), 37.

12. John Gosling, *Waging the War of the Worlds* (Jefferson, NC: McFarland, 2009), 197.

13. Mark Memmott, *Radiolab*, October 30, 2013.

14. Schwartz, *Broadcast Hysteria*, 73.

15. Gosling, *Waging the War*, 199.

CHAPTER 12

1. John Gosling, *Waging the War of the Worlds* (Jefferson, NC: McFarland, 2009), 202.

2. Brad Schwartz, *Broadcast Hysteria: Orson Welles's War of the Worlds* (New York: Farrar, Straus and Giroux, 2015), 74.

3. Gosling, *Waging the War*, 202.

4. Schwartz, *Broadcast Hysteria*, 74.

5. Simon Callow, *Orson Welles, Volume 1: The Road to Xanadu* (New York: Penguin Books, 1997), 402.

6. Guy E. Swanson, *Readings in Social Psychology: Prepared for the Committee on the Teaching of Social Psychology of the Society for the Psychological Study of Social Issues* (Ann Arbor: University of Michigan Press, 1952), 199.

7. Schwartz, *Broadcast Hysteria*, 74.

8. Hadley Cantril, *The Invasion from Mars* (Princeton, NJ: Princeton University Press, 1940), 17.

9. Gosling, *Waging the War*, 202.

10. Gosling, *Waging the War*, 202.

11. Gosling, *Waging the War*, 202.

12. Alex Lubertozzi and Brian Holmsten, *The Complete War of the Worlds* (Naperville, IL: Sourcebooks, Inc., 2001), 36.

13. Schwartz, *Broadcast Hysteria*, 76.

14. "Realistic Radio Play of Attack from Mars Causes Stir Over U.S.: Hundreds of Persons Flee from Homes, Others Pray," *Tampa Times*, October 31, 1938, 1.

15. Gosling, *Waging the War*, 202.

16. Lubertozzi and Holmsten, *The Complete War*, 43.

17. Lubertozzi and Holmsten, *The Complete War*, 203.

18. "Radio Censorship Feared After Nation-Wide Panic: Mass Hysteria Passes Anything Seen Since War," *Bergen Evening Record* (Hackensack, NJ), October 31, 1938, 14.

19. "Radio Censorship," 14.

CHAPTER 13

1. Thomas E. Sanders, *Speculations: An Introduction to Literature Through Fantasy and Science Fiction* (New York: Glencoe Press, 1973), 273.

2. Alex Lubertozzi and Brian Holmsten, *The Complete War of the Worlds* (Naperville, IL: Sourcebooks, Inc., 2001), 44.

3. David Martin Anderson, *Hunting Snipes* (Boerne, TX: ConRoca Publishing, 2020), 245.

4. Associated Press, "Thousands Flee Homes as Radio Drama Too Realistic," *Riverside Daily Press*, October 31, 1938, 1.

5. John Gosling, *Waging the War of the Worlds* (Jefferson, NC: McFarland, 2009), 204.

6. Lubertozzi and Holmsten, *The Complete War*, 46.

7. Howard Koch, *The Panic Broadcast* (Boston, MA: Little, Brown, 1970), 56.

8. Kenneth C. Gardner Jr., *And All Our Yesterdays* (Bloomington, IL: IUniverse, LLC, 2014), 88.

9. Gardner, *And All Our Yesterdays*.

10. United Press International, "War Refugees Flee from Homes Convinced Devastation Is Near," *Racine Journal-Times*, October 31, 1938, 3.

11. Gosling, *Waging the War*, 205.

12. Hadley Cantril, *The Invasion from Mars* (Princeton, NJ: Princeton University Press, 1940).

13. Brad Schwartz, *Broadcast Hysteria: Orson Welles's War of the Worlds* (New York: Farrar, Straus and Giroux, 2015), 77.

14. Gosling, *Waging the War*, 205.

15. Lubertozzi and Holmsten, *The Complete War*, 16.

16. Cantril, *The Invasion*, 100.

17. Gosling, *Waging the War*, 205.

18. Schwartz, *Broadcast Hysteria*, 77.

19. Associated Press, "'Mars War' Broadcast Terrifies Thousands; Federal Inquiry Begun," *Roanoke World-News*, October 31, 1938, 1.

CHAPTER 14

1. Brad Schwartz, *Broadcast Hysteria: Orson Welles's War of the Worlds* (New York: Farrar, Straus and Giroux, 2015), 95.

2. Schwartz, *Broadcast Hysteria*, 96.

3. Alex Lubertozzi and Brian Holmsten, *The Complete War of the Worlds* (Naperville, IL: Sourcebooks, Inc., 2001), 50.

4. Jerome Kroth, *Omens and Oracles: Collective Psychology in the Nuclear Age* (New York: Bloomsbury Academic, 1992), 38.

5. Leonard Broom and Philip Selznick, *Sociology: A Text with Adapted Readings* (New York: HarperCollins, 1958), 276.

6. Simon Callow, *Orson Welles, Volume 1: The Road to Xanadu* (New York: Penguin Books, 1997), 403.

7. Neil Badmington, *Alien Chic: Posthumanism and the Other Within* (New York: Routledge, Taylor & Francis Group, 2004), 15.

8. "People Flee in Terror from Radio Broadcast," *Trenton* (NJ) *Evening Times*, October 31, 1938.

9. "When 'War of the Worlds' Brought a Small Washington Town to a Panic," MyNorthwest.com, October 30, 2023, https://mynorthwest.com/1158440/concrete-war-of-the-worlds.

10. Harold Ross, "Panic from Realistic Broadcast," *New Yorker*, November 8, 1938, 38.

11. John Gosling, *Waging the War of the Worlds* (Jefferson, NC: McFarland, 2009), 209.

12. Noel Keyes, *Contact* (Athens: University of Georgia, 1963), 123.

13. Lubertozzi and Holmsten, *The Complete War*, 51.

14. Lubertozzi and Holmsten, *The Complete War*, 53.

15. Gosling, *Waging the War*, 53.

16. Schwartz, *Broadcast Hysteria*, 79.

17. Gosling, *Waging the War*, 210.

18. Schwartz, *Broadcast Hysteria*, 79.

19. Lubertozzi and Holmsten, *The Complete War*, 52.

20. Robert J. Brown, *Manipulating the Ether: The Power of Broadcast Radio in Thirties America* (Jefferson, NC: McFarland, 2004), 215.

21. Lubertozzi and Holmsten, *The Complete War*, 17.

22. Hadley Cantril, *The Invasion from Mars* (Princeton, NJ: Princeton University Press, 1940).

23. Lubertozzi and Holmsten, *The Complete War*, 48.

24. Schwartz, *Broadcast Hysteria*, 82.

25. Brown, *Manipulating*, 216.

26. Cantril, *The Invasion*.

27. Alan Gallop, *The Martians Are Coming: The True Story of Orson Welles' 1938 Panic Broadcast* (Gloucestershire, UK: Amberley, 2012), 52.

28. Lubertozzi and Holmsten, *The Complete War*, 50.

29. "Fake Radio 'War' Stirs Terror Through U.S.," *Daily News* (NY), October 31, 1938, 1.

30. Gosling, *Waging the War*, 218.

31. Schwartz, *Broadcast Hysteria*, 98.

32. "Panic in City from Broadcast," *New York World-Telegram*, October 31, 1938.

33. Schwartz, *Broadcast Hysteria*, 99.

34. Schwartz, *Broadcast Hysteria*, 99.

35. Steven C. Smith, *A Heart at Fire's Center: The Life and Music of Bernard Herrmann* (Berkeley: University of California Press, 2002), 67.

36. David Thomson, *Rosebud: The Story of Orson Welles* (New York: Knopf, 1997), 105.

CHAPTER 15

1. Hadley Cantril, *The Invasion from Mars* (Princeton, NJ: Princeton University Press, 1940), 100.

2. Alex Lubertozzi and Brian Holmsten, *The Complete War of the Worlds* (Naperville, IL: Sourcebooks, Inc., 2001), 16.

3. Shearon Lowery and Melvin Lawrence DeFleur, *Milestones in Mass Communication Research: Media Effects* (New York: Pearson Longman Publishing, 1995), 61.

4. Cantril, *The Invasion*, 99.

5. Cantril, *The Invasion*, 101.

6. Cantril, *The Invasion*, 101.

7. Cantril, *The Invasion*, 103.

8. Lubertozzi and Holmsten, *The Complete War*, 16.

9. Robert Edwin Hertzstein, *Roosevelt & Hitler: Prelude to War* (St. Paul, MN: Paragon House, 1989), 116.

10. Lubertozzi and Holmsten, *The Complete War*, 16.

11. Cantril, *The Invasion*, 51.

12. Lubertozzi and Holmsten, *The Complete War*, 12.

13. Lubertozzi and Holmsten, *The Complete War*, 16.

14. Frank Brady, *Citizen Welles: A Biography of Orson Welles* (Lexington: University Press of Kentucky, 2023), 191.

15. Cantril, *The Invasion*.

16. Cantril, *The Invasion*, 208.

17. Brady, *Citizen Welles*, 190.

18. Brady, *Citizen Welles*, 189.

19. Brady, *Citizen Welles*.

20. John Gosling, *Waging the War of the Worlds* (Jefferson, NC: McFarland, 2009), 45.

21. Gosling, *Waging the War*.

22. "Demand for Radio Panic Inquiry Grows: Rely upon Papers for True Story," *Windsor Star*, October 31, 1938, 10.

23. "Demand for Radio Panic Inquiry."

24. "End of World Radio Sketch Is Cause of Excitement Here," *Free Lance-Star* (Fredericksburg, VA), October 31, 1938.

25. Associated Press, "Radio 'War' Leaves Jersey with Jitters," *Plainfield* (NJ) *Courier-News*, October 31, 1938, 13.

26. "Fictional 'Invasion from Mars' Panics Listeners, Brings Down Wrath on Radio: Tulsans Also Included; Telephones Are Swamped," *Tulsa Tribune*, October 31, 1938, 1.

27. Brady, *Citizen Welles*, 200.

CHAPTER 16

1. "Fake War on Radio Spreads Panic Over U.S.," *Daily News* (NY), October 31, 1938, 1.

2. "Radio Listeners in Panic, Taking War Drama as Fact," *New York Times*, October 31, 1938, 1.

3. "Radio Listeners in Panic," 1.

4. "Fake War," 1.

5. "Fake War."

6. "Fake War," 1.

7. "Fake War."

8. Fran Capo, *It Happened in New Jersey* (Essex, CT: Globe Pequot, 2012).

9. Capo, *It Happened in New Jersey*, 162.

10. Louis Snyder, *A Treasury of Great Reporting: Literature Under Pressure from the Sixteenth Century to Our Own Time* (Ann Arbor: University of Michigan Press, 1962), 542.

11. "Fake War," 6.

12. "Fake War," 6.

13. "Fake War," 6.

14. "Fake War," 6.

15. "Fake War," 6.

16. "Radio Fake Scares Nation," *Herald-Examiner* (Chicago, IL), October 31, 1938.

17. "'Invasion' of Country Causes Bus Passengers to Become Hysterical," *Asheville Citizen*, November 1, 1938, 8.

18. "Fake War."

19. Brad Schwartz, *Broadcast Hysteria: Orson Welles's War of the Worlds* (New York: Farrar, Straus and Giroux, 2015), 88.

20. "Radio Drama Causes Panic," *Philadelphia Inquirer* (PA), October 31, 1938.

21. "Radio Drama."

22. "Radio Drama."

23. "Radio Drama."

24. "Sturdy Cadets Grow Faint at Radio 'Attack,'" *Asheville Times* (NC), October 31, 1938, 2.

25. Alex Lubertozzi and Brian Holmsten, *The Complete War of the Worlds* (Naperville, IL: Sourcebooks, Inc., 2001), 23.

26. Hadley Cantril, *The Invasion from Mars* (Princeton, NJ: Princeton University Press, 1940), 55.

27. "Radio Drama."

28. "Radio Drama."

29. "Welles Novel Broadcast Panics U.S. Listeners," *Derby Evening Telegraph*, October 31, 1938, 1.

30. Associated Press, "Fictional Broadcast of Rocket Attack on New Jersey by Men from Mars Creates National Panic as Listeners Think End of World Has Arrived," *Knoxville News-Sentinel*, October 31, 1938.

31. "Radio Listeners in Panic, Taking War Drama as Fact."

32. "'War of the Worlds' Radio Broadcast Causes Panic," United Press International, October 31, 1938.

33. "Radio Play Terrifies Nation," *Boston Daily Globe*, October 31, 1938.

34. "Panic Sweeps U.S. as Radio Stages Mars Raid," *San Francisco Chronicle*, October 31, 1938.

35. "Radio War Panic Brings Inquiry, U.S. to Scan Broadcast Stations," *New York Post*, October 31, 1938.

36. "Martians Attack!" *Sarnoff Collection* (Ewing: College of New Jersey), October 31, 1938.

37. "Realistic Radio Play of Attack from Mars Causes Stir Over U.S.," *Tampa Tribune*, October 31, 1938.

38. "Thousands Flee Homes, Pray, or Faint, as Fictitious Radio Program Relates Invasion by Martian Hordes," *Amarillo* (TX) *Globe-Times*, October 31, 1938.

39. "Hysteria Sweeps Nation," *Daily Times* (Davenport, IA), October 31, 1938.

40. "U.S. Probes Radio Invasion Scare," *St. Louis Star-Times*, October 31, 1938.

41. "Thousands Flee Homes."

42. "'Mars War' Broadcast Terrifies Thousands; Federal Inquiry Begun," *Roanoke World News*, October 31, 1938.

43. "'Mars War' Broadcast."

44. Peter Noble, *The Fabulous Orson Welles* (London: Hutchinson, 1956), 116.

Chapter 17

1. Brad Schwartz, *Broadcast Hysteria: Orson Welles's War of the Worlds* (New York: Farrar, Straus and Giroux, 2015), 119.

2. Schwartz, *Broadcast Hysteria*, 119.

3. Schwartz, *Broadcast Hysteria*, 119.

4. "Inquiry Follows Broadcast of H. G. Wells War Drama," *Buffalo Evening News,* October 31, 1938, 14.

5. "Iowa Senator to Ask Law Against It," *Tampa Tribune,* October 31, 1938, 2.

6. "H. G. Wells Says He Gave No Right to Alter Script," *Bergen Evening Record* (Hackensack, NJ), October 31, 1938, 1.

7. Schwartz, *Broadcast Hysteria,* 120.

8. "Reaction of Public to Radio Drama Amazes Welles," *Philadelphia Inquirer,* October 31, 1938, 5.

9. "U.S. Considers Greater Control of Radio After Spook Play," *Allentown Morning Call,* November 1, 1938, 1.

10. Frank Brady, *Citizen Welles: A Biography of Orson Welles* (Lexington: University Press of Kentucky, 2023), 193.

11. This conversation, which continues on subsequent pages, is taken from video of the conference available online at https://www.youtube.com/watch?v=8vbYyDh-BRI.

12. "This Week in Universal News: The War of the Worlds Broadcast, 1938," National Archives: The Unwritten Record, October 27, 2014, https://unwritten-record .blogs.archives.gov/2014/10/27/this-week-in-universal-news-the-war-of-the-worlds -broadcast-1938.

13. Howard Koch, *The Panic Broadcast: Portrait of an Event* (Boston, MA: Little, Brown, 1970), 21.

14. Koch, *The Panic Broadcast.*

15. Brady, *Citizen Welles,* 195.

16. "Radio Program Depicting War of Worlds Causes Mass Hysteria Throughout Nation," *Everett* (WA) *Daily Herald,* October 31, 1938, 5.

17. "Thousands Flee Homes, Pray, or Faint as Fictitious Radio Program Relates Invasion by Martian Hordes," *Amarillo* (TX) *Globe-Times,* October 31, 1938, 1.

18. "Herring Will Demand U.S. Radio Control," *Asheville Times,* October 31, 1938, 2.

19. "Asheville Folk Are Still Puzzled Over Realistic Broadcast," *Asheville Times,* October 31, 1938, 2.

20. "No Men on Mars, Harvard Savants Assure Nation," *Asheville Times,* October 31, 1938, 2.

CHAPTER 18

1. Alex Lubertozzi and Brian Holmsten. *The Complete War of the Worlds* (Naperville, IL: Sourcebooks, Inc., 2001), 18.

2. R. H. McBride and R. A. Springs Jr., "Orson Welles Calls Broadcast 'Terribly Shocking Experience,'" *Daily Princetonian,* November 1, 1938.

3. Brad Schwartz, *Broadcast Hysteria: Orson Welles's War of the Worlds* (New York: Farrar, Straus and Giroux, 2015), 130.

4. Simon Callow, *Orson Welles, Volume 1: The Road to Xanadu* (New York: Penguin Books, 1997), 408.

5. Arthur Pollock, "Orson Welles Does Buchner's 'Danton's Death' Over into a Little Thing of His Own, Enjoying Life as a Boy Prodigy," *Brooklyn Eagle-Examiner,* November 6, 1938, 39.

6. Schwartz, *Broadcast Hysteria*, 132.

7. John Gosling, *Waging the War of the Worlds* (Jefferson, NC: McFarland, 2009), 88.

8. "Tells of Earlier Protests on Radio Terror Programs," *St. Louis Star-Times*, November 1, 1938, 7.

9. Schwartz, *Broadcast Hysteria*, 140.

10. Schwartz, *Broadcast Hysteria*, 140.

11. Schwartz, *Broadcast Hysteria*, 140.

12. Schwartz, *Broadcast Hysteria*, 140.

13. Schwartz, *Broadcast Hysteria*, 140.

14. Schwartz, *Broadcast Hysteria*, 141.

15. Lubertozzi and Holmsten, *The Complete War of the Worlds*, 24.

16. "Fictional Invasion from Mars Panics Listeners, Brings Down Wrath on Radio," *Tulsa Tribune*, October 31, 1938.

17. "FCC Will Probe Panic Broadcast," *Fort Collins Express-Courier*, October 31, 1938, 1.

18. "Two Die in Crashes," *Fort Collins Express-Courier*, October 31, 1938, 1.

19. "The Gullible Radio Public," *Chicago Tribune*, November 10, 1938, 16.

20. David Thomson, *Rosebud: The Story of Orson Welles* (New York: Knopf, 1997), 106.

21. Frank Brady, *Citizen Welles: A Biography of Orson Welles* (Lexington: University Press of Kentucky, 2023), 191.

22. Brady, *Citizen Welles*, 191.

23. "Radio's Biggest Boner," *Courier-Post* (Camden, NJ), November 1, 1938, 10.

24. "All-Time High Reached in Welles' Presentation," *Pittsburgh Press*, November 9, 1938, 12.

25. "National Guard Almost Called Out," *Lincoln Star*, October 31, 1938.

26. Brady, *Citizen Welles*.

27. "Radio Censorship Feared After Nation-Wide Panic: Mass Hysteria Passes Anything Seen Since War," *Bergen Evening Record* (Hackensack, NJ), October 31, 1938, 11.

CHAPTER 19

1. "Curious Crowds Flock to Farm Around Which Radio's 'Scare' Program Revolved," *Seattle* (WA) *Star*, November 1, 1938, 1.

2. "So They Say," *Kokomo* (IN) *Tribune*, November 7, 1938.

3. Alex Lubertozzi and Brian Holmsten, *The Complete War of the Worlds* (Naperville, IL: Sourcebooks, Inc., 2001), 8.

4. Lubertozzi and Holmsten, *The Complete War*, 8.

5. Lubertozzi and Holmsten, *The Complete War*, 8.

6. Brad Schwartz, *Broadcast Hysteria: Orson Welles's War of the Worlds* (New York: Farrar, Straus and Giroux, 2015), 157.

7. "Nationwide Terrorism Created by Radio War Drama Starts Inquiry," *Modesto* (CA) *Bee*, October 31, 1938, 1.

8. "U.S. Says 'No' to All Future 'Wars' on Air," *Daily News* (NY), November 1, 1938, 3.

9. "U.S. Says 'No,'" 3.

10. Mrs. Shirley, letter to CBS, November 1, 1938, University of Michigan, Box 23, folder 21/54.

11. "U.S. Says 'No,'" 3.

12. "Rigid Radio Regulation Likely to Follow Weird Horror Play Broadcast," *Eau Claire* (WI) *Leader-Telegram*, November 1, 1938, 1.

13. "Comment by Press on Radio Fantasy," *St. Louis Star and Times*, November 1, 1938, 7.

14. "Comment by Press."

15. "Comment by Press."

16. "Comment by Press."

17. "Comment by Press."

18. "Comment by Press."

19. Schwartz, *Broadcast Hysteria*, 164.

20. Ray B. Browne and Arthur B. Neal, *Ordinary Reactions of Extraordinary Events* (Bowling Green, OH: Bowling Green State University Popular Press, 2001).

21. David Thomson, *Rosebud: The Story of Orson Welles* (New York: Knopf, 1997), 105.

22. Simon Callow, *Orson Welles, Volume 1: The Road to Xanadu* (New York: Penguin Books, 1997), 405.

23. Donald McQuade and Robert Atwan, *Popular Writing in America: The Interaction of Style and Audience* (Oxford: Oxford University Press, 1988).

24. Howard Koch, *The Panic Broadcast: Portrait of an Event* (Boston, MA: Little, Brown, 1970), 93.

25. Schwartz, *Broadcast Hysteria*, 165.

26. Hadley Cantril, *The Invasion from Mars* (Princeton, NJ: Princeton University Press, 1940).

27. Cantril, *The Invasion*, 93.

28. Cantril, *The Invasion*, 94.

29. Cantril, *The Invasion*, 94.

30. Cantril, *The Invasion*, 94.

31. Cantril, *The Invasion*, 97.

32. David Goodman, *Radio's Civic Ambition: American Broadcasting and Democracy in the 1930s* (Oxford: Oxford University Press, 2011), 265.

33. Paul Heyer, *The Medium and the Magician: Orson Welles, The Radio Years, 1934–1952* (Lanham, MD: Rowman & Littlefield, 2005), 106.

34. Koch, *The Panic*, 93.

35. Royal Commission on Violence in the Communications Industry, *Violence in Print and Music*, Vol. 4 (Ontario, Canada: The Commission, 1977), 59.

36. Koch, *The Panic*, 93.

37. Koch, *The Panic*, 93.

38. Thomson, *Rosebud*, 106.

39. Stephen Shapiro and Mark Storey, *The Cambridge Companion to American Horror* (New York: Cambridge University Press, 2022), 86.

40. Schwartz, *Broadcast Hysteria*, 150.

41. Schwartz, *Broadcast Hysteria*, 150.

42. See "Heinl Radio Business Letter," November 4, 1938, available at https://www
.worldradiohistory.com/Archive-Heinl-Letter/30s/HEINL-REPORT-1938-11.pdf.

43. Schwartz, *Broadcast Hysteria*, 150.

44. Frank Rhylick, "FCC Won't Punish CBS on Welles Play," *Daily News* (NY),
December 6, 1938, 51.

45. Rhylick, "FCC Won't Punish," 51.

46. Schwartz, *Broadcast Hysteria*, 167.

CHAPTER 20

1. Simon Callow, *Orson Welles, Volume 1: The Road to Xanadu* (New York: Penguin
Books, 1997), 419.

2. John Houseman, *Run-through: A Memoir* (New York: Simon and Schuster,
1980), 412.

3. Frank Brady, *Citizen Welles: A Biography of Orson Welles* (Lexington: University Press
of Kentucky, 2023), 198.

4. Alex Lubertozzi and Brian Holmsten, *The Complete War of the Worlds* (Naperville,
IL: Sourcebooks, Inc., 2001), 27.

5. "Campbell Playhouse Makes Good Start," *New York Times*, December 10, 1938.

6. "Orson Welles Given Free Hand in Movies: Wonderboy of 24 Enters on New Career
with Bounding Spirits and Ferocious Energy," *Vancouver Sun*, December 30, 1939, 16.

7. "Orson Welles Given Free Hand in Movies."

8. "Orson Welles Given Free Hand in Movies."

9. "Orson Welles Given Free Hand in Movies."

10. Houseman, *Run-through*, 217.

11. Brad Schwartz, *Broadcast Hysteria: Orson Welles's War of the Worlds* (New York: Farrar, Straus and Giroux, 2015), 196.

12. Schwartz, *Broadcast Hysteria*, 196.

13. "Orson Welles Gives View of Movies Today," *Kansas City Star*, December 5, 1939.

CHAPTER 21

1. Barbara Leaming, *Orson Welles: A Biography* (New York: Limelight Editions,
2004), 288.

2. Brad Schwartz, *Broadcast Hysteria: Orson Welles's War of the Worlds* (New York: Farrar,
Straus and Giroux, 2015), 45.

3. Alex Lubertozzi and Brian Holmsten, *The Complete War of the Worlds* (Naperville,
IL: Sourcebooks, Inc., 2001), 17.

4. Peter Prescott Tonguette, *Orson Welles Remembered: Interviews with His Actors, Editors, Cinematographers and Magicians* (Jefferson, NC: McFarland, 2014), 177.

5. Museum of Broadcasting, *The Radio Years* (Bloomington: Indiana University Press,
1988), 30.

6. John Gosling, *Waging the War of the Worlds* (Jefferson, NC: McFarland, 2009), 218.

7. Hadley Cantril, *The Invasion from Mars* (Princeton, NJ: Princeton University Press,
1940), 199.

8. Lubertozzi and Holmsten, *The Complete War*, 31.

9. Cantril, *The Invasion*, 199.

10. Cantril, *The Invasion*, 199.

11. Cantril, *The Invasion*, 159.

EPILOGUE

1. Peter J. Beck, *The War of the Worlds: From H. G. Wells to Orson Welles, Jeff Wayne, Steven Spielberg & Beyond* (New York: Bloomsbury Academic, 2016), 226.

2. Beck, *The War*, 227.

3. Beck, *The War*, 227.

4. Brad Schwartz, *Broadcast Hysteria: Orson Welles's War of the Worlds* (New York: Farrar, Straus and Giroux, 2015), 200.

5. Alex Lubertozzi and Brian Holmsten, *The Complete War of the Worlds* (Naperville, IL: Sourcebooks, Inc., 2001), 22.

6. Lubertozzi and Holmsten, *The Complete War*.

7. John Houseman, *Unfinished Business: Memoirs, 1902–1988* (New York: Applause Theatre & Cinema Books, 1989), 228.

8. Edward Ruppelt, *The Report on Unidentified Flying Objects* (Norfolk, VA: Project Blue Book Archive, 2008).

9. Simon Callow, *Orson Welles, Volume 1: The Road to Xanadu* (New York: Penguin Books, 1997), 407.

10. Callow, *Orson Welles*, 407.

11. Jerry Belcher, "Orson Welles, Theatrical Genius, Found Dead at 70," *Los Angeles Times*, October 11, 1985, 1.

12. Belcher, "Orson Welles," 10.

Bibliography

Anderson, David Martin. *Hunting Snipes.* Boerne, TX: ConRoca Publishing, 2020.

Asimov, Isaac. "Afterword." In *The War of the Worlds,* by H. G. Wells. New York: Penguin, Putnam, 1986.

Atlantic Monthly. "Martian Canals," vol. 76. New York: John Ballister Collection, 1895.

Badmington, Neil. *Alien Chic: Posthumanism and the Other Within.* New York: Routledge, Taylor & Francis Group, 2004.

Barnouw, Erik. *The Golden Web: A History of Broadcasting in the United States, 1933–1953.* Oxford: Oxford University Press, 1968.

Bartholomew, Robert. *Panic Attacks.* Stroud, Gloucestershire: Sutton, 2004.

Beck, Peter J. *The War of the Worlds: From H. G. Wells to Orson Welles, Jeff Wayne, Steven Spielberg & Beyond.* New York: Bloomsbury Academic, 2016.

Bowen, Ezra A. *This Fabulous Century: 1930–1940.* New York: Time-Life Books, Inc., 1969.

Brady, Frank. *Citizen Welles: A Biography of Orson Welles.* Lexington: University Press of Kentucky, 2023.

Broom, Leonard, and Philip Selznick. *Sociology: A Text with Adapted Readings.* New York: HarperCollins, 1958.

Brown, Haywood. "It Seems to Me." *New York World-Telegram,* November 2, 1938.

Brown, Robert J. *Manipulating the Ether: The Power of Broadcast Radio in Thirties America.* Jefferson, NC: McFarland, 2004.

Browne, Ray B., and Arthur B. Neal. *Ordinary Reactions of Extraordinary Events.* Bowling Green, OH: Bowling Green State University Popular Press, 2001.

Buckland, Warren. *Who Wrote Citizen Kane? Statistical Analysis of Disputed Co-Authorship.* Cham, Switzerland: Springer Nature, 2023.

Callow, Simon. *Orson Welles, Volume 1: The Road to Xanadu.* London: Jonathan Cape, 1995; New York: Penguin Books, 1997.

Cantril, Hadley. *The Invasion from Mars.* Princeton, NJ: Princeton University Press, 1940; New York: Taylor and Francis, 2017.

Capo, Fran. *It Happened in New Jersey.* Essex, CT: Globe Pequot, 2012.

Chaplin, James Patrick. *Rumor, Fear and the Madness of Crowds.* Mineola, NY: Dover, 2015.

Cimone, Marlene. "The Night the Martians Landed." *Los Angeles Times,* October 30, 1979.

Clarke, Arthur C. "Introduction." In *The War of the Worlds*, by H. G. Wells. London: Everyman, 1993.

Colbert, David. *Eyewitness to America: 500 Years of American History in the Words of Those Who Saw It Happen*. New York: Knopf, 1998.

Crespy, David. *Richard Barr: The Playwright's Producer*. Carbondale: Southern Illinois University Press, 2013.

Estrin, Mark W. *Orson Welles: Interviews*. Jackson: University Press of Mississippi, 2002.

Feder, Chris Welles. *In My Father's Shadow: A Daughter Remembers Orson Welles*. Chapel Hill, NC: Algonquin Books, 2009.

Fedler, Fred. *Media Hoaxes*. Ames: Iowa State University Press, 1989.

Flynn, John L. *War of the Worlds: From Wells to Spielberg*. Owings Mills, MD: Galactic Books, 2005.

France, Richard. *Orson Welles on Shakespeare: The W.P.A. and Mercury Theatre Playscripts*. New York: Taylor & Francis, 2013.

Gallop, Alan. *The Martians Are Coming: The True Story of Orson Welles' 1938 Panic Broadcast*. Gloucestershire, UK: Amberley, 2012.

Gardner, Kenneth C., Jr. *And All Our Yesterdays*. Bloomington, IL: IUniverse, LLC, 2014.

Gear, Matthew Asprey. *At the End of the Street in the Shadow: Orson Welles and the City*. New York: Columbia University Press, 2016.

Goodman, David. *Radio's Civic Ambition: American Broadcasting and Democracy in the 1930s*. Oxford: Oxford University Press, 2011.

Gosling, John. *Waging the War of the Worlds*. Jefferson, NC: McFarland, 2009.

Hand, Richard J., and Mary Traynor. *The Radio Drama Handbook: Audio Drama in Context and Practice*. New York: Bloomsbury, 2011.

Harmon, Jim. *The Great Radio Heroes*. Jefferson, NC: McFarland, 2001.

Henry, Neil. *American Carnival: Journalism Under Siege in an Age of New Media*. Berkeley: University of California Press, 2007.

Hertzstein, Robert Edwin. *Roosevelt & Hitler: Prelude to War*. St. Paul, MN: Paragon House, 1989.

Heyer, Paul. *The Medium and the Magician: Orson Welles, The Radio Years, 1934–1952*. Lanham, MD: Rowman & Littlefield, 2005.

Higgins, Bernie. "Battle for the Airwaves: Radio and the 1938 Munich Crisis," interview with author David Vaughan. Radio Prague International, September 29, 2008. https://english.radio.cz/battle-airwaves-radio-and-1938-munich-crisis-8591724.

Hilmes, Michele. *Radio Voices*. Minneapolis, MN: University of Minneapolis Press, 1997.

Houseman, John. *Unfinished Business: Memoirs, 1902–1988*. New York: Applause Theatre & Cinema Books, 1989.

Houseman, John. "The Men from Mars." *Harper's Magazine*, December 1948.

Houseman, John. *Run-through: A Memoir*. New York: Simon and Schuster, 1980.

Jackaway, Gwenyth. *Media at War: Radio's Challenge to Newspapers, 1924–1939*. Westport, CT: Praeger, 1995.

Jackson, Charles. "The Night the Martians Came." In *The Aspirin Age, 1919–1941*, edited by Isabel Leighton. New York: Simon and Schuster, 1949.

Jarrow, Gail. *Spooked! How a Radio Broadcast and* The War of the Worlds *Sparked the 1938 Invasion of America.* New York: Astra Publishing, 2018.

Jenkins, Mark. *Rosebud: The Lives of Orson Welles.* Saint Davids, Wales: Infested Waters, 2004.

Kaltenborn, Hans. *Fifty Fabulous Years, 1900–1950.* New York: Putnam, 1950.

Keith, Michael C. *Talking Radio: An Oral History.* New York: M. E. Sharpe, 2000.

Keyes, Noel. *Contact.* Athens: University of Georgia, 1963.

Kisha, Tim. *A Newscast for the Masses.* Detroit, MI: Wayne State University Press, 2009.

Klass, Philip. "Wells, Welles, and the Martians." *New York Times Book Review*, October 30, 1988.

Koch, Howard. *As Time Goes By.* New York: Harcourt Brace, 1979.

Koch, Howard. *The Panic Broadcast: Portrait of an Event.* Boston, MA: Little, Brown, 1970.

Kovarik, Bill. *Revolutions in Communication: Media History from Gutenberg to the Digital Age.* New York: Bloomsbury Academic, 2015.

Kroth, Jerome. *Omens and Oracles: Collective Psychology in the Nuclear Age.* New York: Bloomsbury Academic, 1992.

Leaming, Barbara. *Orson Welles: A Biography.* New York: Viking Penguin, 1985; New York: Limelight Editions, 2004.

Locke, Richard Adams. *The Moon Hoax.* New York: William Gowans, 1859.

London, Todd. *An Ideal Theater: Founding Visions for a New American Art.* New York: Theater Communications Group, 2013.

Lowell, Percival. *Mars.* New York: Eilbron Classics, 2004.

Lowery, Shearon, and Melvin Lawrence DeFleur. *Milestones in Mass Communication Research: Media Effects.* New York: Pearson Longman Publishing, 1995.

Lubertozzi, Alex, and Brian Holmsten. *The Complete War of the Worlds.* Naperville, IL: Sourcebooks, Inc., 2001.

MacLiammoir, Micheál. *All for Hecuba: An Irish Theatrical Biography.* Berkeley: University of California Press, 2011.

McCarthy, Michael. *The Hidden Hindenburg: The Untold Story of the Tragedy, the Nazi Secrets, and the Quest to Rule the Skies.* Lanham, MD: Lyons Press, 2020.

McGilligan, Patrick. *Young Orson: The Years of Luck and Genius.* New York: Harper Perennial, 2015.

McQuade, Donald, and Robert Atwan. *Popular Writing in America: The Interaction of Style and Audience.* Oxford: Oxford University Press, 1988.

Memmott, Mark. *Radiolab.* October 30, 2013.

Museum of Broadcasting. *The Radio Years.* Bloomington: Indiana University Press, 1988.

Naremore, James. *The Magic World of Orson Welles.* Chicago: University of Illinois Press, 2015.

Noble, Peter. *The Fabulous Orson Welles.* London: Hutchinson, 1956.

Parrinder, Patrick. *Learning from Other Worlds: Estrangement, Cognition, and the Politics of Science Fiction and Utopia.* Durham, NC: Duke University Press, 2001.

Paultz, Estelle. Letter to Orson Welles, October 31, 1938. University of Michigan, Box 24, folder 1.

Poindexter, Ray. *Golden Throats and Silver Tongues: The Radio Announcers.* Conway, AR: River Road Press, 1978.

Posnanski, Joe. *The Life and Afterlife of Harry Houdini.* New York: Avid Reader Press, Simon and Schuster, 2002.

Rippy, Marguerite. *Orson Welles and the Unfinished RKO Projects.* Carbondale: Southern Illinois University Press, 2009.

Robinson, Michael K. *A New Treatise on a Small Blue Planet.* Cambridge: Vanguard Press, 2007.

Roosevelt, Franklin D. *My Own Story: From Private and Public Papers.* New York: Routledge, 2017.

Rose, Alexander. *Empires of the Sky: Zeppelins, Airplanes, and Two Men's Epic Duel to Rule the World.* New York: Random House, 2020.

Rosenbaum, Jonathan. *Discovering Orson Welles.* Berkeley: University of California Press, 2007.

Ross, Harold. "Panic from Realistic Broadcast." *New Yorker,* vol. 64, issues 38–45. November 8, 1938.

Royal Commission on Violence in the Communications Industry. *Violence in Print and Music,* Vol. 4. Ontario, Canada: The Commission, 1977.

Ruppelt, Edward. *The Report on Unidentified Flying Objects.* Norfolk, VA: Project Blue Book Archive, 2008.

Sanders, Thomas E. *Speculations: An Introduction to Literature through Fantasy and Science Fiction.* New York: Glencoe Press, 1973.

Sarnoff Collection. "Martians Attack!" Ewing, NJ: College of New Jersey. October 31, 1938.

Sawyer, Robert. *Shakespeare Between the World Wars: The Anglo-American Sphere.* New York: Palgrave Macmillan, 2019.

Schwartz, Brad. *Broadcast Hysteria: Orson Welles's War of the Worlds.* New York: Farrar, Straus and Giroux, 2015.

Shapiro, Stephen, and Mark Storey. *The Cambridge Companion to American Horror.* New York: Cambridge University Press, 2022.

Sheehan, William. *The Planet Mars: A History of Observation.* Tucson: University of Arizona Press, 1996.

Shirley, Mrs. Letter to CBS, November 1, 1938. University of Michigan, Box 23, folder 21/54.

Smith, David C. *H. G. Wells: Desperately Mortal.* New Haven, CT: Yale University Press, 1986.

Smith, Steven C. *A Heart at Fire's Center: The Life and Music of Bernard Herrmann.* Berkeley: University of California Press, 2002.

Snyder, Louis. *A Treasury of Great Reporting: Literature Under Pressure from the Sixteenth Century to Our Own Time.* Ann Arbor: University of Michigan Press, 1962.

Sterling, Christopher. *The Concise Encyclopedia of American Radio.* New York: Routledge, 2010.

Swanson, Guy E. *Readings in Social Psychology: Prepared for the Committee on the Teaching of Social Psychology of the Society for the Psychological Study of Social Issues.* Ann Arbor: University of Michigan Press, 1952.

Swanson, Guy E. "The War That Never Was." *Starlog,* December 1988. https://www.glenswanson.space/science-fiction.html.

Tarbox, Todd. *Orson Welles and Roger Hill: A Friendship in Three Acts.* Duncan, OK: BearManor Media, 2013.

Terrace, Vincent. *Radio Program Openings and Closings, 1931–1972.* Jefferson, NC: McFarland, 2015.

Thompson, Dorothy. "On the Record: Mr. Welles and Mass Delusion." *New York Herald Tribune,* November 2, 1938.

Thomson, David. *Rosebud: The Story of Orson Welles.* Boston, MA: Little, Brown and Co., 1996; New York: Knopf, 1997.

Tonguette, Peter Prescott. *Orson Welles Remembered: Interviews with His Actors, Editors, Cinematographers and Magicians.* Jefferson, NC: McFarland, 2014.

Torricelli, Robert, and Andrew Carroll. *In Our Own Words: Extraordinary Speeches of the American Century.* New York: Kodansha America, 2000.

Turner, Fred. *The Democratic Surround: Multimedia and American Liberalism from World War II to the Psychedelic Sixties.* London: University of Chicago Press, 2013.

Welles, Orson, and Peter Bogdanovich. *This Is Orson Welles.* London: HarperCollins, 1993.

Wells, H. G. *The War of the Worlds.* New York: Looking Glass Library, 1960.

"When 'War of the Worlds' Brought a Small Washington Town to a Panic." MyNorthwest.com, October 30, 2023. https://mynorthwest.com/1158440/concrete-war-of-the-worlds.

NEWSPAPER ARTICLES

Allentown Morning Call. "U.S. Considers Greater Control of Radio After Spook Play." November 1, 1938.

Amarillo (TX) *Globe-Times.* "Thousands Flee Homes, Pray, or Faint as Fictitious Radio Program Relates Invasion by Martian Hordes." October 31, 1938.

Asheville Citizen. "'Invasion' of Country Causes Bus Passengers to Become Hysterical." November 1, 1938.

Asheville (NC) *Times.* "Asheville Folk Are Still Puzzled Over Realistic Broadcast." October 31, 1938.

Asheville (NC) *Times.* "Herring Will Demand U.S. Radio Control." October 31, 1938.

Asheville (NC) *Times.* "No Men on Mars, Harvard Savants Assure Nation." October 31, 1938.

Asheville (NC) *Times.* "Sturdy Cadets Grow Faint at Radio 'Attack.'" October 31, 1938.

Belcher, Jerry. "Orson Welles, Theatrical Genius, Found Dead at 70." *Los Angeles Times,* October 11, 1985.

Bergen Evening Record (Hackensack, NJ). "H. G. Wells Says He Gave No Right to Alter Script." October 31, 1938.

Bergen Evening Record (Hackensack, NJ). "Hitler Boosts Price of Peace." September 22, 1938.

Bergen Evening Record (Hackensack, NJ). "Radio Censorship Feared After Nation-Wide Panic: Mass Hysteria Passes Anything Seen Since War." October 31, 1938.

Buffalo Evening News. "Inquiry Follows Broadcast of H. G. Wells War Drama." October 31, 1938.

Burlington (VT) *Daily News.* "U.S. Lines Ready to Bring Home All Americans." September 28, 1938.

Chicago Tribune. "The Gullible Radio Public." November 10, 1938.

Courier-Post (Camden, NJ). "Radio's Biggest Boner." November 1, 1938.

Daily News (NY). "Fake Radio 'War' Stirs Terror through U.S." October 31, 1938.

Daily News (NY). "Fake 'War' on Radio Spreads Panic Over U.S." October 31, 1938.

Daily News (NY). "U.S. Says 'No' to All Future 'Wars' on Air." November 1, 1938.

Daily Times (Davenport, IA). "Hysteria Sweeps Nation." October 31, 1938.

Derby Evening Telegraph. "Welles Novel Broadcast Panics U.S. Listeners." October 31, 1938.

Detroit (MI) *Free Press,* October 31, 1938.

Detroit (MI) *News,* October 31, 1938.

Eau Claire (WI) *Leader-Telegram.* "Rigid Radio Regulation Likely to Follow Weird Horror Play Broadcast." November 1, 1938.

Everett (WA) *Daily Herald.* "Radio Program Depicting War of Worlds Causes Mass Hysteria Throughout Nation." October 31, 1938.

Fort Collins Express-Courier. "FCC Will Probe Panic Broadcast." October 31, 1938.

Fort Collins Express-Courier. "Two Die in Crashes." October 31, 1938.

Free Lance-Star (Fredericksburg, VA). "End of World Radio Sketch Is Cause of Excitement Here." October 31, 1938.

Hartford Courant. "Radio Scare Here Spreads Fear, Anger." October 31, 1938.

Herald-Examiner (Chicago, IL). "Radio Fake Scares Nation." October 31, 1938.

Journal Times (Racine, WI). "War Refugees Flee from Homes Convinced Devastation Is Near." October 31, 1938.

Kansas City Star. "Orson Welles Gives View of Movies Today." December 5, 1939.

Kaye, Joseph. "Prodigy of New York Stage Bites Hand That Is Feeding Him during Course of Talk Before Group of Educators—Orson Welles Asserts Movies Have It All Over Stage—Plans Ambitious Season for Mercury." *Cincinnati Enquirer,* August 7, 1938.

Knoxville News-Sentinel. "Fictional Broadcast of Rocket Attack on New Jersey by Men from Mars Creates National Panic as Listeners Think End of World Has Arrived." October 31, 1938.

Kokomo (IN) *Tribune.* "So They Say." November 7, 1938.

Lancaster Sunday News. "Radio Programs." October 30, 1938.

Lincoln Star. "National Guard Almost Called Out." October 31, 1938.

Mantle, Robert Burns. "'Cradle Will Rock' Given Stage Room by New Mercury Theatre." *Daily News* (NY), December 7, 1937.

Mantle, Robert Burns. "'Julius Caesar' in Overcoats Mercury's First Experiment." *Daily News* (NY), November 12, 1937.

Mantle, Robert Burns. "Theme of Two Productions: Negro 'Macbeth,' Ghosts, Futuristic Fantasy Provide Spooky Fare." *Chicago Tribune*, April 26, 1936.

Mantle, Robert Burns. "WPA 'Macbeth' in Fancy Dress: Negro Theatre Creates Something of a Sensation in Harlem." *Daily News* (NY), April 15, 1936.

McBride, R. H., and R. A. Springs Jr. "Orson Welles Calls Broadcast 'Terribly Shocking Experience.'" *Daily Princetonian*, November 1, 1938.

The Mercury (Pottstown, PA). "Sudetenland or War, Says Hitler." September 27, 1938.

Miller, Webb. "World Doubts Europe Peace Is Permanent: England Continues to Arm in Spite of Hitler's Recent Statements." *Hammond Times* (Munster, IN), October 6, 1938.

Modesto (CA) *Bee*. "Nationwide Terrorism Created by Radio War Drama Starts Inquiry." October 31, 1938.

Morning Call (Allentown, PA), October 31, 1938.

Newark Evening News. "Too Real Radio Drama Gives Nation a Bad Case of War Jitters." October 31, 1938.

New York Post. "U.S. Probes Invasion Broadcast . . . Radio Play Causes Wide Panic." October 31, 1938.

New York Times. "Campbell Playhouse Makes Good Start." December 10, 1938.

New York Times. "Radio Listeners in Panic, Taking War Drama as Fact." October 31, 1938.

New York Times. "A Wave of Hysteria." October 31, 1938.

New York World-Telegram. "Panic in City from Broadcast." October 31, 1938.

Philadelphia (PA) *Inquirer.* "Radio Drama Causes Panic." October 31, 1938.

Philadelphia (PA) *Inquirer.* "Reaction of Public to Radio Drama Amazes Welles." October 31, 1938.

Pittsburgh Press. "All-Time High Reached in Welles' Presentation." November 9, 1938.

Plainfield (NJ) *Courier-News.* "Radio 'War' Leaves Jersey with Jitters." October 31, 1938.

Pollock, Arthur. "Orson Welles Does Buchner's 'Danton's Death' Over into a Little Thing of His Own, Enjoying Life as a Boy Prodigy." *Brooklyn Eagle-Examiner*, November 6, 1938.

Riverside Daily Press. "Thousands Flee Homes as Radio Drama Too Realistic." October 31, 1938.

Roanoke World-News. "'Mars War' Broadcast Terrifies Thousands; Federal Inquiry Begun." October 31, 1938.

San Francisco (CA) *Chronicle*, October 31, 1938.

Seattle Daily Times. "US Launches Inquiry into Radio Panic." October 31, 1938.

Seattle (WA) *Star.* "Curious Crowds Flock to Farm Around Which Radio's 'Scare' Program Revolved." November 1, 1938.

Seattle (WA) *Times Courant*, October 31, 1938.

St. Louis Star-Times. "Tells of Earlier Protests on Radio Terror Programs." November 1, 1938.

Tampa Times. "Realistic Radio Play of Attack from Mars Causes Stir Over U.S.: Hundreds of Persons Flee from Homes, Others Pray." October 31, 1938.

Tampa Tribune. "Iowa Senator to Ask Law Against It." October 31, 1938.

Time. "The Brightest Moon Over Broadway." May 9, 1938.

Time. "The Theatre: Marvelous Boy." May 9, 1938.

Trenton (NJ) *Evening Times.* "People Flee in Terror from Radio Broadcast." October 31, 1938.

Trentonian. "Radio Show Stops Hospital Work." October 31, 1938.

Tulsa Tribune. "Fictional 'Invasion from Mars' Panics Listeners, Brings Down Wrath on Radio: Tulsans Also Included; Telephones Are Swamped." October 31, 1938.

Vancouver Citizen. "All Hail Julius Caesar." December 8, 1937.

Vancouver Sun. "Orson Welles Given Free Hand in Movies: Wonderboy of 24 Enters on New Career with Bounding Spirits and Ferocious Energy." December 30, 1939.

Washington Post. "Church Services Interrupted by Panicked Parishioners." October 31, 1938.

Windsor Star. "Demand for Radio Panic Inquiry Grows: Rely Upon Papers for True Story." October 31, 1938.

INDEX